FIRING A SHOT F

The Memoirs of

With a Foreword and Afterword
by
Angela Jackson

THE CLAPTON PRESS
LONDON E5

First published 2020 by:
THE CLAPTON PRESS LTD,
38 Thistlewaite Road, London E5.

ISBN: 978-1-913693-00-8

Angela Jackson – Biographical Note

Angela Jackson's research for her doctoral thesis included many interviews with women, including Frida Stewart, who had been involved with the civil war in Spain. These formed the basis for her book, *British Women and the Spanish Civil War,* and for a novel, *Warm Earth,* which fictionalises some of the women she met and their true stories.

In 2001, after moving to the Priorat in Catalonia where she lived for fifteen years, Angela became a founder member and President of *No Jubilem la Memòria,* an association for the recovery of events and memories of the civil war in the region. Further books followed, exploring the interactions between local villagers and the International Brigaders who were stationed in the area for many weeks before the Battle of the Ebro.

Letters between civil war nurse Patience Darton and the International Brigader Robert Aaquist inspired Angela to write a full and moving biography of Patience entitled '*For us it was heaven'.* The publication of *Firing a Shot for Freedom* has at last brought about the fulfilment of a project Angela shared with Frida in the months before her death in 1996.

Dedication

To Paul Preston for his huge contribution to the understanding of modern Spanish history and for providing encouragement and support for the publication of this series of memoirs.

Contents

Frida Stewart as a young woman

List of Illustrations

Foreword by Angela Jackson

When Frida's ashes fell amongst the warm, dry grass, the sound was like the rustle of fallen leaves on a crisp autumn day beneath the old trees she loved in Cambridge. But the historic bridges over the river in her home town do not have such a recent past of blood and death as the bridge which now loomed above us, the *Puente de los Franceses* in Madrid. Those who had died defending the bridge during the Spanish Civil War would have known the songs we sang in memory of Frida, *los Cuatro Generales*, *Viva la Quince Brigada* and the *Internacional*. She had hoped to return to Spain in 1996 to join in the events arranged for the International Brigaders on the sixtieth anniversary of the war, but died too soon to see the welcome they received.

The last time she had been in Spain was after her escape from an internment camp in France, and she was looking forward to seeing the many changes that had taken place since then. Her death took me by surprise, for although she was old and frail, she had overcome serious illness many times before and I had begun to take her ability to survive for granted. She would probably have been amused to see me clutching the little wooden box containing her ashes as I sat on the plane to Madrid, fearing to lose them or to be searched at customs, but the idea of a symbolic return to Spain at last would have pleased her. Certainly she would have rejoiced to see so many people with Republican Flags by the river Manzanares, young and old, Spanish veterans and International Brigaders, all gathered together to say a last goodbye to her as the sun was setting. Perhaps her spirit was with us, I may never know, but I do know that I have been irrevocably changed through my friendship with her and that I continue to feel her presence, not just in happy memories but also sometimes prodding at my conscience, as if her vitality remains although her ashes are scattered and gone.

In Cambridge a few weeks afterwards, her family and friends arranged a meeting to celebrate her life. In her later years the tiny but indomitable figure of Frida had become a familiar sight in the town, determinedly making her way on crutches, disdaining the use of a wheelchair whenever possible. But it was not only local friends and fellow campaigners who came to the meeting, they came from far and wide to share their recollections of a memorable woman and to listen to some of her favourite music. The hall was filled but still more people came and congregated in an extra room where they too could listen to the musicians, the choir and the speakers, each chosen to represent an aspect of Frida's life and work. One after the other, people from different walks of life paid tribute to her, not just because of the work she did and the example she set, but because she offered true friendship and whatever help she could to us all, despite her own physical frailty, sharing our troubles and making us laugh.

However, her memoirs give no hint of the profound impact she had on the lives of those around her; nor, apart from the brief final chapter, do they cover the years after the Second World War. As the fragile, yellowing pages we discovered in various drawers of her bookcases attest, they were written when her recollections of the civil war in Spain and her escape from France were still fresh so, unlike many others written later in life, they vividly capture the spirit of the times, without being filtered through a retrospective eye casting a modern perspective on the past. Her attempts to find a publisher for the memoirs shortly after the Second World War failed, in part due to paper shortages, though her small book, *Dawn Escape* had found its way into print. She showed me a surviving copy, detailing her experiences of internment complete with her own illustrations drawn in the camps. Due to increased public interest in the Spanish Civil War thanks to the forthcoming 60th Anniversary Commemorations, we discussed the possibility of finding a publisher for the memoirs. With this end in mind, we eventually managed to gather all the dispersed chapters together and I was given the task of typing them on to computer, together with her handwritten corrections. She intended to dictate further chapters on to tape for me to transcribe but, always busy with broader issues and more urgent causes, or with welcoming friends and visitors, she never found the time. However, she had spent many hours helping me in my research on the involvement of British women with the Spanish Civil War, during which we talked at length about her life. After her death, I helped to sort out the vast but chaotic collection of her papers, and began to realise the true extent and the diversity of her interests. This led me to write an Afterword which was printed and given out at the celebration of her life at the Friends Meeting House in Cambridge. It is included at the end of these memoirs for readers who would like to know more about this remarkable woman, how she sustained her commitment to the ideals in which she believed, what influences contributed to the formation of such a determined character, and why she came to be remembered so fondly by so many people.

Frida in her later years

Chapter 1 – Wartime in Cambridge

O grasses wet with dew, yellow fallen leaves,
Smooth-shadowed waters Milton loved, green banks,
Arched bridges, rooks and rain-leaved willow-trees,
Cambridge my home...

Frances Cornford, *A Glimpse*

When the First World War broke out in August 1914, I was three years old, so I don't recollect much about the peaceful days sometimes called the 'end of an era'; but a few shadowy figures and scenes still haunt me – a wondrous man with a monkey on his shoulder who played a hurdy-gurdy at the front door one day; a little hunchbacked blind woman who sat begging at the corner of our road; and a big white owl which perched on the silver birch tree in the garden and scared me with its mysterious hooting. And I have faint memories of toddling about the big playroom of the house where we were brought up – my brother, three sisters and me – in one of the greenest and most pleasant corners of Cambridge, looking across the river by Newnham Mill to the unspoilt Fen beyond. How fortunate and privileged we were I did not realize till many years later.

The old malt house building facing the mill pond was bought and converted by my grandfather for our parents when they married in 1902, and it was an ideal place for a young family, with lots of space upstairs, and underground passages and cellars (perfect for hide and seek) and the playroom which had once been a storage barn for the malt. With a raised platform at one end this made a natural hall for plays, meetings, gatherings and games of all kinds, and it gave scope for my mother's artistic and organising gifts; she was indefatigably involved in social and fundraising events for good causes whose supporters used the playroom freely. Her hospitality never failed and the house was open to relatives and friends of all descriptions – as is testified by the many volumes of 'Visitor's Books' which anybody staying in the house was expected to sign. As a 'university wife' my mother now and again had to give formal dinner parties, which I suspect were less congenial to her democratic spirit; older daughters were allowed to attend these, but the 'little ones' were segregated in a nursery well out of earshot of grown-ups, which we would have preferred but for the fearsome nurses, 'Chappie' and Jessie Porter – nannies in name but dragons by nature – who kept us under strict control.

I was always getting into trouble with them, and probably *was* a very naughty child. Two occasions which prove this come to my mind, faint but clear: one, when at the age of 3-plus I was taken, dolled up in a white muslin frock printed with little red rosebuds, to dance in a charity garden fête in Madingly Road. Just before the performance began I lost sight of my mother, panicked and began to howl. Chappie took me in hand and brought me home, still bawling, in a horse-drawn cab, to be put to bed without supper in utter disgrace. A second disgrace was when this 'holy terror', as Chappie called me, pushed over the grandfather clock which stood in the entrance hall of our house; this, I'm now sure, was only done to draw attention to myself away from my baby sister Margaret, who I thought was getting more than her share of mother love. The action certainly achieved its objective: the big clock toppled on to the tiled floor with an almighty crash which brought people out from every room in the house, startled and curious. To my surprise, nobody punished me; they probably realised that the three year old didn't know the value of clocks and was just showing off in a rather unusual way.

On the whole I was a happy infant, surrounded and cherished by people I loved and trusted; even the chilly disciplinarians of the nursery could not spoil the comforting warmth of our peacetime home.

Then the War came. For a time, life went on more or less as before. But gradually even we small children came to realise that something was very wrong. In spite of all our parents' care, the happiness and security we knew was clouded perpetually by the fears of the unknown outside, and the hints and rumours of tragedy that filtered through to us.

We (at any rate the 'little ones') were told the minimum and knew nothing about the causes or events of the War, though of course we pretended we did; we played war games, pretending to be Haig or Kitchener or Foch, in the garden, or fought naval actions with tables as warships and the nursery carpet as the North Sea. You could be Jellicoe if my brother was kindly disposed, or Von Tirpitz if he wanted to take you down a peg; the worst disgrace was to be cast as the Kaiser or 'Little Willy', the Crown Prince. We never heard about military setbacks but were always told of Allied successes and of course joined in the general rejoicing on those occasions.

One celebration I remember was the christening of a baby in my grandfather's village, who was born at the time of a victory and impressively named Verdun Goodenough; and I wondered whether the next babies would be blessed with grand names like Gallipoli or Mesopotamia – till someone explained that those suggested disasters and not victories at all.

Our favourite uncle, Maurice Crum, once came to see us when on leave from the Front where he had been under fire; but he never spoke of his experiences there. Instead, being a great humourist, he cracked jokes dating from the Boer War (where he fought in 1899), such as the old chestnut, 'Why does the Kaiser wear galoshes? – To keep De Wett from De-feat.' It seems strange now to have lived through that terrible period so unaware of what was happening – the holocaust in Flanders, the 400,000 deaths at Ypres, the disastrous campaign in the Near East; but those were pre-radio, pre-television days, and the world's disasters did not come into our front room as they do now; the war was much farther away.

In those days of 'localised' war, childhood was surprisingly normal as regards daily life; our middle-class, middle-income family suffered little, though there were minor hardships. Wartime diet was unappetising – parsnips instead of potatoes, strange substitutes for butter and jam. The garden was mostly turned into a chicken run, the lawn dug up to plant vegetables, and the playroom became a temporary barracks for half a platoon of Welsh Guards due to embark for France and in the meantime kipping on the Malting House floor and cooking in a corner of the garden. We children found the operations fascinating and wickedly used to creep up when the Tommies' backs were turned and surreptitiously drop bits of grass into their stewpot.

My mother did not have an easy time with the uninvited guests; she had to wage a private war with squalor, blocked drains and rats as a result of the soldiers' mess; another group of visitors, Belgian refugees, gave her a lot of hard work (which she did not grudge – she even added to her tasks the organising of concerts to raise funds for poor little Belgium in exile) – however they were not with us for long. They were succeeded by a family of displaced Greek Russians who stayed for many months and finally settled in Welwyn, quite anglicised. They were enterprising people, once well off, very choosy about food; my mother spent hours trying to cater for them and for their enormous tabby cat, which they insisted had to have fresh liver every day. She regarded all this as her share of war work, along with looking after the hens and rabbits and vegetables, and in the holidays helping to milk cows and run the electric plant at my grandfather's house at Longworth, where most of the farm hands had been called up.

My father was too old for active service, and being a minister of the Church would anyway not have entered the Army, but he contributed to the war effort by taking on much more than one teacher's work at the University, in the absence of younger staff who were mobilised. He went to France several times to help out the army chaplains, and gave lectures to the troops, showing slides on a 'magic lantern' which included pictures of Joan of Arc. The fact that Joan was no friend of the English did not worry my Dad, who was passionately francophile and always believed in burying hatchets.

Family life went on otherwise fairly normally: Jean and Katharine went to the Perse High School, won prizes and played hockey; Jean, gifted and vivacious, acted in plays, Katharine, lovely as a Boticelli angel, excelled on the piano; they got glowing reports and passed exams which would get you into university (for which both were clearly destined). Brother Ludovick, being exceptionally musical (even as a very small boy he would compose tunes, and could play them on the violin) and having a lovely voice, was packed off in 1917 to St George's choir school at Windsor, where he was bullied by the masters and was always hungry, but had the honour and glory of singing in the Royal Chapel every Sunday to King George and his family – at least that's how it seemed to me from the accounts he gave us in the holidays. (His voice did not break till he was thirteen, so they kept him on, poor boy, up to 1922 when he joyfully left for a happier life at Eton.)

My sister Margaret and I had our war-time education at Mrs Berry's Dame School, ten minutes' walk from home; the only things I can recall about it are the writing lessons, when we wrote our words ending in neat tails or elegant flourishes with scratchy nibs, between 'tram-lines'; and the witch-like but worthy headmistress telling us over and over again that 'there's no such word as *can't* in the English language.' I have never forgotten that useful tip. Goodness knows if we learned anything else useful apart from picking up the three Rs, and some scraps of poetry and songs which still sometimes run through my head; but it was a nice friendly school which has left a warm memory to many Newnham children.

War was a long way off – or so it seemed: nonetheless, one never forgot its distant but menacing presence. At family prayers which my father led every morning – the six of us at one end of the dining-room, the maids at the other – Almighty God was always implored to 'Give peace in our time'; it puzzled me that He allowed the war to go on; as there was 'none other that fighteth for us but only thou, O Lord', why didn't He call it a day and put an end to the fighting? In 1918, Margaret and I would gaze anxiously at the night sky, and when we said our prayers we put in special appeals to God 'not to let the Zeppelins come this way tonight,' and 'to bring Uncle Maury and all our friends safe back from the war.'

No Zeppelins came over Cambridge, and we did not lose any close relatives, but my mother had a brother and cousins at the Front and lived in dread of bad news; and I shall never forget the shock of seeing her in tears over a letter from a friend whose young son had been killed on the Somme. I had never seen a grown-up crying, or thought it was possible – and my mother's tears brought home the tragedy of war to me more sharply than anything else I remember. After that it was almost unbearable to say goodbye to anyone leaving for the Front; and one of the traumatic moments of those days was the departure of the Tommies billeted in our house, who had teased and petted us so good-humouredly (in spite of their grassy soup). Corporal Turney, a curly-haired young Welshman, gave me a goodbye hug, at which I burst into tears, wondering if he would ever come back – which of course he never did.

Other vivid impressions of the war background aroused uneasy childish curiosity: one, the sight of bedraggled grey figures filing across Coe Fen after dredging a muddy stream or toiling at some other dirty work. They were German prisoners, and there was something sub-human about them and their dejected procession which was disturbing even to a six year old.

Another memory is of the wounded English soldiers who were brought by the local Red Cross to a garden party in Grandfather's grounds at Longworth; they wore bright blue hospital clothes, some had an arm missing, or a bandaged head, and were pushed about in wheelchairs, others limped on crutches having lost a foot or leg at the Front. We children were part of a pageant, produced supposedly for their entertainment, and each of us represented one of the Allies. I was Japan, and brandished a red and white flag with the circle and rays of the Rising Sun. It might have been fun to parade about in a scarlet kimono, but the sight of the mutilated spectators in blue spoiled any possible enjoyment that afternoon.

It must have been towards the end of the war – early 1918 – that I heard the Russian Revolution being discussed by the Dragons in the nursery while we ate our tea – bread and margarine and carrot jam (unless it was the equally revolting 'honey-sugar' substitute for syrup). 'That Lenin and Trotsky,' Chappie would say to Caroline, the housekeeper, 'they're no better than beasts!' The word 'Bolshevik' conjured up untold horrors (and I think now that lots of my contemporaries must find it difficult to discard the image of the Revolution implanted by their nannies at that tender age). The famines in East Europe were brought home to me by terrible pictures of children with swollen bellies and stick-like legs, and it didn't help when Chappie used them to blackmail us into swallowing our pet abomination – 'frogspawn' (sago or tapioca pudding) or 'greens': 'just think 'ow lucky you are beside them poor starving Serbians,' or 'Wot wouldn't them Russians give for them nice sprouts!' At least, I thought, the Serbians didn't suffer from 'Chappy-rule', threats of spanking (if you don't eat that sago you'll have a taste of my bunch of bananas on your B-T-M), or being stood in the corner of a dark box room with the door locked for some petty offence.

But these were minor miseries compared to our awareness of the war, which seemed to be going on for ever. At last, though, hopes rose and as my eighth birthday approached I began to add a special plea to God to arrange for the war to end that day. Two days before – 9th November – the Kaiser had abdicated and the German Republic was set up; the air was full of talk of surrender and peace, though we were warned not to be too hopeful. I redoubled my pressure on God and, when the news came through on the 11th at midday that the Armistice had been signed that morning, I felt immensely responsible and as important as if it had been all my own work!

Our French *mademoiselle* (who had replaced Chappie and was supposed to talk French to us at meals) took Margaret and me into the town to see the celebrations. It was announced that there would be two minutes' silence in memory of our heroic dead, at 11 am, and we hurried to get to the centre in time. The signal went just as we were passing Macfisheries in Petty Cury, and we were stuck beside the wet cod and haddock on the stall for the whole two minutes, inhaling the strong smell of the good fresh fish. To this day, every time I pass a fishmonger's I am back in November 1918 outside that shop (long since gone), bursting with frustration and impatience to join in the peace celebrations in the market place. After the silence we ran down the street and were just in time to see the students scrambling up the fountain in the square (now disappeared) and fixing a huge Union Jack on top, while the jubilant crowd shouted and cheered. Then the students went surging along the streets with banners and flags which they planted all over the town; a small gang of patriots turned their attention to the Pacifist bookshop in King's Parade, whose owners were considered to be traitors to King and Country. The windows were smashed and books hurled about, and the shop never recovered.

My mother who was no pacifist, but strong on human rights and an admirer of Bertrand Russell who patronised the bookshop, was indignant at the vandalism. I wondered vaguely, hearing her, why the Cambridge Magazine (as the shop was called) should be so badly treated. What on earth could *books* have to do with war?

However, nothing was going to spoil the joy of the glorious occasion or my personal pride in being eight that day. How marvellous to have peace – no more wounded soldiers, no more Zeppelins, no more parsnips or carrot jam! Everything seemed suddenly to be sorted out – everybody was going to live happily ever after, without war or rations or newspapers. It was a great surprise on the next morning to see, as usual, the top of my father's head peeping above *The Times* at breakfast. 'But Daddy,' I said, 'now there isn't any war how can there be any more news?'

Chapter 2 – A Taste for the Arts

Come, come, come, let us leave the Town
And in some lonely place,
Where Crouds and Noise were never known,
Resolve to spend our days.

Thomas Betterton, *The Fairy Queen*

Strange as it seemed to me, the newspapers that arrived on 12th November continued to come – *The Times* for my father, the weekly *Statesman* for my mother, and occasionally (for she was broad-minded and even considered 'rather a red') the weekly *Herald*. The Great War was over, but little wars were going on – no less bitter or savage for the fact that they were civil or colonial wars. The newspapers had plenty of material with these and the problems of peace treaty making, demobilisation, unemployment, labour troubles, the situation in Central Europe and in Russia, where interventionary armies were fighting the forces of the new Soviet Republic tooth and nail.

I only vaguely recollect hearing of the war of intervention in Russia, but very vividly remember the horrifying pictures in the newspapers of crowds of starving peasants and pot-bellied children, and the hair-raising stories told by émigré aristocrats, cultured and charming, who arrived in England about then and naturally swayed our elderly relatives and their circles to sympathy with the White Russians. But of what it was all about I really had not a clue.

The truth is that back in Cambridge the troubles of the outside world passed us by, along with the political struggles nearer home. The University town might have been an island in the South Seas, so little did social upheavals seem to affect our lives.

When the war ended, the wheels of culture and learning began to turn normally again. Students poured back to the colleges, demobilised dons resumed their courses, festivals of music and drama were planned, the playing fields were reoccupied by cricketers and rugger teams, and the river swarmed with rowing eights.

The University had its own political battles, of course, in which my parents were sometimes involved – the debates on the new English Tripos, and on the Music Board, of which my father was chairman, left him tired out by the strenuous diplomacy required.

There was the great battle of Degrees for Women, which was waged periodically, and painfully. Round after round was won by the obscurantist misogynists in Cambridge; although Oxford had two months before secured caps and gowns and places in the Senate for its women, even titular degrees were refused to the women of Newnham and Girton when the matter was brought up in the Cambridge Senate House in October 1921. My mother was an ardent feminist, and fired her small daughters with her enthusiasm and her fury at the injustice of mankind. We waited as anxiously as she did for the result of the fateful Senate meeting, and when we heard that there was some excitement outside Newnham we ventured out to watch from a distance. A crowd of anti-feminist undergraduates had rushed to the college to demonstrate their delight at the women's defeat, and we saw them trying to get in through the Clough Memorial entrance. These handsome bronze panelled gates were shut and barred, so the flower of Cambridge manhood broke into a yard, took a hand cart as a battering ram and bashed through the elaborate carved panels, smashing and largely destroying them, to shouts of 'Down with women! No votes for girls!' and so on. Miss Clough, the Principal, and Jane Harrison, the distinguished archaeologist (my mother's friend and mentor) stood by 'and saw those young wild beasts break down the beautiful gates,' as Jane wrote later, and they called on them to stop – but ineffectively till the Proctors and the police arrived, and the hooligans scattered. Women were officially admitted to full membership of the Cambridge University only in 1947.

Apart from such incidental excitements, Cambridge was calm, and an ideal place for children to grow up in, with its lovely scenery and buildings, the College Backs, the gardens. What more could any child want than all these, the river to row and punt and swim along, the fields and woods nearby to explore, the fens for nature study in summer and skating in winter, the plays and pictures and museums of all sorts, and music *ad lib*?

Besides all this culture on the side, our lives proceeded in a regular routine. Every Sunday we went to the College Chapel and sat beside my father who took the service. I never got much uplift from this, but felt proud of Daddy and enjoyed studying the stained glass saints and the young men in white surplices, and listening to the organ and to the intoning of the Master, Sir J. J. Thomson (which was irreverently described by someone as 'a cataract of tin pots and pans.') I wondered how such a small person could have such a big voice, and why everyone called him 'the Great Man'.

We usually went for holidays to my grandfather's house in Berkshire, or to Scotland where my scout master uncle ran a camp for small ragamuffins from Stirling and let us help the scouts serve out soup and mince (no knives were allowed the little terrors) and we sailed on the lochs and climbed the nearest hills. But we were always happy to get back to Cambridge.

Although there were many limitations in a university childhood (we were sheltered and protected, and knew nothing of the stern realities of life) our home was a very happy one; I adored my father, who I still believe was one of the world's wisest and best men, and my mother – an angel if ever there was one with such enthusiasm and energy as hers.

I can't remember one moment of tension or hostility between my parents, and the house was peaceful except for the occasional squabble between sisters or between nurses and housemaids. If the turmoil arose from noisy children or too many visitors, my father withdrew to his oast house study, or to his room in Trinity.

He was happy in his vocation or research and writing on Pascal and other religious philosophers, and he enjoyed his teaching and chapel services and innumerable university 'boards', exhausting though they were; while my mother led a very full life, and a happy one (in spite of her regret at having to give up her beloved archaeology), organising a lively household, doing all sorts of good works, helping to run the Cambridgeshire Music Festival, seeing to our education, producing plays and concerts in the various clubs under her wing, and entertaining countless visitors to an open house. I never heard her say no to any request of ours to put up a guest, however unwelcome, or inconvenient the occasion; as a result the house was always teeming with people; bishops, boy scouts, singers, students, foreign musicians, friends, relations or complete strangers.

On one embarrassing occasion an unknown gentleman came into the dining-room as we were sitting down to Sunday dinner, and my mother, assuming he was a friend of one of the family, planted him down among us, pressing him to eat. It was not until the meal was over that we discovered that he was in fact the 'young man' of the cook down the road, and had come to the wrong house, but had not liked to refuse my mother's hospitality. In those days it was possible for such things to happen, as large lunch parties were quite usual and most university families had help in the house.

As a playground we had the fen, just across the road on the other side of the millpond. It was like being in the country: there were still kingfishers flashing down the river, streaks of blue lightning, and many quite rare birds among the reeds and willows of the swampy fen. One winter morning we picked up a heron, frozen to death by the side of a stream. My father had it stuffed and it still stands with great dignity on one leg in a glass case on my mother's staircase.

The only disadvantage of the proximity of the river was that the Cam had in those days a tendency to flood in wet seasons, and would rise and flow across the road and through our front door into the entrance hall. One year the water on the ground floor rose to a foot deep, and stilts came in very useful; we waded about the hall just above the surface of the muddy river, with dead fishes floating around our feet.

Luckily the living quarters of the house were all on the first and second floors, well above the damp ground level, and so was the big playroom. Here we played riotous games and ran wild whenever it was not occupied by one of the many clubs or classes to which it was continually lent out, and to which my mother insisted on sending us as a gesture of courtesy to the borrowers.

Margaret and I attended one class or another almost every day of the week – Bible class on Sunday, country dancing on Monday, Brownies on Tuesday, Dalcroze (the then fashionable Eurhythmics) on Friday; and on other evenings we watched, fascinated, the rehearsals of plays or concerts which went on in the room. Sometimes there were lectures or recitals; I remember lantern lectures (the old magic lantern was one of the great thrills of our unsophisticated pre-cinema youth) and talks by many eminent people. The two that made most impression on me were the lecture on Everest by Mr Wollaston, a member of the 1921 expedition, and one by Dr Schweitzer about his newly started hospital at Lambarene. He was like a specially nice ready made uncle, I thought, as he patted my head and wrote in my autograph album his good wishes to a small English girl, *'pour sa vie et son bonheur'*.[1]

The most exciting thing that ever happened in the playroom was the production of *The Fairy Queen*, Purcell's opera which had been dug out of obscurity by my father's friend Professor Edward Dent, and which was eventually staged by the University Musical Society with Clive Carey as producer. The lovely music (the loveliest in the world, I still think) became familiar and ran in our heads for months. They gave me a tiny part (Titania's Indian boy) which meant only walking on, lying down and going to sleep beside the fairy queen, but which entailed having my face painted black, mixing with real live actors and facing the footlights of a real theatre. What greater thrill could there possibly be for a child of nine?

The Fairy Queen was our first introduction to opera, and for me the beginning of a devouring love of music which dominated my existence for so long that it can't very well be left out of this account. Purcell reigned over our lives for years, but Mozart was a close runner-up, as our musical education was in the hands of my aunt Daisy, who was married to the University Librarian, and had a sort of mystical devotion to Mozart whom she claimed to have 'discovered' for herself long before he became well known among musicians. She celebrated his birthday every 27th January with a party, where we sang and played Mozart, and drank his health in Atholl Brose – a very potent Highland concoction from an old Stewart recipe based on whisky, oatmeal, honey and cream! She was a pianist of extraordinary perception and a unique sense of interpretation, and played Couperin, Rameau, Scarlatti and Purcell harpsichord pieces years before the general public had ever heard of them, and with a rare understanding. She was convinced that her way of playing Bach was the right way, and as confirmation would recount how John Sebastian had paid her a visit one night – 'A big tall man with a curly wig, all dressed in brown.' He had patted her gently on the shoulder, and said kindly, 'Never mind what they say, my dear. You and I know how it should go.'

My aunt gave us all piano lessons, but except for my sister Katharine – who, like herself, was exceptionally gifted – we were not very rewarding pupils, and must have caused her a good deal of suffering. She used to insist that we must all learn music, for if everybody did there would be peace in the world; but even this powerful inducement to practise could not make a pianist out of me, and I was allowed in the end to take up the violin instead, which was more to my taste (though perhaps even harder on the ears of the long-suffering family) and opened up a new world of orchestral and chamber music, with its supreme and inexhaustible delights.

In 1922, our family had an unforgettable experience – a six months' emigration to the South of France, ordered by the family doctor. Sun and complete change of air were essential for my father, who had just undergone a lengthy treatment for TB in Papworth Hospital – the famous institution with its pioneer 'colony' of resettlement for discharge patients, who worked in ships and studios in the village and produced, under the 'Papworth Industries' scheme, furniture and fittings of all kinds while awaiting complete recovery. My poor father had endured the dreary period of open-air treatment with great patience, lying for months in an open hut, forbidden to utter a word. His only solace had been reading the Classics (he went through *The Odyssey* and *The Iliad* from beginning to end), long letters from his friends, particularly from 'Q' (Sir Arthur Quiller-Couch), and my mother's daily visits; she made these on a small motor bicycle called a Vellocette, causing her children much trepidation.

Daddy emerged from hospital almost completely cured, but had to sleep out of doors for months afterwards with an evil-smelling disinfectant mask over his mouth. The convalescence on the Riviera restored him to normal activity, and he went back to a full life in Trinity (giving his lectures at first in a whisper into a microphone) and thereafter became ever more active until he finally retired from work at eighty years of age.

For us children, the half year at Vence was sheer paradise. We lived in a big white villa ('Les Agaves', in honour of the enormous aloes that flanked the front door) which was secured for us by our friends the artists Jacques and Gwen Raverat, who lived next door, and introduced us to the loveliest walks and to the nicest shops and people in the little town.

'Les Agaves' was within five minutes of the main square, the church, and the handsome circular fountain which spouted such delicious drinking water that it was well worth a visit with our pitchers every day. And in ten minutes' walk in the other direction we could be up on one of the mountains.

My younger sister and I were sent to the local Dame school, where we wore black pinafores, soon bespattered with green luminous spots from the purple ink which spluttered from the thin scratch French nibs. We loved the school and made great friends with the other children. The only fly in the ointment was the headmistress, who alternately smothered us with kisses – 'Ah! Ces chères petites Anglaises!'[2] – or threatened us in a high-pitched shriek, 'Aaah! Je te tirerai les oreilles!'[3] In fact she never did pull our ears, but we lived in constant apprehension of the humiliating chastisement.

We spent every possible minute out of doors, in the bright winter and spring sunshine, exploring the countryside and the little towns and villages within twenty miles – the fantastic fortress-like Tourettes, Saint Paul perched on its miniature peak, Gourdon, clinging to sheer rock face, and accessible only by a madly zigzagging road up the edge of a precipice: the dark narrow alleys and slit-windowed houses, and the castellated walls over which rubbish was thrown, regardless of who was sitting down below, all this struck us as very picturesque, and it never occurred to us that these relics of Saracen hygiene and culture really represented an appalling poverty and destitution.

What we liked best of all was roving about the hills that lie behind Vence – the four great lumpy limestone cliffs, known as Les Baous, that rise up out of the plain and are I suppose the first of the foothills of the Alpes Maritimes proper. As soon as school was over for the day we used to snatch our *goûter* (tea-time treat) of bread and chocolate and run out of the town and through the olive groves, shot with the pink of the autumn roses and the scarlet of the big wild anemones (Solomon's lilies of the field), out into the open hillside, rough and stony but unbelievably fragrant with wild thyme and aromatic herbs and small cistus plants whose cream or coral flowers dropped in showers of petals under the hot sun, but were always magically replaced by a thousand others.

We were fascinated by a small grey stone tower high up on one of the Baous which, we found on exploring it, was occupied by a strange group of people who went about half naked, with sandals on their feet and gold bands in their hair, and who proved to be a colony of disciples of Isadora Duncan, the dancer.

Sometimes our expeditions took us so far afield that we came home to find my parents distractedly wondering whether to send out a search party; but we never came to the slightest harm, and although we stopped to talk to every labourer, stone-breaker, wood-cutter and charcoal burner we met on the hills and highways we were never, needless to say, molested in any way by these friendly, decent and terribly hard-working Meridionals.

Visitors used to come out from England to stay at Vence, and we dragged them panting up the hills to our favourite haunts. One new arrival at once outstripped us in our walks – Peter Scott, a small boy then, later a naturalist of world renown, who came with his mother and Commander Hilton Young for a few days to the hotel in the square. Here he had to be given a special room fitted with meat-safe windows to house the collection of creatures which he was taking back to the London Zoo.

He showed them off to us with great pride: there were several scorpions, a tree frog, lizards, and salamanders and innumerable spiders. We helped him to collect a supply of the local variety of trapdoor spider, digging them and specimens of their dwellings out of dry mud banks up one of the mountain paths.

Peter was my idea of the complete boy hero, with his yellow hair and tanned face and his firm intention of being an explorer like his father – not to mention his way of pulling snakes and scorpions out of his pockets to my great delight, but to the horror of most of the company.

We made a lot of friends among the people of Vence, from Monsieur Jabot, who gave me fiddle lessons, and the *curé* who discussed theology with my father, to the butcher Monsieur Rollin, whom my maiden aunt Edith, the most tender hearted of women, did her best to convert to her view that it was a major crime to kill song birds for the table – but alas, the festoons of skylarks and blackbirds and blue tits still hung in his window after several months' campaign.

The nicest people of all were our *femme-de-ménage* Marcelline and her husband, peasants from the hinterland, who invited my sister Margaret and me to spend Easter in their village, Isola Bella.

Isola is right up in the mountains, almost on the Italian border, and is one of the communities over which there was friction between Italy and France just before World War II, owing to its position on the frontier, rather than any civic importance of its own. It is a long way from anywhere, and took hours to reach, so the journey made an indelible impression on me; we were packed like sardines along with swarthy peasants breathing garlic and smoking strong black tobacco, in the very hard carriage of a little train which crept twisting and climbing through the wild and desolate country, more majestic, mountain-ous and remote every mile, till it reached Isola, a tiny town of grey stone and purple slate roofs at the foot of high rocky crags. Marcelline's home, where we lived for a week with her family of brothers, sisters, cousins and in-laws, all talking patois nineteen to the dozen, was in the main street, and we had the fun of seeing the yearly spring clean of the town on Easter Day. This consisted in a sort of purification ceremony, the floodgate of some mountain river being opened so that the water rushed down through the town, swirling away the accumulated muck of the past year – and as almost everything was thrown out of the windows into the street there was plenty.

The house itself was perfectly clean inside, and everyone was quite content with the municipal hygiene arrangements and satisfied with this drastic annual action.

I had another exciting journey that winter, as my maiden aunt who was a gifted artist wanted to go to Florence, and took me as her companion for a few days' sightseeing. It was just before Mussolini's bid for power, and I don't think Aunt Edith realised what a state of near revolution Italy was in, or we probably would not have gone. Owing to the country's acute economic crisis, poverty and hunger were widespread. The Communists were by far the strongest party and they alone had a programme for social reconstruction: but the enormous influence of the Roman Catholic church had been thrown behind the Fascists who were on the verge of seizing power, and Florence was seething with unrest. I remember seeing walls chalked with slogans (I had no idea what or why) and hearing shopkeepers discussing politics and excitedly telling my aunt in broken English how bad things were.

The political situation didn't worry me unduly; I was much too thrilled by the marvels of Renaissance Italy to take any interest in present-day Italian politics. The first sight of the Duomo and the Giotto Campanile was something quite unforgettable; but though the picture galleries and the frescoes and statues inside palaces and churches impressed me, it was the beauty of Florence as a whole, fountains, carved doorways, archways, every corner of almost every street, that stuck in my mind. (And one of the minor worries of the Second World War was whether the Della Robbia babies and the Donatella sculptures would still be in the Piazza when peace came.)

Our six months in Venice came to an end in the summer of 1923, and back in Cambridge my sister and I were sent as day girls to the Perse School to catch up on our neglected studies.

My school career was very far from glorious, and the less said about it the better. During my two years at the Perse I learned shockingly little; this was of course my own fault, as can be seen from the subsequent academic successes of some of my contemporaries there, but the teaching was not calculated to inspire dullards and lazies like me. Our headmistress and most of her assistants were in their last year before retirement, and repeated their well-worn lessons punctuated with 'Is that quite clear, girls?' when nothing could have been more obscure, till I could have cried with boredom.

Any general or useful knowledge that came my way was picked up through reading outside school, and from the many cultural activities in Cambridge – public lectures, film shows, the plays at the Festival Theatre (then at the height of its fame, with Flora Robson among its stars) and of the Marlowe Society; not to mention the concerts to which I sneaked off whenever possible and on any excuse.

I went through a feverish bird-watching stage too, and spent every spare moment (and many hours which should have been devoted to homework) in the fields and copses near our new home at Girton, and on the edge of the town sewage farm which abounded with divers and other water birds – undeterred by the nasty smells and unsalubrious association of that stretch of grey water.

Miss Turner, the famous 'Lone woman watcher of Scolt Head', befriended me and my younger sister and took us to stay in her houseboat on the Broads to see the bitterns and grebes, and to the bird sanctuary at Scolt Head, a desolate spread of sand dunes and mud flats off the east coast, where she would point out birds almost invisible to the naked eye, but which she recognised instantly thanks to her arduous training plus a uncanny instinct or second sight. For quite a long period I was determined to follow in Miss Turner's footsteps and become a professional bird watcher – if not a famous violinist (my dearest but most improbable dream).

Best of all, of course, would be to combine the two, I thought, and entered my 'teens' cheerfully, unaffected by the family's discouraging comments on my shocking school reports, and fortified by a clear vision of a glorious career as a super musico-ornithologist.

Chapter 3 – Teenager in the Twenties

Home is where one starts from. As we grow older
The world becomes stranger, the pattern more complicated
Of dead and living.

T. S. Eliot, *East Coker* in *Four Quartets*.

These grandiose projects were nipped in the bud, as it happened, because in the autumn of 1925 I was ordered to bed for several months and stayed there for nearly a year with a cardiac condition which could only be cured by complete and prolonged rest.

My ornitholigico-musical hopes, not to mention my general academic prospects, dwindled and all but disappeared. Still, it was a fine opportunity for reading and for listening to music, and I spent the long weeks not unhappily, thanks to the supply of records and literature provided by my angelic aunt who looked after me at our grandfather's house in a remote corner of Berkshire.

Grandfather Crum had retired years earlier from the calico printing business to this big manor and farm in a tiny village, and it was there that we spent all our holidays – rambling in the fields, helping with the hay, swimming in the stripling Thames – along with his other grandchildren. He was a grand old Liberal with a tremendous social conscience, and he kept up his good works and his interest in public affairs till he died, aged nearly ninety, in late 1926. I remember his agitation when faced with the choice of candidates in the 1924 election: a Liberal whom he disliked and mistrusted personally, or a Tory friend and neighbour. An individualist if ever there was one, he plumped in the end for the 'good man with a bad policy', groaning, as he pulled his patriarchal white beard, at having helped to put in a Protectionist 'after voting for Free Trade all my life!'

He was extremely tender hearted and generous, and constantly assailed by appeals from all sorts of charities; and would embarrass everybody by refusing to eat his dinner after hearing some case of hardship: 'How can I sit here guzzling while so and so's starving!' till my aunt persuaded him that to make himself ill would do nobody any good.

He was deeply distressed by the industrial and social troubles that darkened the months I was staying at the house; and although it bored me dreadfully, I read *The Times* every day so as to be able to talk to him about something serious and grown-up when he visited my bedside. And together we shook our heads over the sad state of Britain's affairs.

It was obvious even to a callow ignorant teenager that there was a great deal of misery and unrest, particularly in the mining areas. Grandfather explained that the war had caused economic disruption, and that unemployment and poverty were inevitable; he thought the government could put everything right, 'given time.'

'Given time' – but the problems were desperately urgent, the miners were not prepared to wait indefinitely, they were demanding immediate improvements and reorganisation of the pits, if not the nationalisation they had long been promised; instead they were offered economy measures in the form of longer hours, wage cuts or the sack.

During April things came to a head. We read of negotiations between the government and the miners' leaders, which dragged on for weeks and ended in deadlock. The Trades Union Council, representing the whole Labour movement of the country had declared it would call a general strike if the miners were not given satisfaction; and for several anxious days at the end of April the country waited in acute suspense, hoping against hope for a settlement.

I remember the mounting tension of those days, as we listened to the radio news reports of cabinet consultations, of labour conferences, of preparations for a possible show-down. Ministers came and went to emergency meetings, Trade Union leaders scurried to and fro between Downing Street and Transport House, trying desperately to find a compromise.

The little radio was the centre of interest at the manor. Like most wireless sets of that date it was a primitive crystal set, given to much crackling and wailing, but we were not fussy, and friends and relatives clustered round at news time, to hear the latest developments, each listener crowned with a pair of earphones which framed faces drawn in lines of anxious expectation. The personalities in the drama aroused strong feelings: Baldwin was much admired for his firmness, A. J. Cook the miners' leader and his misguided followers reviled, and the TUC leaders applauded for their attempts to get peace at almost any price. Mr Clynes, with his mixed metaphor, 'we will leave no step unturned,' was hailed as a model of common sense and good will, unusual in a working man, and Mr Thomas's remark that 'I never begged and pleaded like I begged and pleaded all day today' aroused universal sympathy. But for all the begging and pleading it seemed clear, on 2nd May, that neither the miners nor the Government would give way. And on 3rd May we learned that the strike was on. By midday all the workers in the most vital services had come out: railwaymen, transport workers, dockers, printers, and of course the miners, 100 per cent.

'The country will be paralysed,' somebody said, sending a chill down my spine. Comments at Longworth Manor varied from my aunt's lament: 'Everybody sympathises with the poor miners – but why are they so impatient?' – to the angry indignation of an ex-army cousin: 'Strike, indeed? What would have happened if the men at the front had gone on strike?! A spot of army discipline, that's what they need.' To this cousin it was excellent news that the government a day or two later, had called out the troops to break the strike. Army and navy were mobilised, and great numbers of armoured cars appeared at 'trouble spots' to protect the soldiers and deal with the pickets. A special constabulary was formed from 'reliable' civilians, who were given emergency powers and orders to arrest individuals engaged in agitation such as distributing leaflets or indulging in inflammatory remarks. (One youth received three months' hard labour for calling out 'Don't shoot the workers!')

Appeals were made to the patriotism of middle-class people, who volunteered in their thousands to unload ships, drive trains and buses and to man newspaper offices and presses. We heard stirring stories of the exploits of Cambridge students, some of them my father's pupils, who went off to Hull or Liverpool, cheerfully abandoning their studies to become dockers and save their country in her hour of need. They thoroughly enjoyed themselves, particularly those in charge of express trains, whose boyhood dreams of driving a real engine came true for one blissful week, and the amateur bus drivers who altered their routes so as to pick up or deposit pretty girls on their doorsteps.

Individual car drivers were asked to give lifts, and my twenty-year old girl cousins sallied forth in their little cars and taxied people to work, much to my admiration and envy. What wouldn't I have given to emulate them in their contribution to the national salvation. They would rather have liked the 'emergency' to continue indefinitely. The strikers on their side were prepared to see it through to the bitter end; their organisation and morale were very good and any sort of surrender was out of the question.

It was a great surprise to both sides to learn on 8th May that the TUC leaders were already negotiating with Baldwin again; it seemed that they at any rate were anxious to bring the strike to an end as soon as possible. On 11th May, it was announced that the General Council had accepted a new Memorandum (a face-saving document on much the same lines as the original Samuel proposals) and though it seemed obvious that this would not satisfy the miners, on 12th May, we heard that 'the general strike is to be terminated forthwith, so that negotiations may proceed.'

At first, nobody believed it: the strike was at its height, and apparently completely solid. But it turned out to be true, to the astonishment and disgust of the workers, who had made great sacrifices in the belief that victory would be theirs if only they held out long enough. To them it seemed that all their effort had earned them nothing but a bad let-down by some of their leaders.

The end of the strike was greeted with a sigh of relief by the government's supporters. The household at Longworth breathed again. The lower classes had been put in their place. Thank heaven for Mr Baldwin and Mr Thomas! I echoed the general satisfaction in a three act play which I composed (in verse) on the subject of the General Strike, with the Prime Minister as hero, and Messrs Cook and Saklatvala (the Communist MP) as the double-dyed villains.

My secret doubts as to the rights and wrongs of the struggle emerged in one or two lines where Mr Thomas bemoaned his difficult position, and Cook voiced the miners' case. But these waverings were suppressed in favour of Baldwin's stand for the public weal in the face of anarchy and red revolution. The play ended in a paean of praise for the Prime Minister uttered by a chorus of cabinet ministers headed by Lord Birkenhead, and the rout of the trouble makers. This disreputable piece of doggerel delighted my conservative relatives, and it somehow found its way to the House of Commons, where it earned high praise from a Liberal Member ('remarkable for a fifteen year old'); when I found a tattered copy, years later, I blushed to re-read it, but there it was: those sentiments reflected not only my ignorance but that of the kind people who surrounded me. It never struck us for a moment that perhaps the workers were not entirely in the wrong, but had in fact been fighting for a principle and the right to live a decent life.

Then, as now, in most middle-class eyes there could be no two ways about it; the striker can never – well, hardly ever – possibly be right!

'Lay your doubts and fears aside, and for joy alone provide,' Jove tells Semele, in Handel's opera, staged by the University Musical Society just at that time. This struck me as very sound advice, though I certainly needed no encouragement to join in whatever was going on.

The Cambridge generation of 1927 reflected the mood of the youth of the country, which had pushed away memories of the war of ten years before, and was determined to get the most out of life. The frivolous found escape in jazz – the Black Bottom and Charleston were all the rage – and in musical comedy; the more earnest indulged in the folk dance revival, and in the cinema and experimental theatre. There was much dancing, a great deal of sport, amateur dramatics both high and low brow.

Those were the days of Gershwin, of *Porgy and Bess*, of *Tea for Two*; the heyday of Suzanne Denglen and Helen Wills, Jack

Dempsey, Jack Hobbs; of Marlene Dietrich, Emil Jannings, Rudolph Valentino, and a spate of great comedians – the Marx Brothers, Harold Lloyd, Eddie Cantor, Buster Keaton, and of course, Charlie Chaplin. Galsworthy, Somerset Maugham; P. G. Wodehouse wrote, in serious or ironic or humorous vein, just what the common reader wanted; and Virginia Woolf, E. M. Forster and T. S. Eliot reflected the intellectual's attitude: one of escape from basic social questions, unconcerned with politics, occupied with exploration of personal individual problems.

Of course there were the pessimists and the agitators: Robert Graves and Siegfried Sassoon writing on war, Shaw sharpening his pen on social injustice, D. H. Lawrence crying out against conformism and preaching revolt against bourgeois morality. But on the whole, art and literature sought to re-establish a standard of values that were not different, not disturbing, to return if possible to the happy pre-war days where all (we liked to imagine) was well with the world.

Chapter 4 – Time on the Wing

Let us drink and sport to-day,
Ours is not to-morrow.
Love with youth flies swift away,
Age is nought but Sorrow.
Dance and sing,
Time's on the Wing.
Life never knows the Return of Spring.

John Gay, *The Beggar's Opera*

In September 1928, Katharine and I set off for Frankfurt – a very different Frankfurt from today, before the bombings of 1942, an attractive city full of picturesque houses, including Goethe's home (which he described in his memoirs) and ancient monuments; the *sehenswürdigkeiten* (sights) included the handsome Gothic cathedral, a pretty old quarter, the Romerberg, with its market full of lights and music and toys and coloured cakes at Christmas, a Jewish cemetery famous throughout Europe, and a fine memorial to Heine.

Frankfurt was still suffering from the economic and social disruption of the Great War and its population was rent by political quarrels. It was typical of post-war Germany which was in acute crisis, deprived of many of its richest areas – the Saar in the hands of the French, East Prussia cut off by the Polish Corridor and seething with resentment against the Versailles Treaty; poverty and unemployment were rife, and although the Weimar Republic governments had restored much in the way of education, social services and culture, there was deep discontent, which both the extreme left and right exploited. One didn't have to be an economist to see the distress below the surface, the hungry shabby people in the poorer streets, the scores of shops announcing closing down sales ('*Ausverkauf*' was almost the first word I learned from seeing it in so many windows). The students whom we met were often nearly penniless; many were sympathetic to the Communists if they had not joined the National Socialists out of sheer disgust and hopelessness – for the latter offered an outlet for their frustration and a scapegoat in the shape of Germany's enemies – Reds and Jews.

Katharine and I stayed in a respectable middle-class home which had not been too badly hit by the economic blizzard; we, and a hired upright piano, squeezed into a room crowded with heavy mahogany furniture, aspidistras and ornaments of sentimental value. One knick knack which seemed to me the incarnation of *kitsch* was a pair of tiny boots, formerly belonging to Heini, our landlady's son, which, complete with every crease, wrinkle and bootlace, had been cast in bronze for use as ashtrays. As we were non-smokers, this did not even serve a useful purpose.

Whatever her taste in internal decoration, our old lady was kindness itself and she mothered us unmercifully, inspected all our visitors, and stuffed us with good wholesome food – frankfurters of course, but *Nudeln* and *Sauerkraut* and *Wurst* unlimited. She talked no English, so our German improved rapidly from zero to passable, and she detailed her son to take us round the town and show us the sights. Heini was a kind, pasty-faced, bald, stodgy law student who had the statistics of the local building projects, drainage electrification and all at his fingertips, and reeled them off as he pointed out the new *Siedlungen* housing estate on the outskirts of the city. He was justifiably proud of this municipal enterprise; the buildings were most impressive, towering up in their blocks of concrete and glass and steel.

'They are all-electric too,' said Heini, adding as an after-thought, 'It is only a pity the workers can't afford to use the electricity.' This was a typical example of Weimar Republic window-dressing; it also applied to cultural matters like the Opera and municipal theatres which staged lavish productions with expensive decors and highly paid conductors while the musicians in the orchestra were semi-starving, and many under-waged actors would have gone hungry if they had not taken jobs sweeping the streets or the like, to keep the wolf from the door.

Workers' flats and welfare schemes were an inadequate

41

palliative, and the growing poverty and unemployment had given rise to strong political passions. The Nazis were not yet much in evidence, but the Brownshirts were waiting in the wings, and there were occasional clashes between them and the Communists, and also between the latter and the Social Democrats who each had remedial programmes for the crisis but were unwilling to co-operate in a common cause against the Right. Demonstrations often took place in the Hauptwache (the big square near our lodgings) and were broken up by the police.

These sharpened my vague interest in politics, and it was a great thrill to meet some real live Communists at a Faschings ball during Carnival week. They were, unlike what Heini and his conservative Catholic mother had led us to believe, cultured, intelligent people, young actors on tour with an avant-garde theatre group inspired by the pioneer producer, Piscator. They tried to indoctrinate us, but we were not ready for the treatment. Though I fell passionately in love (or imagined I did) with one Dietrich, he evidently did not think me worth cultivating for I never saw him again; but I often wondered what became of him when the Nazis came to power.

National Socialism at that time showed few signs of becoming a serious factor in German life, and in Frankfurt the university, schools, and Konservatorium were largely staffed by distinguished Jewish teachers. I had lessons with the brilliant violinist, Adolf Rebner, who later fled to London, and we played in the Jazz class (which was of course abolished when jazz came to be considered un-German), and sang in the choir conducted by Hermann Schmeidel, a lively Viennese Jew. Many of our friends outside the college were non-Aryan, and Paul Hirsch, a prominent banker and musicologist friend of Professor Dent, invited us to his library to look at first editions of Beethoven and Brahms; we wandered round the treasures overawed, little thinking that a few years later they would have to be removed to Cambridge for safety from the 'Aryan' vandals.

My last impression of pre-Nazi Germany was a walking tour through the Schwabische Alb (the beautiful district south of Stuttgart) with Luise, a German friend of left-wing tendencies and an exceptionally fine sense of humour. For a week we footed it over the hills and dales of this delightful stretch of country, staying at some of the *Jugenherbergen* hostels, newly built by the Weimar government for the open-air minded, clean-limbed post-war youth. The *Wandervogel* movement was in full swing, and we felt very friendly towards the bare-legged, fair-haired girls and boys we met hiking through the woods that lovely Whitsuntide of 1930.

I went back to England soon afterwards filled with a great feeling of international goodwill, a smattering of German and an improved bow-arm, plus a grounding in the elements of music. Obviously I would never shine, or even twinkle, as a violinist. As Bernard Shaw remarked, 'Those who can, do; those who can't, teach.' I was quite happy to be a teacher, if by accepting that fate I could go on studying for a while, reach a certain standard, and hear all the music available. My parents wisely and kindly agreed to my entering the Royal College of Music in London for a two years' course in the autumn of 1931.

The privilege of becoming a student of the RCM meant giving up many outside interests: music demanded one's whole time and attention. My budding interest in politics went into cold storage (to use a clumsy metaphor) and most of the crucial events of 1930-32 passed me by, though letters from Jean, travelling on a Commonwealth Fellowship in the United States, revealed the extent of the economic crisis there which was already hitting Britain, and Katharine (who went back to Frankfurt and Hoehn for another eighteen months) described the mounting unrest in Germany, and occasionally newsreels from Russia gave glimpses of the massive changes in the countryside, peasants 'dizzy with success' as Stalin sternly said, kulak expropriation, vast areas collectivised; the Japanese and Italian governments were flouting international treaties while the League of Nations piously disapproved but took no action – and the average Briton couldn't or wouldn't see the threat of fascism looming ahead.

I was all too average at the time, and concerned mainly and immediately with getting through the course at College; time enough to bother about world affairs later on. For the next two years, life was a hard slog of study – the simplest exercises in counterpart and harmony took me hours, scales and arpeggios half the day. My violin teacher, Maurice Sons, a tiny fragile old Frenchman, though becoming dim-eyed and a little deaf, was an exacting master. His hand shook and his voice quavered as he exclaimed, 'Ve must 'ave no vibrato': but he was very firm in other respects and insisted on three hours' practice daily.

Frida as a music student

I suffered a good deal from his conservative approach, but found great compensation in the chamber music classes led by Ivor James, and occasionally the brilliant Isolde Menges, and in orchestra rehearsals where I was lucky enough to be put at the back of the first fiddles, and even to be conducted once or twice by Sir Thomas Beecham. It was a quite terrifying experience to have his eagle eye on you; 'I galvanise my players' he once said, and indeed his dynamism sent an electric current through even the College amateurs. Sometimes Sir Hugh Allen, our Principal, took over the baton, and was much kinder, not so exciting, but sympathetic to young players and with an ever ready wit: when we presented him with a box of cigars on his birthday he made a delightful speech thanking us, but regretting that his efforts on our behalf would be going up in smoke.

There were plenty of 'perks' for students, the best value being tickets, free or at absurdly low prices, for concerts and opera; I remember sitting through the first act of *Tristan* on a painfully hard seat in the Gods, but slipping into the Stalls for the rest of the evening – not being a Wagner addict it's unlikely I'd have lasted out otherwise; with *Otello* and *Don Giovanni* I did not mind how hard or how long the session, and to hear Chaliapine in Boris Godunov I would willingly have sat up all night.

After taking the diploma exam I should have left College, but somehow managed to stay on for the spring and summer term of 1933, combining musical life in London and Cambridge by commuting, and earning a pittance by taking a violin evening class in Camberwell. The smell of the fried fish and jellied eel shops is what I mainly remember of those journeys into a very poor part of Camberwell, along with the difficulty of getting the undernourished children to tackle the techniques of fiddling. I loved them and wanted to help but the problems – lack of musical background, decent instruments, and physical fitness – seemed insuperable and in the end put me off teaching beginners for many years.

Frustration in Camberwell was compensated by a feeling of fulfilment in Cambridge, where there was any amount of music for an amateur violinist; following Purcell's *King Arthur*, came another production of *The Fairy Queen*, Handel's *Semele*, and a staged performance of Honegger's *King David* which the composer came from Paris to conduct. My father, as President of the Musical Society CUMS, had been asked to put him up, and I remember poor Honegger arriving in a very sorry state after a bumpy air journey; he was too sick to conduct *King David* but recovered his vitality enough to supervise the production. I did not much care for the music but remember him, with his curly black hair, twinkling dark eyes and warm smile, as one of our nicest guests: we were lucky in having visitors such as Honegger and other musicians to stay. One who because a treasured friend was Zoltan Kodaly, who came from Budapest with his wife, Emma, to conduct the *Psalmus Hungaricus* in 1927 and returned several times; and Alban Berg, invited for the International Contemporary Composers' Jury which Professor Dent presided over in the winter of 1933. Berg was extremely handsome, and somewhat awe-inspiring, like a benevolent eagle. I learned later, to my horror, from the letters to his wife published some time in the 1960s, that he suffered dreadfully from our cold draughty house. Since my father's treatment in Papworth we were fresh air fiends, and poor Berg found the small gas fire in his room most inadequate, after continental central heating. But he seemed to have liked the view over open fields, and was impressed by my father ('the Reverend') and by my mother's overflowing kindness. All in all he did not care for wintry Cambridge, not even for the dinners in Trinity Great Hall to which Dent took him. My parents invited him to come back for the summer music festival, when the weather would be more clement, but he never returned, and died – much too young – in 1935.

Professor Dent sent us another friend for that festival – a very solid silent Swiss, Werner Reinhart; he turned out to be one of three wealthy brothers who had made a fortune in oriental spices and were internationally known patrons of the arts. Werner, who had created a famous music centre in his home town, Winterthur, invited the whole of the Trinity Musical Society to perform in his grand concert hall in September, and Margaret and I, who played in the college orchestra, joined the party and, after the concert, spent an idyllic week in Reinhart's *Château de Muzot* in the Rhône valley. My dear friend Sylvia Spencer, a gifted oboist, came with us, and James Robertson and Mervyn Horder, and it was perhaps the best of many good holidays of my student days; we walked in wonderful Alpine country around Muzot, made music, laughed and talked in the rough comfort of the tiny castle where the poet Rilke had once stayed as a guest of the millionaire, Reinhart. I had slight twinges of conscience about our host; nobody, I thought, ought really to be so rich! But if he was so generous – to the Arts and to students? I learned many years later that he had given refuge to anti-fascists such as the conductor, Scherchen, and always supported worthy causes.

The years 1929 to 1933 are to me now a haze of endless

music making – on top of study, lessons and concerts, summer schools where we played quartets all day, competition festivals (organised by my mother who roped one in to conduct a girls' choir), university orchestra practices conducted by Dr Rootham (known as Roothoven) and once – unforgettably – by Vaughan Williams, a towering figure with an almost unfollowable beat; there were camps with indefatigable enthusiasts, who lived in tents and played through operas and symphonies in a barn from early morning till late at night; and madrigal parties in a converted windmill on the Norfolk coast, as guests of Professor Frank Cornford, who joined us in our attempts at chamber music. A most distinguished Professor of Greek philosophy, Frank had taken up the viola in middle age so as to play with his children (our contemporaries, John, Christopher and Helena), but they had dropped music in favour of politics, painting and ballet dancing respectively; he welcomed us to his mill, took us for walks along the beautiful wild shore, pointing out plants and birds and recounting local history and folklore – a marvellous companion, modest, warm and accessible for all his great learning.

Then there were tours – always making music – in Britain and abroad; apart from the Swiss trip, an expedition in the cause of Anglo-German friendship to Frankfurt an der Oder in 1931, organised by Rolf Gardiner, a famous Cambridge aesthete, disciple of D. H. Lawrence, and great believer in *Wandervogel* ideals.

I was still a confirmed germanophile, and delighted to go on this mission. We sailed from Harwich and were met at Hamburg by Rolf, a picturesque figure in *Wandervogel* costume (velvet shorts and bright blue shirt), golden hair flying and arms full of daffodils, who conducted us through Berlin to the Frankfurt Musikheim; this cultural centre, housed in the latest Weimar-style building with a fine concert hall, was our base for ten days' music, much more seriously undertaken than we English amateurs expected: we worked at madrigals, motets, modern choral works, under the meticulous direction of Georg Goetsch, till our voices gave out; the viol consorts and recorder groups were equally hard driven. For relaxation we were given marionette theatre, and for exercise folk dancing led by Rolf Gardiner.

The musical side of this visit was very interesting and worthwhile. I felt much more doubtful about the ideological background. Rolf and Georg were dedicated to building Anglo-German friendship, and though not openly anti-communist, it was clear that socialism was anathema to them. I could not accept the theories they propounded, which seemed suspiciously like those of the young National Socialists I had met in 1928, nor the expressions 'flaminess' and 'feeling with the blood' nor the semi-religious symbolism of dancing by firelight and such like ritual. It seemed an excellent idea for people of different nations to meet and make music, but why were Rolf's goodwill tours not extended to include non-Teutonic countries – France, Italy and even Russia? But when I suggested this to one of the German singers, (Walter, a handsome blonde Aryan) it was received with shocked silence – that was not the idea at all.

However, the Musikheim fortnight was great fun, if one did not take too seriously the dancing in circles and processions, and musically profitable; and I made friends with several gifted musicians who had come for the music and not for the ideology. One of them was called Karl Marx, a charming small dark Bavarian, of no political affiliation, who must have been most unfairly embarrassed later on by his unfortunate name.

The next year, 1932, some of the singers paid a return visit to England for a tour of Yorkshire towns. I joined them for a week's rehearsal at Ormesby Hall, a big beautiful mansion near Middlesborough, where our hosts, a retired Indian Army major, Jim Pennyman and his artistic wife Ruth, entertained us with most lavish hospitality. They were old friends of Rolf's though not really in sympathy with his ideas, and I remember the major muttering disparaging remarks about 'pasty-faced German wenches', and the dignified butler pouring wine with a rather disapproving face into the foreigners' glasses, while the 18th century ancestors looked down on us with po-faced tolerance.

The Hall was turned into a sort of *Collegium Musicum* and the garden a practice ground for folk dances such as Sellengers Round on the lawn and Helston Furry down the paths. When

Rolf and Georg considered that a high enough standard had been reached we set out to sing in cathedrals and churches of the region, such as Guisborough, Ripon, and Selby, and to dance (clad in yellow and white) through the streets and round the squares of the grimy northern towns.

It certainly provided some entertainment for the population, and I for one thoroughly enjoyed the tour, especially when the local Sword Dance group joined us, and when we stayed in villagers' homes, but whether it succeeded in endearing the Germans to the British populace is doubtful. Whatever results Rolf hoped to achieve were, I fear, largely annulled by events in Germany a few months later.

Chapter 5 – Darkness over Germany

The sky is darkening like a stain,
Something is going to fall like rain
And it won't be flowers.

W.H. Auden and Christopher Isherwood, *The Dog Beneath the Skin*

The German singers did not come to England after the summer of 1932. Rolf organised a tour round the Baltic in 1933 with a band of faithful followers, but I felt I had had enough of this kind of spiritual uplift. It was becoming clear, too, that Anglo-German friendship was not a simple issue; the Germany of Bach and Buxtehude, even of Weimar and the original Musikheim, was one thing – but the *Deutschland* that was starting to take over at the beginning of 1933 was something very different. Even I, naïve as I was, could grasp that strange and sinister things were happening there with official sanction, and that one should think twice before getting involved in any activity blessed by the right-wing Von Papen government, however purely *kulturel* it might appear to be.

Goetsch and his followers had never talked politics during their stay in England; but another visitor from Berlin, in the autumn of 1932, was ready to discuss anything and everything to do with his country and proved a mine of information. This was Wolfgang Stresemann, the son of Bruning's one time Foreign Minister, introduced to us by Professor Dent who thought highly of him as a musician. Wolfgang stayed with us for several weeks, and I liked him very much though he was not the gayest of guests; he was a diabetic, tall, deathly pale and painfully thin, and suffered from extreme pessimism about the fate of Germany and his own future. He sat at the piano playing Beethoven for hour after hour with the tips of his long white fingers, then flopped into an armchair to talk endlessly about the crisis of the Weimar Republic. Now under Bruning's Christian Democrat government things had been going from bad to worse;

unemployment had risen from six million in 1930 to a fantastic nine million in 1932. Stresemann senior had died earlier that year, an unhappy, thwarted man; Bruning had been deposed by Von Papen who was conducting affairs in a dictatorial manner, unsuccessfully attempting to hold the balance between Communists and National Socialists.

Wolfgang was thoroughly gloomy about the prospects for democracy, and was convinced that success for the Nazi Party would mean disaster: 'Ze beeg Beesness wiz ze Arms makers would like it to vin' he said, 'but zis means fascismus and Krieg if it 'appen.' His alarm about the rising militarism and growing anti-Semitism in his country, along with the threat to progress and culture, gave me a fairly good idea of the situation there, and when I read of the Reichstag fire in December it was fairly obvious that there was something fishy about the way it was so promptly blamed on the Communists, and that the 'red coup' was being made a pretext for suppressing the Left and installing the Nazis in government. Hitler was almost immediately appointed Reich Chancellor by Hindenburg, with virtually unlimited powers 'to restore law and order,' and the assurance, for what it was worth, that elections would follow later.

I was politically very innocent, but keenly interested in Germany, and followed the rise of the Nazis, and their gradual murder of democracy, in the press. It all read like a horror comic – the Reichstag trial with its faked evidence and sentences, followed by the wholesale elimination of trade unionists, Communists, Jews and even liberals from German life by pogroms, concentration camps and exile.

My sister Katharine, who went back to Frankfurt in the summer of 1933 to study again with Alfred Hoehn, had a front seat at the autumn election campaign which finally established Hitler; she wrote to us describing how our middle-class friends had been 'got at' by the Nazis, who blamed all Germany's troubles on Jews, Marxists and Freemasons, and appealed to patriots to claim back the Saar, Danzig and the Rhineland so ruthlessly torn from the motherland. Owing to the general frustration and despair, this propaganda succeeded widely, partly owing to the theatrical staging of Nazi activities; Katharine saw the sinister side: 'Very few Jews about, but a lot of young Brownshirts swaggering through the streets; the *Hakenkreuz* (Swastika) very prominent and red white black flags everywhere. Familiar shops have gone, and the fine memorial has been removed; remaining shops display big photos of Hitler, medals, emblems and Nazi Youth knives inscribed *Blut und Sturm (Blood and Storm)*.'

There were no end of spectacular demonstrations: 'A parade of school-teachers and pupils today, in preparation for a grand *Fest* (celebration) on Saturday; today also a *Fest* for the anniversary of *Türkenbefreiung*[4] *(*the siege of Vienna!) A week later a *Kundgebung* (rally) in the Opera House, in honour of some Italian minister; Katharine reports 'an immense crowd, estimated at 75,000, there, the SA (Storm Troopers) in the centre'; a band played patriotic songs, rockets were fired – red, white and green in the Italians' honour, along with floodlighting of the *Opernhaus*. 'The speakers appeared on the roof to cries of "*Heil*", the speeches, more Bravos, Heils, Deutschland uber Alles, Horst-Wessel Lied and Giovinezza. The crowd dispersed after a cannon shot, the troops marching off with flags and bands and torches.'

Two days later, 'an immense procession of all the Frankfurt children (except the Jews) as a protest against the Versailles Treaty... all kinds of fancy dress. Each group carried some placard saying '*Wahrheit ist wahr'*, '*Deutsch ist die Saar!*'[5] or allusions to Danzig, Silesia and so on... the effect was immensely exciting for the children.' (The Nazis certainly set out to 'catch 'em young'.) A few days later there was a *Volksfest–Sturm-Abteilung* with choirs, patriotic solos, the SA brass band and long speeches. 'My neighbours at the concert were half-enthusiastic, half-mocking; they boomed out the songs but someone whispered to me that they were sick to death of everlasting festivities.' No wonder – while the bands were playing, people were having to tighten their belts, as Katharine saw and informed us.

'Appeals for *Winterhilfe* (winter relief fund) are made in the Opera House every night; door-to-door collections are continuous and are made at all public gatherings... All Germany is eating *Arische* (Aryan) stew for lunch – value not to exceed 50 *pfennig* per head. A collection is made afterwards of the amount which would have been spent on an ordinary meal, and this is given to the poor.' Hitler's claims to have solved unemployment were fraudulent, according to well-informed friends: 'The unemployed are given temporary occupation patrolling the streets, doing physical jerks, marches, espionage, Jew-baiting etc, and filling vacancies caused by mass expulsions of Jews and left-wingers from any public office whatever.' And of course most women got the sack surrendering their jobs to men while they returned to *'Kuche and Kinder'* ('Kitchen and Children') to raise more children for the Führer's future cannon fodder.

The anti-feminist laws passed by Hitler, when he became dictator in late 1933 particularly enraged our friend Luise, with whom I had hiked so happily in 1929; she had completed a four years' social science course and now found no openings. Since she had married her cause for complaint was twofold: Jochen, her husband, a law student, had to go for three weeks' physical training before his final exam and was forced to join the Storm Troopers in order to get a government job. There was no way out, no form of protest allowed, and no way of saving the persecuted; good people like Alfred Hoehn risked dire penalties by organising private concerts and lessons for friends who had lost their jobs – dozens of them: almost all the best teachers of the Konservatorium had been sacked, and a high proportion of university professors – for the crime of being non-Aryan – and this was only the beginning.

Katharine's eyes (and through her, ours) were opened through visits to an old friend, Dr Eichwald, living in a village near Frankfurt; she wrote with indignation that 'because he is Jewish with an English wife they have suffered many insults in the village. At a meeting, people get up and refuse to sit at the same table with a Jew... the worst sufferer is Dick, the eldest son, a medical student... Many Jewish students gave up at once. Those who persevered were given red tickets (other students grey) and made to sit apart and not in the front row.' The climax came when, after a lecture, a meeting was announced. 'As the Jews hesitated whether to go or stay, someone called out loudly, *"Nichtaryer mussen den Saal lassen."*[6] They tried to leave at the back – door barred by a student – and had to turn and walk through the room amid stamping and booing (this had been pre-arranged) – friends of the victims being unable to do anything. Hope of employment is practically nil – only Jewish hospitals would be open to them. Jewish doctors may not even be appointed as assistants to Aryans...'

We read Katharine's letters with a mixture of horror and incredulity. But many far worse stories than hers soon reached us and it became clear that Hitler was encouraging all the worst elements of the nation to share in the assault against culture and science: all writers of liberal, left or pacifist tendencies (Jewish or not) were refugees, in jail or living in constant fear; musicians, poets, scientists, communist and Trade Unionist workers were arrested by their thousands, beaten, tortured and thrown into concentration camps surrounded by electrified barbed wire. Our friends' stories of atrocities were substantiated by the official reports of the Committee for the Victims of Fascism which was formed in late 1933 to help them.

The thought of what was happening in the Germany which I had loved and which now seemed to have gone mad, kept me awake at nights. In the small hours Hitler's lunacy threatened to engulf the world in war. (*Mein Kampf* was proof of his intentions, and he obviously had the backing not only of big business and the Arms Kings, but of great numbers of the German people). But in broad daylight one's fears were pooh-poohed by friends and relations, sensible decent people who took the line that Germany was putting her house in order, dealing with anarchists and extremists, and if a few intellectuals suffered in the process they had only themselves to blame for condoning pro-Soviet activity: Uncle Maurice, Chief Scoutmaster of Scotland, as kindly and decent as he was, even admired the 'healthy regime' of the German Youth Movement and affirmed that a little nationalism was not a bad thing for the young.

Travelling back to Cambridge from my music lessons at the RCM, I heard two elderly businessmen discussing how useful Hitler would be in the battle against Bolshevism which was bound to come; many British lives would be saved if the Nazis took over the job of defending Western civilization – and this was not an uncommon view. But a great many middle-class

English consciences were shocked and moved by the personal tragedies of so many harmless Germans, and although hundreds of thousands of working-class and political men and women were abandoned (because an influx of active socialists would have been unacceptable to the Home Office), professional people and academics were saved by being invited to individual homes in Britain, and vouched for by hosts who would guarantee that they would not be dependent on the taxpayer.

Dozens of people we knew or had only just met wrote to my parents appealing for help in leaving Germany, who responded immediately and generously whenever they could, offering hospitality or passing on names to sympathetic colleagues; they were rewarded by the lasting friendship of some wonderful people and it was clear that we had all gained from Germany's loss in getting them out, though far more could and should have been done.

Among our own guests, one of the most notable was Benno Elkan – a Jewish sculptor famous for his great Frankfurt war memorial (which had been condemned by the regime as decadent, pacifist and judeo-communistic, and stuck in a camp for non-Aryan art as its granite bulk had withstood all attempts to break it up). Benno was very small and fat, and arrived wearing a massive fur coat which made him look like the New Yorker's Little King; he had enormous energy and soon landed commissions for Oxford and Cambridge colleges, and religious foundations, including a fine candelabra in Westminster Abbey, and a tombstone in Buckfast Abbey.

Other exiles from Frankfurt were Paul Hirsch, the banker, who brought the priceless collection of manuscripts and first editions which we had admired in his home in 1929, and presented it eventually to the British Museum Library. And there was Rebner, my teacher from the Konservatorium, with his pianist son, for whom we tried to fix up concerts and pupils; but this was not easy, as so many Germans were asking for the same thing – a chance to start a new life away from the nightmare of National Socialism. The Rebners in the end went and settled in America, I hope successfully – we never saw them again.

These people's accounts of what was going on in Germany

brought the horror of it home to us very forcibly. Like a great many others who were not much interested in politics but desperately upset by the German scene, I started looking for the reasons for this state of things. A friend, Fania Pascal, who gave me German lessons at the time, pointed out some basic principles and set me on the right path with elementary books of modern history and political economy. I read right through Paine's 'Rights of Man' with enormous enjoyment, managed a few chapters of Hegel, and a few pages of Marx (Fania advised me to wait a bit before talking 'Capital!'), G. D. H. Cole and the Hammonds gave me a glimpse into working-class history, and Shaw taught me quite a lot about Socialism relatively painlessly. Fania recommended Ludwig Renn and Arnold Zweig as classics which fuelled my fury about Hitler's war propaganda, and large doses of D. H. Lawrence confirmed my vague feelings that our social conventions were not much more than a blind, to protect the bourgeoisie.

Like other girls of my class and age I had no first-hand experience at all of working-class life or problems, and no connection with the Labour movement to show the way, through some form of action, to a solution of (or an attack on) the problems which I dimly discerned but didn't understand. In my half-baked, semi-educated state, beset by anxiety about war, pricked by a guilty conscience about fascism in Germany and unemployment in Britain, worried about finding worthwhile work, I badly needed some political activity, education, organisation. Cambridge offered every sort of cultural delight, but it did not appear to provide that sort of guidance. One never heard social problems discussed, although plenty of high power talk went on at the many parties in college rooms. The brilliant young men of the 1931 to 1933 generation followed in the tradition of those of the 1920s who were poets and philosophers, and contributed to journals concerned in the main with questions of art and aesthetics.

My sister Jean's contemporaries – Jacob Bronowski, William Empson, Kathleen Raine, Humphrey Jennings, and the rest of the galaxy which produced *Experiment* and *Encounter* – wrote and argued away in a rarefied atmosphere above the majority of heads; at the turn of the thirties, art, music and sport seemed to me the main preoccupations in the university and I floundered on the fringe, wondering how to find my way, how to learn the facts of life, how to join the ranks of people who were *doing* something.

Then, suddenly it seemed, in the middle of 1933 there was a strange and wonderful awakening in the university: it dawned on the student population high and middle-brow alike, that politics were important – almost as important as philosophising, rowing, or swotting for exams – and much more exciting. When this happened, a flood of activity seeped through the university gradually involving students in time-consuming occupations such as welcoming and feeding Hunger Marchers, holding anti-fascist meetings, organising (or trying to organise) college porters and 'bedmakers' into trade unions, to the disgust of some of the elderly dons who saw all this as a wicked waste of university time.

My father, who disliked politics but in view of the German scene was prepared to concede a certain amount of gentlemanly discussion, shook his head sadly over some of the outstandingly intelligent Trinity pupils leading the left-wing movement – John Cornford, James Klugmann, Guy Burgess, David Haden-Guest; he felt they would get over this childish ailment, but in the meantime what a thousand pities that they would not win the academic honours they deserved! As it happened, his anxieties were unjustified, for almost all the leading student politicians got double Firsts notwithstanding the long hours devoted to the University Labour Federation or Socialist Club and to pamphlet-eering and debates.

The Cambridge undergraduates' political movement deserves a book to itself, and it would be an inspiration for today's and tomorrow's students, if it could recapture that zeal and enthusiasm, which I remember watching from the sidelines, and wondering how somebody like me could join in when all I had to offer was my music and motivation.

Chapter 6 – Music and Miners

From street and square, from hill and glen,
Of this vast world beyond my door,
I hear the tread of marching men,
The patient armies of the poor.

T. W. Higginson, *Heirs of Time*

What aroused the students and their like in 1933 was not only the atrocities in Germany, but the appalling state of things on our own doorstep. The slump had now well and truly crossed the Atlantic, and there was no shutting one's eyes any longer to the distress and unemployment which had settled like a blight on the industrial areas of Britain.

The National Government, composed of right-wing Conservatives and a bobtail of former Labour leaders, hardly less right-wing, had no remedy or even palliative to offer; on the contrary, wage cuts and the reduction of social services were introduced, in the name of economy in the hour of national crisis; instead of work men got the dole, accompanied by the Means Test, whose chief effect was to break up homes where members who still had work and contributed to the family budget were no longer allowed to do so.

The Labour Party had no viable alternative to offer, and could not be said to give hope or encouragement to the unemployed men who were struggling to organise themselves to fight for a square deal. Luckily for the jobless there were men among them who were determined not to be defeated, and the story of the Unemployed Workers Movement, under their leadership, is an inspiring one.

Agitation against the Means Test and for a decent rate of relief began and grew to great proportions. Marches were organised in all the areas suffering from the depression – Scotland, Lancashire, Cumberland, Wales – and thousands of men set out from North, South, North-East and West, to converge in London with their demands.

The marches were immensely impressive and aroused great sympathy all over the country; in Cambridge the men received a terrific welcome from the left-wing students, many of whom joined the ranks and marched with them to London.

It was good to see the rising tide of protest and to know that people were up in arms against the state of things, but I must admit that the sight of the dark-coated, cloth-capped, tired and footsore file of marchers made my heart ache as did the many solitary and individual unemployed on the road past our house, (some of them genuine seekers after work, others professional tramps) who throughout the day knocked on the door asking for a tinful of tea.

I got very depressed at the feeling of personal helplessness in the face of so much misery and injustice, and longed to be able to do something about it. I envied the students who at least had given a fine show of solidarity with their well-organised welcome – but what was someone who was a mere musician, and barely on the fringe of socialist activities, to do?

Dismally wondering what next, I applied half-heartedly for several teaching jobs. While waiting for replies I got a letter from the Pennymans whom I hadn't seen since the German singers' tour. They needed help with the music of the summer work camp which they had organised at one of the mining villages in the Cleveland hills.

This camp was part of a scheme for subsistence farming among the unemployed workers of the iron ore mines; when the depression had first hit the North East, Jim Pennyman had worked out a plan for reclaiming some of the moorland around the most affected villages; one of these was a tiny place called Boosbeck, whose population of about five hundred was almost entirely dependent on the mine, and now almost to a man living on unemployment benefit.[7]

Jim had put his plan forward to the miners, and offered to raise money and supply equipment to get it going. Although they looked on the idea with suspicion at first, eventually they agreed to co-operate: and after some months' strenuous labour breaking up the bit of moor and tilling it, twenty-odd acres were successfully planted with vegetables which were a valuable addition to the men's families' diets, and were even sold to put a few precious shillings in their pockets.

Frida (front row) with miners and students at Stanghow Mines, grouped around Major and Mrs Pennyman and their Daimler Car.[8]

The whole project meant a lot of hard physical work, more than the local inhabitants could tackle if it were to be done within the foreseeable future. Jim solved the labour problem by getting, through Rolf Gardiner and through international student organisations, groups of foreign students to come and work there for short periods in the summer.

Ruth organised camps to house them, and provided for their entertainment by getting plays and operas produced among them. She drew on talent from far and near, and some interesting and even exciting ventures resulted. Michael Tippett, then a young and unknown student of composition at the RCM, was one of Ruth's helpers, and he produced 'Hugh the Drover' for her one year, and the following summer a ballad opera of his own, based on the Robin Hood story. For this we collected a miniature orchestra of strings, oboe and horn, with James Robertson (then a Cambridge undergraduate, and later the conductor of Sadlers Wells Opera) as the mainstay at the piano, under Michael's baton.

Thanks to these gifted people we put on a quite respectable musical performance; we blamed the village piano, with its many missing notes, and the Boosbeck stage, which creaked and rocked beneath the weight of the chorus for any failings, and if it wasn't right up to Covent Garden standards, everyone enjoyed themselves.

The cast were miners and their wives and children – everyone who could utter a note or articulate a word was roped in – plus a few foreign students and volunteers from the digging, from the South of England. The musicians stayed at Ormsby Hall, and drove out to the moorland village every day to rehearse; the digging party lived in Boosbeck and came to the Hall on Sunday to lunch.

Conversation at these meals was lively and uninhibited; I remember Len, the left-wing Cockney, looking round the dining-room with its carved Adams' mantelpiece and its Reynolds and Gainsboroughs, and saying in a loud sorrowful voice, 'Blimey – wot a bleedin' shime these baronial 'alls 'ave got to go!'

The dignified butler who waited on us (much against his will, I'm afraid) nearly dropped the decanter at this outrage, but luckily the master of the house, for all his family pride, had a great sense of humour and was much tickled. He enjoyed the mixed house parties almost as much as his guests did, and made everyone feel extraordinarily at home.

For all his Eton and Army upbringing, Jim was essentially a liberal, with one of the warmest hearts that ever beat beneath a gruff Indian Army manner. In spite of being a large scale landlord and pillar of the local Conservatives he felt acutely for the dispossessed and underprivileged, and devoted a great deal of thought and energy and money to schemes for the down and out and jobless to help themselves. It would have been too much to expect him to support a socialist revolution, but within the limits of social service under capitalism he did a very fine and generous job.

Whether or not his schemes made any material long-term difference to the villagers I never discovered, but they certainly made a great and lasting impression on me. The visits to

Boosbeck and contact with the miners and their families revealed to me, ignoramus that I was, some measure of the sufferings that had come with mass unemployment to those already miserable places – relics of the worst period of the industrial revolution.

The first impression of Boosbeck village – a row of squalid little houses, just like any back street in Leeds or Manchester, planted down in the middle of the wild beautiful moors – was unforgettable. The people themselves were immensely impressive, standing up to their poverty and to the insult of a society which had thrown them on the scrap heap, with an independence of spirit and a sense of humour that amazed me. I could hardly believe that men and women living under the indignities of the Means Test would be so unaffected and proud. They were not very highly educated nor particularly polite, but how much more interesting than some of the cultured and polished people of Cambridge and how much nearer the realities of life!

After the experience of getting to know them, the idea of teaching music in the soft South seemed out of the question, and I firmly determined that if any jobs were going among these people or others like them, that was the kind of job I'd like.

But music and acting and a smattering of languages were not the ideal qualifications for work in the industrial north, and I went back to Cambridge and its delights, feeling that it was useless to hope to fit oneself into a working-class society. I was pessimistic and disgruntled, miserable about the unemployed, sick about Germany and wretched because there seemed to be nothing useful for me to do.

My mother, miracle worker that she was, had at least a temporary cure for the doldrums. An Austrian family had asked to send a son for four weeks to Cambridge in exchange for two daughters staying a fortnight in Vienna in August. Why shouldn't I go with Katharine, who had had a very hard year's work teaching classics and music at a secondary school in Nottingham, and certainly deserved a holiday. And so we went, stopping in Salzburg en route, for an orgy of music and Reinhardt productions, and after two weeks in Vienna, on to Hungary where we had a long-standing invitation to stay with the Kodalys.

The world crisis had not affected the beautiful villa on the hills outside Budapest, and we spent an enchanted week seeing the city and the surrounding countryside, treated like pampered nieces by our generous friends. But in Vienna the atmosphere was tense, and though it was interesting, and the capital as outwardly impressive and attractive (its palaces, parks and monuments exuding an aura of slightly decaying past glories) as we expected, unhappiness pervaded the place. Economic distress was widespread and under a gay façade the Austrians were suffering much misery and anxiety. The Jewish family with whom we stayed were desperately worried by reports of persecution in Germany, and feared that communist tendencies in the working-class might be made the excuse for a National Socialist coup in Austria. Not long after, the Dollfuss government smashed the workers' organisations and their fine new flats, and opened the way to Clerical Fascism, which in its turn let in the Nazis, justifying the Lowenstein's worst fears. If we could have seen four years ahead, we should have enjoyed our visit to Vienna even less; perhaps it is just as well that one has not the gift of prophecy.

When we got back to England, there was some good news waiting for me. My brother, who was living in Manchester and teaching at the Grammar School, had happened to hear that someone was needed at the University Settlement in Ancoats to organise music and drama there that autumn. The work involved taking classes in the Settlement and producing plays with the unemployed men of the Pilgrim Club and other groups there. Lack of training and experience was no objection, they said, if I was enthusiastic and prepared to take on what might be an arduous job. Of course I was enormously enthusiastic and ready for anything – the more arduous the better – that combined music and some form of contact with the industrial proletariat! I jumped at the offer, and travelled north to start work in Manchester two weeks later.

Chapter 7 – Opera in Ancoats

A dreary place is Ancoats
'Tis full of smoke and fogs,
The lasses wear shawls on their head
Their feet are shods with clogs.

Roger Oldham, *A Manchester Alphabet*

As the train chugged farther and farther north, my enthusiasm for the assignment began to wane, and a gnawing worry crept up on me; by the time we drew in to the black smoke-wrapped station of London Road, I was consumed with secret terror by the thought of directing the activities of a lot of Lancashire working men. They might well be quite different from the simple semi-rural miners in East Yorkshire. I began to imagine them as extremely tough and anti-middle-class, jeering at my 'refeened' accent and bizarre ideas. How on earth would I ever bridge the abyss of class and background, I wondered?

My heart was pretty well in my boots as I made my way through the driving rain, so typical of Manchester, to the Settlement 'residence' at Ancoats Hall. This is an old mansion, which used to be the family seat of the Mosleys, who had obtained estates in Collyhurst and Ancoats back in the sixteenth century ('In 1596 a Mr Oswald Mosley bought the land on which Manchester now stands for £3,500', according to *The Town Labourer*). In 1856, the family sold the land for £200,000 and moved to a more salubrious neighbourhood. For the industrial revolution and the newly built railways had, while filling the Mosley pockets, transformed the green fields bordering the Medlock into a waste of black brick and iron, far too sooty and noisy for a self-respecting ancient family.

The house was now used partly by the Settlement, partly by the town as a local museum. It was still a rather impressive building with a fine view over the canal and a far-reaching vista of back-to-back houses one way, and dominating Ancoats Street with its cobbles and trams and railway arches the other. The noise of the shunting wagons in the adjoining goods yard, and the rattle of the trams almost literally never stopped.

Apart from the noise and gloom of the area, I liked the house very much; it was spacious inside and warm and friendly, even if it did need a new coat of paint. (The Settlement was always on the verge of bankruptcy, and expense on non-essentials was out of the question.)

The bulky, cheerful warden and his neat efficient wife welcomed me and introduced me to the residents – a nice lot, quite unlike my idea of typical social workers, whom I had always (most unfairly) envisaged as rather grim people, terribly earnest and devoid of humour.

The Warden's wife, or Co-Warden as she was called, gave me a cup of strong tea, then took me round the Settlement estate; we looked all over the residents' quarters and into the Museum next door, which was a cross between an old curiosity shop and the Victoria and Albert in miniature, and boasted a stage and a dressing-up wardrobe which was lent out to local children three nights a week (and very good use they made of it, with blood and thunder dramas of their own invention). Then we proceeded through the downpour up the dark and mean thoroughfare known as Every Street, to the Settlement proper – a square of early-nineteenth century houses used mainly as offices; next to it was a large round hall (which had been built a hundred years earlier as a non-conformist chapel, and used often for Chartist and other public meetings) with a fine big stage in three sections, plus a beautiful silver cyclorama. Passages led off from the hall to rooms and basements which served as wardrobes, dressing rooms and club premises.

Across the large yard, which must have been the church burial ground and was now a children's play centre, were more buildings where the Old Clothes Shop and a rather primitive clinic were installed and equipment was stored. The 'Shop', a sort of permanent jumble sale, was a real boon for the 'out of work' wives, who had to count every halfpenny and found it a great problem to keep their families clothed and shod.

That night happened to be the occasion of the annual Hot-

Pot Supper, at which the supporters and members of the Settlement foregathered for a social evening in the big round room. Huge helpings of Lancashire hot-pot were served to about eighty people, seated at long trestle tables; they were the rank and file of club members, a good cross-section of the population of Ancoats, working-class men and girls in their Sunday best, old dears in shawls, gnarled ancients who looked like Chartist veterans, social workers from the Hall, and a number of supporters from the town and University of Manchester. Professor Stocks, the then Vice-Chancellor, was pointed out to me with baited breath. He and Mary Stocks were the moving spirit of the Settlement Council at the time, and she had long provided the inspiration behind its dramatic efforts as well as much of the drive behind its social experiments in Ancoats and in the new housing estates at Newton Heath and Wilbraham.

Mrs Stocks was already famous as a scholar and a wit, and I was dying to hear her speak; but during her after dinner speech I would gladly have sunk through the floor, for she concentrated on giving me an enthusiastic and undeserved public welcome as a second Lilian Bayliss, whom everyone present counted on to build up a sort of Old Vic in Ancoats. This was the last thing I had expected, but I had to rise to my very cold feet and stammer out some sort of thanks, assuring the party that I would do my best. It was one of the worst ordeals of my twenty-three years, because I knew very well that the Settlement had a great tradition of acting and production, and that my efforts would inevitably be compared with those of my predecessor, the brilliant Miss Casmore.

However, everybody was in a good temper and very friendly and moreover, obviously prepared to give support and to make allowances for youth and inexperience. I could only hope to meet the challenge without letting everyone down all round *too* disastrously. It was far too much to dream one might actually succeed!

The first thing to be done was to get to know Manchester and the people, and during the first few weeks there I made friends with many of the Ancoats folk. They were easy to get on with and talked to me not as a stranger, but as somebody they had known all their lives. They were nearly all having extremely hard times, many of them on the dole or else working short time in the few factories nearby that were still turning over.

Manchester was of course the centre of one of the hardest hit of the depressed areas. The blight of mass unemployment had descended on the cotton industry in 1930, and had become steadily worse until 1933; during 1931 and 1932 there had been great marches of protests against the workers' conditions, and against the National Governments' proposed remedies – cuts in benefit for the unemployed, and in wages for the cotton workers, and proposals for 'more looms per worker' as an economy measure in the mills. The marches had ended in clashes with the police. I heard a good deal about the 'Battle of London Road' (in October 1931) when they used batons and water hoses on 50,000 of us, demonstrating against cuts and the Means Test. And about the arrests of unemployed men's leaders at a later demonstration. There were over 40,000 unemployed in Manchester, 12,000 in Salford, 16,000 in Oldham, 11,000 in Bolton, during 1934; some 80,000 in the four centres of Lancashire (a tenth of the total unemployed figures in the North of England. There were over 67,000 out of work in cotton, 15% of the industry, which meant stagnation for the whole area, in which cotton was the overwhelming provider of work.

Unemployment did not seem to have depressed them as much as might have been expected, and they were full of jokes and stories about themselves. I found it cheering but at the same time slightly shocking that they took it comparatively un-tragically; it may of course have been their Northern pride which prevented them from complaining of hardship or hopelessness to me.

The friendliness of the people more than made up for the general gloominess of the city, though at first it was difficult to get used to the monotony of the streets, the fog, the soot, the whole murk-ridden atmosphere; it could hardly have been more different from Cambridge – that grimness, those smoky black gaunt industrial buildings looming out of the mist and rain above row upon row of small grimy dwellings. I kept on thinking of Blake's dark satanic mills, and feeling I was living 130 years ago.

Most of the Ancoats streets did indeed date back to the industrial revolution when houses were built back to back, in endless lines, with never a blade of grass or green leaf to brighten the gloom.

Later on I got used to the lack of light and colour, and almost enjoyed the effects of factory chimneys soaring against stormy skies, the belching of smoke into windy patterns, the harsh black and grey symphony of a great industrial town. I well realised though, that for me there was always an escape from the darkness to the green radiance of Cambridge, or the Lakes, or Derbyshire, where we used to go for weekends. And it was difficult not to revolt against the fact that a whole population of two million people had no other landscape than the stark ugliness of Manchester, Stockport, or Salford.

However, that was the background for better or worse. Having settled into it, I started on an ambitious programme of classes and plays with the clubs, rejoicing in the full backing of the wardens and the blessing of Professor and Mrs Stocks. There were to be three big productions during the 'season', i.e. one every two months, which was a considerable undertaking but, as Pedrillo says in *Il Seraglio*, '*nur der feige Kerl versagt*' or 'Nothing ventured, nothing gained.'

Besides day and evening rehearsals and choir practices, we arranged classes for speech-training, dancing, dressmaking, stage carpentry and scene-painting, all of which came in useful to the final productions. Although everything had to be done on a shoestring we were in fact much luckier than most amateur companies. We could draw on resources outside our clubs – musicians from the College of Music, students and staff from the university, electricians from Ferranti's factory to help with the lighting. The unemployed men's club which met at the Round House assisted in a hundred capacities, fixing the scenery and lights, getting out publicity, making scenery, and best of all, playing the chief parts in most of the plays we put on.

There was an amazing amount of talent in the club, particularly on the comic side; we had a superlative comedian in Jack Orchard, an unemployed wire worker, who took the main part in *The Bourgeois Gentleman* (freely translated from Molière's play), acted Bottom most admirably and many minor roles to perfection. He was an extraordinarily intelligent man, who learned his lines extremely quickly and grasped the essence of a part at once, though he had never been on a stage before our first production in 1934. During my time at the Settlement he wrote a three act play about a strike, based on his own experiences – with some highly dramatic moments and excellent dialogue in scenes where the unemployed man, torn between his need for work, and his revulsion to strike-breaking is involved in sharp conflict with, in one act, his family, in another, his mates, the picket at the factory gates.

Mrs Stocks later on revised the play, and it was produced by the Northern Region BBC, but unfortunately with some of Jack's sharply tendentious passages toned down on broadcasting principles.

In contrast to Orchard there was a somewhat tragic figure, Harrison, who made a noble Brutus, and took other serious parts; there was McCarthy, an almost illiterate Irishman, who was so pleased with his first speech-training lesson that he told the Warden, 'It was champion. I'll soon be telling you to b—— off without saying b——, I'm b——d if I won't!' then there was Tom Johnson, thin, pale-eyed, sandy-haired and slightly insignificant off-stage, but with a surprisingly rich baritone voice, who mastered the difficult solos of Winter and Hymen in *The Fairy Queen*, and sang to my mind, as well as any professional.

Apart from the soloists there were dozens of people ready to play small supporting parts, solemn old men and gay young mill girls who looked splendid when made up as court ladies, and scores of small children whom we brought into every play to add life and gaiety to the scene.

The crowd scenes in the Settlement plays were usually very effective indeed: in Mrs Stocks' *Dr Scholefield* it seemed like the real thing when the mass of Chartist demonstrators in the black (cardboard) top hats, and carrying flaming torches, surged up from the back of the hall through the auditorium to acclaim the old Doctor (who practised in Every Street) and his guest Feargus O'Connor after their victorious encounter with the police of 1848. In *Julius Caesar* the rabble were superbly realistic too, in the second act, and equally good as Roman soldiers in the third; and as Prince Charlie's supporters in *Blue Bonnets in Manchester*, my father's Jacobite ballad opera, written specially for Ancoats.

Our idea was to get as many people into the productions as possible, and to give them the maximum amount of fun with their 'culture'. The plays were as varied as they could be, and we refused to be put off by technical difficulties. Apart from the plays already mentioned we tackled de la Mare's *Crossings*, Haring's *Rehearsal*, Molière's *Le Médecin malgré lui*, John Gay's *The Beggar's Opera*, and Purcell's *Fairy Queen* – quite an under-taking with its double cast of players and musicians – and the American anti-war play *Peace on Earth* (Sklar and Maltz) which demanded elaborate lighting effects (supplied by our friends from Ferranti's) and split-second timing in the exciting crowd scenes.

In spite of the appalling hitches and heart breaking rehearsals when a third of the actors failed to turn up (sometimes a man would get a job on the night of the dress rehearsal, which was a cause for general rejoicing, but did not simplify the producer's task!) the show never failed to go on, and nearly always got a packed house and a good write up in the local press (which, after all included the *Manchester Guardian* whose praise was well worth having).

The production of these plays was enormously stimulating, and I felt exhausted but elated on the last night, when everything had gone well (as it almost always, miraculously, did); but after the players had drifted home and the lights were out and the stage lay empty and dead, I used to wonder what was the good of it all. We'd taken the men and their wives and children out of their grim, hopeless lives for a few hours; we'd given them a glimpse of a different world, and they had avidly seized it and made the most of it – but that world of colour and light and – yes, though it seems an overworked word – of beauty, that world evaporated as soon as the curtain fell, and the hard facts of life were all that was left. Facts of the UAB, of damp and dry rot, of hungry children, of the eternal battle against dirt and soot, of queues at 'the Labour', of life on the dole, ('the terminus of hopes and sorrows' as a contemporary poet said). Every time I went off on a holiday, or even for a weekend to the Lake Country or the

Dales, this existence of theirs haunted me and revolt so overcame me that I swore I wouldn't go back to the make-believe, palliative job of social work of this sort.

But the pull of the little theatre and a deep fondness for the people of Ancoats dragged me back. And I even put in for a job of organising drama groups in outlying clubs for unemployed men, in Bolton, Salford, Oldham, under the National Council of Social Services; I didn't get it, due partly I believe to the fact that I had connections with 'subversive' organisations in Manchester, and had introduced Communists from the Manchester 'Theatre of Action' into the Settlement productions.

The reason for this supposition was that we had produced the left-wing American play *Peace on Earth* in Ancoats in 1935, and I had been in touch with the Left Theatre in London for advice about it; moreover, we had been helped by the Theatre of Action Company (a small avant-garde Manchester group which eventually was to grow into Theatre Workshop) in our production which needed considerable crowds in scenes of striking dockers, demonstrating students and other such seditious scenes. I well remember Joan Littlewood bring some of her actors to help us out, and the evident scorn with which they looked upon my social-democratic ideas. I was too left for the Social Services people, but not nearly left enough for the future Theatre Workshop enthusiasts.

Although I was very ignorant about politics and rather chary of revolutionary ideas it was becoming obvious to me, as to many of my equally well-meaning friends, that the words 'economic crisis' and 'class struggle' were not mere clichés, but expressed certain realities. The hunger and unemployment due to overproduction in capitalist countries (where I learned to my astonishment that wheat was being burned and coffee thrown into the sea), the abyss between the haves and the have-nots, the persecution of socialists and liberals on the continent, were all hard facts which had to be faced; and it began to dawn on me that the solution for the chief problem of our time – how to abolish poverty in an age of physical plenty – was not to be found in palliatives or by applying the soft soap of social service.

Drama for the unemployed, I suddenly realised, was all very

well as a means of diverting their attention from real life; but how much better if it could be used contrariwise, to turn their attention to their personal problems and to stimulate them to thinking about finding a real way out.

After a good deal of internal argument I decided to carry on with the Settlement plays, (a) because the people of Ancoats were now my best friends and I didn't want to quit, and (b) because from this time on I hoped to be able to put on plays with real social point, which might help the players and their audiences instead of just lulling them or entertaining them. There were plenty of agit-prop dramas which I longed to produce in true Piscator style: Ernst Toller's *Draw the Fires* (which incidentally, was staged at the Manchester Repertory that year, and for which we got free tickets for our club members), the works of Brecht, O'Neill, Friedrich Wolf, O'Casey. But excuses were made by the Settlement authorities that such plays were too advanced and difficult (what they meant was 'too revolutionary') and I had to be content with doing *Peace on Earth* and *The Beggar's Opera* in as socially significant a way as possible – after all, it was never intended as a dainty drawing-room piece, and I believe we got nearer the spirit in which John Gay wrote it than the elegant Hammersmith Lyric ever did.

Chapter 8 – A Trip to the Soviet Union

Our neighbours in Russia 'belong' at least
No landlord impugning their worth;
Have much consolation of goods increased
If not the sole havings of earth.

H.H. Lewis, *Farmhand's Refrain*

In my enthusiasm for left-wing drama and my dawning interest in socialism, I signed on for a trip organised by the British Drama League to the Theatre Festival in Moscow, in the summer of 1935.

I shall never forget the pleasures of that voyage – nor the woes of the after-effects of too much caviar. Among the pleasures were the endless conversations with the sailors, men and women, and the most attractive female radio operator (somehow one always managed, with or without an interpreter, to understand and make oneself understood by these friendly people); and the talks which the burly captain gave us in the evenings, crew and passengers mixing on the deck of the classless ship, as we sailed through the Kiel canal and out into the Baltic, shining and calm in spite of forebodings inspired by my father's nickname for *Kattegat and Skagerat*, 'Cataract and Skattergut'.

Lewis Casson and other eminent actors in the BDL party provided a high level of culture with play and poetry readings, we played deck tennis and sang madrigals and sat and talked about the theatre and society and life for solid hours. It was sad when it all came to an end, but we quickly forgot the joys of the sea in the excitement of seeing land – and what a new and surprising land. The first sight of Leningrad harbour was a brightly lit port with a crowd of sailors swarming like ants about the dock sides. To our general surprise a good many of them seemed wildly tipsy; as we had been informed by the captain of the Smolny that alcoholism had been eliminated in the Soviet Union, the pro-Capitalists of the party began to crow over the left-wingers who believed all they were told. But they were soon deflated when, on landing, a very drunk fellow rolled across to us, waiting beside our baggage to go through the customs (an inordinately lengthy business) with a 'Hey budd! 'Sgrand to shee a fellow-Britisher!' In fact we never met any Russian drunks, though were ourselves often well and truly pickled by the unfamiliar and lavish drinks we were given.

We spent a day in Leningrad sightseeing, looked at the marvellous collection of Impressionist paintings in the Winter Palace, and wandered about the great wide avenues. Although the city had not been redecorated since the civil war, and the plaster was flaking off the palaces, giving their long-lost grandeur a rather moth-eaten look, I still think of it as one of the most beautiful cities in Europe that it has been my luck to see – Budapest, Paris, Edinburgh, Vienna, even Venice, not excepted.

We travelled to Moscow through the night, on one of those typically Russian trains, crammed to the roof with passengers, and blessed with a locomotive of extraordinary spasms and with a peculiarly piercing whistle; 'listen to the mating-call of the locomotivniks,' said one of our party, as the high-pitched squeal was echoed by other friendly engines while we roared through the darkness across the seemingly endless northern plain.

In Moscow our party stayed at the New Moscow Hotel, (where in spite of travellers' warnings there actually was hot water *and* a plug to every bath) looking across the Neva river to the turrets and cupolas of the Kremlin, gleaming gold and white in the July sun.

We lived in a whirl of sightseeing for seven days – rushing from state factory to collective farm, from pioneer palace to the Park of Culture and Rest, from museums to metro stations. The famous underground had only just been opened, and was one of the show pieces of the town – it was certainly a fantastic dream of a metro, even with its few stations (today there are a dozen more even finer); the breadth of the stairs and platforms and the walls faced with different coloured marble, and the illumination by hidden lights or fairy-like lamps made it all seem more like a dance hall than a place of public transport. Best of all was the lack of advertisements such as disfigure our own Underground –

no sign of the suspender belts and bras which adorn the moving staircase in London – and I for one didn't particularly regret it! This absence of commercialisation in public places was perhaps one of the most striking things, to a Westerner, about the town. The few posters there were seemed well-designed and only advertised cultural or social events, or were slogans about work and health, exhorting the Muscovites to support this or that government effort for their own welfare. This also applied to shops and cinemas, where of course private enterprise and its products were not advertised, much to the improvement and general restfulness of the surroundings. I tried to imagine London without huge hoardings and gaudy advertisements, and wondered, if they were all to vanish overnight, would we be any worse off?

The theatres were the main interest for our party; we had booked up, along with our boat and train tickets, seats for twelve or thirteen performances, and I for one was determined not to miss a single show. They were all exciting, but perhaps the most exciting of all was the *King Lear* of the Jewish theatre (played in Yiddish) with black and white costumes and sets; the most beautiful, in a traditional, classic style was Ostrovsky's *The Storm,* at the Arts Theatre; the most spectacular, Shostakovich's opera *Lady Macbeth of Mtensk*, the most colourful, the National Gipsy Theatre, in a lively comedy about the organising of the gipsy community into a Trade Union. The most inspiring of all the shows perhaps, was the Children's Theatre.

For this last, we had seats scattered among the crowds of children who packed the auditorium, chattering and laughing till the play began, when the silence was suddenly complete, the youngsters concentrated absolutely intently on the stage. The children were bright and healthy, very tidily dressed, and extremely friendly. A young teacher interpreted for me when my neighbour, a boy of about twelve, told me that he came regularly to this or another children's theatre, seats being allocated centrally, so that every child in Moscow had a chance of seeing an absolutely first-class production quite frequently; and they certainly had the very best of everything in their theatres, if this one was anything to go by: a cast of outstandingly good actors, décor and staging worthy of the Arts Theatre, a fine professional orchestra, a play full of excitement and interest, very intelligently produced. To make them feel it was their own special show, the children were asked to give comments, and criticism and suggestions – which were usually adopted and acted upon by the producers. There was a children's club attached in the adjoining foyer, which was beautifully decorated, and where their own work and model theatres and puppets were displayed.

I sighed to think of the Manchester children whose only theatre was the local music hall and the rough stage and worn-out wardrobe of the Ancoats museum, and I longed for the day when we could provide continual treats like this for the English schools.

When we were not in theatres or sightseeing we were free to wander about Moscow, taking photos, talking to anyone; people came up at once on seeing an obvious foreigner, and showed great friendliness and interest, patting one's clothes and feeling one's leather handbag with noises of surprise or approval; the pity was that we couldn't speak enough Russian to tell them what they wanted to know – the price of our clothes, the jobs we did at home, our impressions of the Soviet Union and so on. But some of us managed to get some conversation with English-speaking Muscovites freely and privately. My sister and I made friends with a violinist in one of the big orchestras, who took us to his flat and gave us Russian tea and toast and jam, and talked about his life as an ordinary musician in the USSR. It seemed that things were a good deal better for him than for his opposite numbers in England, as there was an unlimited demand for music in Russia – from a public hardly tapped in England, the working-class population who were being provided with musical education and concerts of good music for the first time in history and who were determined to take advantage of the opportunity. Our friend said that although the music schools and academies were bursting with students, he was sure that there would be more jobs than players for a long time to come; and that there would be an ever-increasing demand: 'The more music people have, the more they'll want,' said our violinist, 'and the more they'll get.'

We felt somewhat ashamed of having to admit that in Britain there were only two regular opera companies, very few municipal orchestras, and that musicians were hard put to it to make ends meet. At which he said pityingly, 'Well, England is a capitalist country, what else can you expect?'

Among other Russians, we met Prince Dmitri Mirsky, the writer and literary critic of noble origin, who had after years as an émigré in Bloomsbury made a fine gesture by returning to Russia. He was then living in a room in some hotel, a melancholy bearded intellectual doing his best to adapt himself to the proletarian revolution. One felt somehow terribly sorry for him, he just didn't seem to fit in. But he was an honest, courageous person, and it was extremely disturbing to hear that later on he had 'disappeared' in the period when most bourgeois individuals with present or past connections with the West became suspect. If Mirsky was 'liquidated' it was a cold-blooded crime, one of many – far too many – that can hardly be exonerated and that one must devoutly hope will never be allowed to recur. It is hard to believe that Mirsky could have been a danger to the regime – he was certainly neither a spy nor a criminal, nor had he any aspirations towards changing the intellectual climate. I suppose there was the fear that he might be 'used': above all there was Stalin's phobia about imaginary enemies, which led to excesses that the Soviet Union's best friends could not believe happened at the time, and now deeply deplore.

Yet, after seeing a glimpse of that brave new Russia, struggling to win through to an existence of safety and security in a hostile world (because, at that time, most of the world *was* hostile) one can understand a little how vital it was to protect the young State and how careful its guardians had to be to keep out hostile elements.

Among other interesting characters we met Kapitza, the physicist, who had lived for years in Cambridge, just down the road from our home. He had revisited the Soviet Union several summers in succession, and returned, enthusiastically impressed each time to the Cavendish Laboratory. But one year he had not come back. Cambridge reacted with righteous indignation – it was outrageous! He had been kidnapped! He could never do his work under Soviet conditions, even if he were allowed to try! Everybody sympathised and condoled with black-eyed Mrs Kapitza and her two little boys, and it was another shocking surprise to hear one day that she had quietly packed up and followed him over there. Anyway, when we met him in Moscow he was certainly no captive slave, but in fine form, obviously enjoying life, and as full of quick-fire talk and funny stories as ever.

We joined up in Moscow with my younger sister Margaret, who had been on a student organised tour of distant parts of the Soviet Union. How I envied her! She had travelled to Kiev, and Kharkov (a real live city of the future, all white concrete and glass and steel, she said) and had stayed in a People's Palace at Yalta – one of the many great mansions of the former aristocracy standing in superb grounds on the Crimean coast, which had been taken over after the Revolution as a rest home for workers and their children.

Moscow was a microscopic fraction of the USSR I realised, listening to Margaret's descriptions of her travels, and resolving at some future date to visit the centre of the country and do even better than her by exploring remote Soviet Asia – Uzbekistan, Turkestan, Turkmenia, places straight out of the *Thousand and One Nights*, transformed into modern socialist states.

Although my sightseeing was so limited and our time so short, the experience of seeing Russia with one's own eyes was electrifying, and I felt I'd had a glimpse of a new world – an unforgettable periscope peep into the bright future of the Soviet children and young people, with its promise of plenty for all of them (if only peace prevailed) and of health and culture and equal chances. They had a long way to go, the Russians, we could see that from the shabby houses, the poor clothing, the restrictions on consumer goods, the long queues for often non-existent essentials. But from all we saw and heard and read, it was clear that they were determined to go ahead and build up their new society, aiming at the abolition of want through the use of science, and applying their country's vast resources for the benefit of the whole people, and not for a small minority at the top.

Two things stuck out a mile: they believed firmly in what they were doing, and they would fight and die if they had to, for their beliefs. The history of the next ten years proved this, but even then, nobody who visited the country could fail to see or share with them their overwhelming desire for peace. The idea of this splendid social experiment being destroyed by war was too horrible to contemplate, and I think most of us who visited Russia during those years in the mid-thirties inwardly pledged ourselves to work for British-Soviet friendship as a small contribution towards the peace that they so desperately needed.

Most of the Drama League party, though there were few 'reds' among them, were impressed by the spirit of the people and by their great friendliness; but apart from the theatres (which astonished even the most blasé) they were less enthusiastic than I was about the overall picture. They tended to judge Moscow by London (or rather, West End) standards, and deplored the lack of glamour in the shop windows and the monotony of the women's clothes. They forgot that twenty years earlier there had been chaos and illiteracy, and that only super-human efforts and sacrifices had achieved the very substantial results of order and planning and universal education.

One of the old actors in our party grumbled incessantly at the delays and apparent inefficiencies of the travelling arrangements in Russia, the hours of waiting between trains, the lack of comfort on the railways. He even blamed the squealing locomotives on the 'system'. 'Let them have their theatres and give me our English trains,' he groaned. He would probably have been happier in Mussolini's Italy where the tourist was treated to trains that ran on time, and fine new stations which were put up with bankers' money while much of the Italian population lived in caves. Or in Hitler's Germany, where the streets were scrupulously clean and military spit-and-polish but hid the poverty and mass unemployment.

The real difference between Socialist Russia and National Socialist Germany was not one of efficient versus hopelessly inefficient train services, as one easily saw if one spent a few days in both countries that summer. I disembarked at Kiel on our return journey, and went to stay with my old friend Luise in

Hanover. After carefully closing all the windows and doors, she told me in a whisper about her experiences of Nazi domination, and the atmosphere of terror in which ordinary people lived, and how many of her former colleagues and friends, Jewish or mildly left-wing, had 'disappeared'.

Wandering about the streets of Hanover, I saw for myself any amount of lurid Nazi propaganda. It made one feel quite sick to see the loathsome and sadistic newspaper, *Der Stuermer*, displayed at street corners (and worse still, being read by queues of young people) plainly inciting violence and vandalism. My relief at shaking the dust of Nazi Germany off my feet was proportionately as great as my regrets had been at leaving Moscow. After the sea journey from Hamburg in S.S. Bremen, surrounded by monstrous more than life size photographs of Hitler and Goering in every lounge and cabin, and the fat, complacent bald cigar-smoking German businessmen doing very nicely out of the regime, it was very delightful indeed to be back in England.

Chapter 9 – Fighting Fascism

Now is a darkness gathered on the deep
And all the winds a hurrying to war;
The thrush of peace is silent in her sleep,
The lark of liberty will sing no more.

Robert Nathan, *Ethiopia*

After Moscow, Manchester seemed very grim, even in the sunshine of the beautiful Indian summer of 1935. Remembering my fellow tourists' comments on the dowdiness of the Russians, and the dark dull clothes of Soviet women, it occurred to me that the standard of dress in Ancoats was certainly no higher, and the people themselves looked dejected and unwell. I missed the vitality of the shining-faced Russians, and the sense of hope and purpose which had struck me so forcibly in Moscow.

Pessimism and frustration seemed to pervade Lancashire, and particularly the Pilgrim Club, where the men were still hanging about without jobs. Most of them had become pretty cynical about the chance of getting work which was as short as ever – except in firms which had been 'fortunate' enough to get government orders for arms; Baldwin had that summer launched a great £300 million rearmament programme, in complete violation of the promises of disarmament on which he had won the general election earlier in the year.

Jack Orchard, our best actor, had been offered a job in a factory making barbed wire, which had suddenly become extremely busy. He was one of the lucky ones, envied by McCormick and the rest, but 'Ah'd sooner be in the play,' he said, in his rich Lancashire, 'Ah don't like the job. And this 'ere bloody wire's going out to Musso, ah wouldn't be surprised, to 'elp finish off they poor Abyssinians.'

Mussolini's war was in everybody's mind, and the question asked everywhere was what were we going to do about it. It was clear to anyone who could read a headline that this was the most

81

bare-faced aggression against a fellow-member of the League of Nations, and something that should be stopped as quickly as possible. It was also clear to anyone who could read between the headlines that this was proof of the nature of Italian fascism; and that Italy, with an unbalanced budget, an inflated currency, and a huge number of unemployed – 600,000 was said to be a low estimate – was on the verge of bankruptcy, and that it was to divert the attention of her working people and peasants that she had mobilised two million men to despoil Abyssinia. Mussolini's remarks about living like a lion sounded very hollow beside Haile Sellassie's brave words, 'It is better to die as free men than live in slavery,' and his lion-hearted warriors massacring the Ethiopian archers with tanks and aeroplanes and gas were a poor advertisement for the new Italy.

As reports of the slaughter came in, and Mussolini's son boasted of the joys of bombing the natives and the beauty of shells bursting over villages – 'like roses blossoming in the desert' – the British people, who were on the Emperor's side from the start, expressed their horror and disgust in no uncertain way. Public opinion, shown in hundreds of meetings and demonstrations, letters and resolutions, and above all in the furore over the Hoare-Laval pact, was extremely effective. The government was forced to throw Sir Samuel Hoare overboard, and to pay lip service to the League, by loud noises about applying sanctions (every sanction except cutting oil supplies to Italy – the one thing that would have made a difference). And public opinion could have probably stopped the war if it had been backed by mass working-class action.

Real solidarity in the Labour movement, with strikes against loading supplies for the aggressor, and token strikes against Baldwin's policy, and mass demonstrations up and down the country, might have ended the Abyssinian war and finished off Mussolini; but the Labour leaders refused to call the strikes and demonstrations, refused to do anything to embarrass the Government, failed as over and over again in the thirties, to take effective action.

Baldwin got away with doing nothing to hinder the Italians, and Mussolini marked up the first major triumph, since 1918, of force over international law, which was to be the pattern of international politics for the next few years.

The failure of the League of Nations, through Britain's and France's betrayal to its principles, was a deep disappointment to older people; to the young it showed that those in control of the League were more concerned with keeping reaction in power, appeasing the dictators and checking the advance of the USSR and the popular forces everywhere, than in furthering the cause of world peace. It was clear to us, even then, that our government's policy would be a fatal boomerang, that buying the Fascists' good will by selling out the defenceless victims, meant eventually that they strengthened the dictators at their own expense.

Italy's operations in Abyssinia, the growing threat of German militarism, the disintegration of the League – Italy had walked out, Germany was about to do so, the US had never come in – and our Government's acceptance of the situation, aroused much alarm and anger among peace lovers; the increase in unemployment, the growth of fascist tendencies at home, the brutalities of the Nazis, on the one hand, and the success of the Popular Front in France (where working-class unity had driven back the fascists and was achieving encouraging social results – 15% rise in average wages, the 40 hour week, a fortnight's paid holidays) stirred all progressives to an urgent desire for positive action against our reactionary government and in support of the anti-fascists all over Europe. There was a tremendous surge of left-wing anti-war activity from the spring of 1935 onwards, which drew in peace lovers and mildly progressive people and turned them into ardent campaigners in social and political fields where many of them would never have expected to find themselves.

Activity was nationwide and extremely lively, and chiefly obvious among the young. It took the form of meetings and demonstrations up and down the country, in anti-war groups supporting the Peace Ballot (eleven million strong) of mid-summer 1935.

At the same time, artists and writers and actors determined not to be left out, threw themselves into creative work for the anti-fascist cause, and, encouraged by a vigorous left-wing movement in America, combined to produce exhibitions and plays and pageants against war and fascism in halls and theatres all over the country. Culture suddenly came alive and had a big contribution to make to society. Poets realised this was an exciting time to be living, and found something new and important to say: Cecil Day Lewis, Stephen Spender, and Louis MacNeice proclaimed their suddenly discovered faith in humanity in poems like *The Magnetic Mountain*, and *Noah and the Waters*, and *Vienna*. Rex Warner's lines, even if not great poetry, expressed the feeling in the air:

> Come then, companions. This is the spring of blood,
> Heart's hey-day, movement of masses, beginning of good.[9]

Auden and Isherwood were bright planets among a galaxy of young writers, and their verse dramas, studded with angry epigrams and vivid social comment, shone out against the vapid entertainments of the West End theatres. What fun it was to go to the performance of *The Dog Beneath the Skin*, and hear the things we believed in declaimed in poetry and with the conviction of angry young actors! *The Ascent of F6*, and *The Peace* (by Aristophanes) productions that made me feel we might even have something to teach the Russians – because, after all, their theatres had the blessing of the government, while ours had the stimulus of struggling and the joy of rebellion.

Enterprising young men launched periodicals packed with vigorous anti-fascist sentiments. In the most flourishing of these journals, Hogarth Press's *New Writing*, John Lehmann discovered and published the work of talented young authors whose poems and stories reflected what so many of our generation wanted to say, or hear said. They were mostly extremely left-wing, as Lehmann himself claimed to be, and many joined the Communist Party; whether their work was great or lasting, it was certainly lively, and had a point and positiveness which gave it immense value for its time.

But perhaps the most important sign of the times was the Left Book Club, launched by Victor Gollancz at the beginning of

1935. This was a stroke of genius, both as a business proposition and an educational project: there was an immense demand for topical readable information, and the books, chosen by Gollancz, John Strachey and Harold Laski, on some burning topical issue every month, came as manna to the thirsty – food for thought within everybody's means. Fat, solid books like Dutt's *World Politics*, Strachey's *Theory and Practice of Socialism*, and *The Coming Struggle for Power*, and Spender's *Forward from Liberalism*, normally published at prices which few could afford, were made available at two shillings and sixpence to members of the Club. All you had to do was sign your name on a form and undertake to buy the monthly choice. It was as simple as that.

How we looked forward to those orange covered packets of dynamite every few weeks! There were 'supplementary books' as well, which could be bought by the more affluent and passed round to friends who couldn't afford the extra half-crown. But in fact most of the club members bought all the books they could get hold of, and would have welcomed even more.

Mr Gollancz had to start a complete department to deal with the thousands of applications for the books, which became tens of thousands as time went on. The scheme was flexible, as was the format of the volumes – yellow cardboard to begin with, turning to stiffer orange covers, which gave way later to cherry red boards – and new ideas from friends and readers were always considered and often used.

The Club's activities were by no means only literary; quite soon after its inauguration readers were getting together all over the country to discuss the books, and, acting on the assumption that theory must join with practice to have any useful effect, (and that our duty was not only to contemplate the world but to change the world) they formed groups which became active in all sorts of ways, organising meetings (often addressed by the authors of topical books, or by Gollancz or his staff), and demonstrations, raising money for good left-wing causes, distributing news-sheets and pamphlets, circulating petitions, winning new readers, starting new branches. The club reached a membership of almost 60,000, and held giant rallies in all the big cities of Britain, before its inevitable decline at the beginning of the war; by then it had certainly made a lasting mark on multitudes, and opened the eyes of millions of people.

It can be said that the Left Book Club did not achieve its objective, which was, I suppose, the attainment of unity between all parties, organisations and individuals of the left; had it done so, if it had won over the rank and file of the Labour Party and forced the Party to adopt a progressive policy during those years, Fascism could have been defeated probably without a blow being struck, certainly without the nightmare of World War II.

But the Labour rank and file followed its leaders; and the leaders were determined, come what might, not to co-operate with the Left, not to embarrass the government, not to alter the status quo. They heartily disapproved, and consistently frowned upon the sudden political enthusiasm of masses of young people clamouring for a dynamic and united socialist policy. Because of course it was the young who were the most energetic and vocal.

In spite of every discouragement from officialdom, including the suppression of the Labour League of Youth, the angry young people insisted on raising their voice and waving their brave banners. In the universities in particular there was great political enthusiasm. Cambridge, for instance, resembled a political ant-heap, its inhabitants scurrying hither and thither in a constant stream of activity. I had a lot of friends 'up' at Cambridge at that time, and heard a good deal about the goings on of the flourishing Socialist Society, and the University Labour Federation to which most left-wing students belonged.

The ULF was the centre of things, with its lively pamphlets and publications and its meetings which were often noisy and sometimes ended in a free fight between conservatives and socialist students. One that will long be remembered by those present, was that at which Attlee spoke, and which was attended by young fascist hecklers who kept up a steady chorus of 'We want Attlee's pants, we want Attlee's pants...' till forcibly ejected by the stalwarts of the left.

Students themselves often addressed meetings, and were baited unmercifully by the opposition; John Cornford, a gifted young Marxist, was a frequent orator and often suffered at the hands of hecklers. His failing as a speaker was that he tended to get so excited that his tongue ran away with him, so that he became almost unintelligible and his enemies favourite trick was to goad him on: 'Speak faster, John! Faster, faster...' till he was gabbling away against a torrent of laughter and abuse. However he would usually finish by demolishing his opponents through sheer strength of personality. Ram Nahum, another brilliant student, on the contrary, expressed himself slowly and with some difficulty, but won over doubters by his sincerity and the sense of his arguments.

These two boys, perhaps the most outstanding of their generation were tragically prevented from developing their gifts. They were both killed at the height of their promise by wars which they had put their whole hearts and strength into preventing – John in Spain, Ram by a Nazi bomb. But they had lived their short lives to the full, and left an indelible impression on the student movement which they did so much to found and foster.

Faced with the clear cut issues of unemployment, Mussolini and Hitler's Fascism, and international aggression and possible war, it seemed to me strange that anyone should fail to choose the socialist solution; odd that anyone should be a conservative; and extraordinary that anyone could turn to fascism – but the economic distress was affecting the lower middle-class people in England and Blackshirt propaganda might have its appeal to them as the Nazi's had to their equivalent class in Germany. Most of us, up to 1935, had thought of the British Union of Fascists as a rather poor joke, but in the autumn of that year it all at once seemed to become serious: Sir Oswald Mosley had started organising mass meetings and marches through the Jewish quarters of Manchester and London – which were highly provocative and certainly not funny when they ended in violence and even bloodshed. Talking to ordinary people, I found they were slightly shocked at such goings on, but vague about the nature of the movement; at a sewing bee in the Settlement, attended by worthy old women, I heard one good lady ask another 'Wot is this 'ere Fassism?' She was told 'Something like Communism, dear. Free love, free everything and mess up all round.'

When it was announced that Mosley was going to speak in the Free Trade Hall, there were discussions in the Club as to whether he should be allowed to. 'Them Blackshirts is rotten', was the general opinion. 'They get paid a quid a time to go to these 'ere meetings,' Mr McCormick, unemployed since 1932, confided to me. 'And the uniform and truncheon thrown in,' added Creasey, his pal.

The thought of the money brought a wistful look to their worn faces, and I thought that if they had been less fundamentally decent it would have been a considerable temptation to enlist, as a change from the dole. I asked if anyone would be going to the meeting and was sharply told it would be a waste of time.

Nonetheless, I was too curious to resist going along to the Free Trade Hall, and imagine it was mainly curiosity which drew the audience, that wet November evening. Outside in the rain, Mosley's supporters were giving away leaflets entitled *Mind Britain's Business!* and inside they lined the sides and gangways of the hall looking sinister, I thought, in their jackboots and high-necked black shirts. We had to wait in an atmosphere of nervous anticipation for quite a while till the Leader came on. In spite of the elaborate stage management and theatrical effects (borrowed from Hitler) he was very unimpressive. He came forwards to the front of the platform, illuminated by a glaring spotlight and stood stock still – an uninteresting figure, with his sallow foxy face and smooth black hair emphasised by the gloomy fascist uniform – for a long stagey pause before raising his arm in the Mussolini salute and beginning a dreary speech full of clichés and empty phrases.

If anyone in the audience fidgeted or commented, the stewards moved towards that row, peering toward the possible troublemaker and ready to pounce. Several people were grabbed and removed struggling between two toughs during the first half hour, and I didn't stay after that, not wanting to get mixed up in any trouble that might follow.

In fact, the Manchester meeting finished without bloodshed but this was a rather rare event. More typical was their rally at Olympia, which hit the headlines in the press because of the ferocious manhandling of spectators by the stewards.

Several friends of mine were involved in it and gave eye-witness accounts for publication afterwards. Young Christopher Cornford described how he was treated after he had ventured some uncomplimentary remark: 'One of the Blackshirts made a dive at me and got me by the foot and pulled me down into the gangway where about six or seven of them dragged me along the floor, hitting or kicking me, and when they got me outside, twelve or more of them set on me, hitting me, and then dragged me along the floor by the feet... I left Olympia with my eye cut and bleeding, and my body covered in bruises.' Christopher added that he saw many other acts of brutality and 'several people with their faces reduced to pulp by the Blackshirts.'

There were a lot of protests to the press from eminent and respectable persons, including the novelist, Storm Jameson, the Reverend Dick Sheppard and two Conservative Members of Parliament, Geoffrey Lloyd and T. J. O'Connor, and I thought to myself that this would surely open everybody's eyes to what Fascism meant, and unite more and more of us against it; surely Mussolini wouldn't get away with it in Abyssinia now? Surely Hitler would not be allowed to get the Saar and the Rhineland? Surely the Labour Party would call a great anti-fascist campaign and expose Mosley and drive out the Tory government who were so kindly allowing fascist goings on, in the name of free speech? But the call didn't come from the Labour leaders, and, alas, the Fascists continued to get away with it.

Meanwhile the cloud of the Depression still hung over the north of England. It seemed to me more than ever that social service was not the solution for the unemployment trouble, and that I was in a false position working in a charitable organisation; there was not even the satisfaction of being able to do good plays really well in Ancoats, for the Settlement was deep in debts and our cultural activities had to be cut down as they did not bring in the money. With the strictest economy we managed to put on *The Beggar's Opera*, in a Hogarthian setting – it did not need much outlay to clothe highwaymen and beggars – the Round House rang to the strains of *Fill Every Glass* and we all felt very jolly. But it was clear that opera in Ancoats was at an impasse: without money we couldn't expand, and without expanding we could not get any more money.

I felt it best to resign and try for a new job on a rather more professional basis. There was one being offered by the Yorkshire County Council, in conjunction with the extra-mural department of Hull University College, which had a livewire at its head and an enterprising programme for presenting drama and opera in rural areas, through evening classes. Between applying for the job and being accepted for the autumn of 1936 I would have to do a lot of reading and preparation, and I went back to Cambridge in May, determined not to be distracted by its pleasures or its politics whatever the temptations.

Chapter 10 – The Popular Front

A lorry halts beside me with creaking brakes
And I look up at waving flag-like faces
Of militia men staring down at my French newspaper.
'How do they speak of our struggle, over the frontier?

Stephen Spender, *Port Bou*

Before settling down to exile in the North (which despite its
charms began to look to me like a country of banishment, all too
far from the many attractions of London), I persuaded my father
to take me with him for a short holiday in France. He was
planning to go to Pontigny, the Burgundian village where his old
friend Paul Desjardins was holding his annual series of *décades*
– ten day 'intellectual' house parties; and though I might be a
very small fish out of very deep water at the Abbaye de Pontigny,
it seemed a good chance to see something, en route, of *Front
Populaire* France, which looked from conservative England like a
bright beacon amid the gloom of European reaction. Every
country from the Netherlands to Greece was led by timid semi-
fascist, or completely Fascist governments, and although there
were gleams of light from Czechoslovakia (still strongly democratic) and from Spain, (where a Republican left-wing government
had recently been voted into power) it was France which had
raised the torch most bravely and which was giving us new heart
for the future at that moment.

It was always great fun crossing the Channel with my father,
who was transformed the moment he set foot on French soil
from a staid University cleric into a gay Francophile, tourist and
guide combined. He took off his dog-collar, donned a beret, and
would at once get into conversation with fellow passengers on
trains, and with people in cafes, making a great impression on
everybody with his beautiful French accent and carefully turned
phrases.

This time it was an especially delightful trip, for there was an infectious happiness among the ordinary people, and we shared the jubilation which was still in the air after the May elections that had brought the Popular Front its great victory and ensured that its programme would become law at last. I may have imagined this general happiness, being carried away by enthusiasm myself, but it certainly seemed that people were cheerful and proud of themselves and their achievement in a way not seen in such countries as Belgium, Switzerland, Holland, Greece (all of which I had visited within the last two years), and certainly not in Germany and Italy. Russia, of course, was of another world.

English left-wingers had eagerly followed the progress of the *Front Populaire* during the previous two and a half years, and it had been an inspiration to us all. If only our so-called Socialists had been willing to follow that example, we might be in a very different position today (but then – if only pigs could fly!).

The pioneers of the Popular Front, the combined Socialist and Communist workers of Paris, had routed the Fascists after the Stavisky scandal and the February riots in 1934, had formed a united Trade Union movement (the CGT) in September 1935, had continuously demonstrated and campaigned, had forced Laval's cabinet to resign in January 1936, and had virtually sealed the fate of Laval's successors, Sarraut and Daladier, by publishing the *Front Populaire* programme of long overdue social and economic reforms.

This programme was supported by organisations 'sworn to defend democratic freedom, to give bread to the workers, work to the young, and peace to humanity as a whole.' The demands, under the headings, 'Defence of Liberty', 'Defence of Peace', and 'Economic Demands', were clearly exactly what the French people wanted, as they showed at the May elections, where the Popular Front candidates were voted in by a majority of 138 deputies over the combined Right and Centre parties.

Léon Blum became Premier in a government of Radicals and Socialists (not including Communists, though backed by them), pledged to carry through the programme in its entirety. There was some disquiet when he spoke of doing so 'gradually', and went out of his way to reassure the bankers. To make sure there would be no evasion or betrayal to big business or to resisting employers, and to bring pressure on the new parliament, the workers demonstrated their strength and their determination to have the programme made law, by a series of giant 'stay-in' strikes, which shook not only the French employers but the whole capitalist world, and filled the newspapers for two or three weeks.

It certainly was a sensational story. Over a million workers were 'out' (or rather 'in') on strike by the beginning of June, in nearly all industries, from the shop assistants in great department stores, hitherto unorganised, to the entire personnel of Renault's motor works.

Their system was simple, unique and highly effective. They occupied their premises, spent the night there, organised committees, arranged food supplies, kept everything clean and in order, amused themselves with impromptu entertainments – but just refused to work. So vast was the movement, so irrepressible and tenacious the workers, that it was impossible to stop it by blacklegs or strike breaking. The employers had no choice but to surrender and accept the demands in full. The strike ended with the signing of the Matignon agreement in the middle of June, and the *Front Populaire* programme went full steam ahead, beginning with wage rises, collective agreements, and holidays with pay, towards a future of peace and prosperity – so we hoped.

That July, the political atmosphere in Paris was as warming to the spirits as was the bright sunshine pouring down on the café terraces along the Boulevards. We stayed two or three days, and promised ourselves another halt in the city on the way back from Pontigny; in the meantime my ever-punctual father was anxious to press on to the opening of the *décade*, where he was due to read a paper, and where it would have been considered extremely discourteous to be late.

We boarded a south-west bound train, and found ourselves travelling with the distinguished philosopher, Professor Brunschvig and his scientist daughter, Madame Weill, and various other eminent scholars all bound for the Abbaye and ten days of high intellectual discussion. M. Desjardins, looking exactly like a Dürer scholar with his frail saintly white-bearded face and black skull cap, met us at the little station, his hands outstretched in welcome, with his impressive energetic wife. Madame showed us our rooms and told us the timetable.

The house parties were organised down to the smallest detail; and much in the programme of each *décade* had become traditional ceremony, which seemed to fit well into the setting of the stately Romanesque abbey, with its white pillared refectory, its magnificent library – high vaulted and lined deep with precious volumes – and the garden with its ancient trees (great yews, acacias and limes), its formal flower beds and pleached alley.

There were usually twenty to thirty visitors at a *décade*, at least half of them very eminent people. M. Brunschvig came most years, sometimes with his famous wife who was Minister of Education in Blum's government (and naturally too busy with affairs of state to leave Paris this summer); André Chamson, Jean Martin du Grard, André Malraux (invariably putting the cat among the pigeons) sometimes came, and members of the Tolstoi family and Berdayeff the philosopher. This year, André Gide was there, and Martin Buber and Jean Wahl, among many others to discuss *La Volonté du Mal*, and I was petrified at the thought of mixing with such eminent people. Madame Desjardins allotted places at the long tables for meals, and for three days running, to my great alarm, I found myself sitting next to Gide, tall and impressive, with the high cheekbones and tilted inscrutable eyes of a wise old mandarin. Actually he was extremely kind and soon put me completely at ease with his reminiscences of Cambridge and his English friends; when I tried to draw him out about Russia, though, he shut up like a clam. In revenge I had the pleasure of beating him at deck tennis, which, for a man of over seventy (who might on balance be considered to be more of an aesthete than an athlete) he played with great agility, jumping about the place at extraordinary speed.

The serious part of the *décade* was away up above my head, but everyone was expected to sit through the discussions, however lengthy and abstruse. They were terribly important to those

94

taking part, but I personally felt they were just a very rarefied form of word spinning, and that they could not contribute substantially to the ultimate happiness of mankind. Social and political questions were carefully avoided, as it was felt, no doubt rightly, that too much controversial dust would be stirred up, and the general harmony of the party would be spoiled by the introduction of immediate and burning issues. I believe that in the early days of the Pontigny experiment the discussions were livelier and more realist, but then Paul Desjardins was younger and more actively involved in the progressive movements of his time. It is true that, at a later date, one or two *décades* were devoted to specifically social problems, but these were somewhat exceptional and not directed by him.

However, nobody who was privileged enough to go to a *décade* could have failed to enjoy the experience: the company of unusually interesting people, the life in the beautiful monastic buildings, the drives and walks through the undulating Yonne countryside surrounding the great Cistercian building – it was all very stimulating.

In the evenings, there was music, or charades by the younger guests (who rather dreaded having to perform, but, after all, could hardly refuse to make some humble contribution to the general cultural feast) and romantic strolls through the lush and scented garden in the moonlight. It all seemed to me a delightful escape from a sordid world into a sphere of not too plain living and very high thinking – even if escape was not exactly what one was seeking at that moment in 1936.

There was a different kind of pleasure in staying in Paris on the way home. I was determined to find out all I could about French politics, and dragged my father round with me from meeting to meeting, from exhibitions to demonstrations, and even to the *Cabaret du Front Populaire*, which was housed in the rather drab bare premises of some local political committee and decorated entirely with topical posters. Here, in spite of hard benches, we spent a hilarious evening listening to well known artists and to some very funny comedians giving free rein to satire against the Two Hundred Families, Colonel de la Roque (leader of the Fascist *Croix de Feu*) and half-baked Radicals.

After seeing the outspoken Paris workers, it was a little disappointing to be told of the comparative silence of French intellectuals. Our friend Madame Laurent and her sister Andrée Viollis (a vivacious white-haired journalist who had travelled all over the world reporting crises and wars) bemoaned the fact that so few of the non-Communist intelligentsia were prepared to commit themselves. 'We have some of the best,' said Mme Viollis, '*la crème de la crème* among the scientists: Langevin, Perrin, the Joliot-Curies: and among the writers, Éluard, Aragón, Chamson. They are always ready to speak for peace, and sign the manifestoes. But many well known writers, and *les universitaires* prefer to remain in their ivory towers and let others do the work of saving freedom.'

It was surprising to hear this, as in the British universities – at least in Cambridge and London, the only ones I knew well enough to compare with Paris and Pontigny – there was plenty of support even from the most eminent, for the anti-fascist campaign.

This struck me more than ever coming back in July 1936; our movement was not only gathering strength every day, it was gathering all kinds of people, from top scientists and writers to the most lowly, in a vocal and insistent demand for left-wing unity. And although the Labour Party leadership turned down all proposals for a popular front, on the grounds that it would only benefit the Communists, nonetheless Labour speakers often shared platforms with Liberals and Communists and stressed their belief in joint action to bring down the Tory Government.

A good meeting ground for all shades of opinion was the Left Book Club, which by now had a membership of over 12,000 – it had been 6,000 in May. (No wonder Lloyd George referred to it as 'the most remarkable movement in the political field in two generations.') It was a reflection of the tremendous sense of urgency and the desire to be equipped with facts, with knowledge by which we could analyse situations, expose evils, propose remedies.

I remember the applause from about seven thousand people at the first Book Club rally in the Albert Hall, when one of the speakers quoted Lenin's words, 'I do not know how long the capitalist powers will allow us the opportunity of learning, but every moment we have free from war we must devote to study.'

The Book Club was by now an embryo Popular Front, engaged in political as well as literary activity. Its groups of specialists flourished and multiplied: there was a Scientists' Group, a Medical Group, a Poetry Group; there was a Professional Actors' Group, whose members included Sybil Thorndike, André van Ghyseghem, Beatrix Lehmann, Miles Malieson; there were groups of Clerical Workers, Lawyers, Film Workers, Taxi Drivers. All over the British Isles people were reading, learning, discussing, preparing to take an active part, even as far away as Ben Lomond, where a friend one day came upon a shepherd sitting on the hillside reading an Orange back!

The widespread success of the Book Club, described as 'a great crusade' by Dr Lewis, was a cause of considerable annoyance to the Conservatives and to the right-wing Labour leaders, whose idea of a quiet life was definitely not 'a great crusade' of which they themselves had not got control.

Members of the Club were threatened with expulsion from the Labour Party, and would certainly have been thrown out, had not most of them been the pillars of the local parties, the most keen, energetic and indispensable.

In some cases Book Club members were disgusted with the attitude of the official Labour Party and left of their own volition; many joined the Communist Party which was a great deal more dynamic and offered more chance of action. But this was a later development, one of many that inevitably followed the events of the high summer of 1936.

These events were, of course, the rising of the rebel Junta in Spain, and the spontaneous resistance of the Spanish people to Fascism; and they sooner or later affected every one of us in the left-wing movement, and proved a turning point in many lives. In Spain, all the issues of our own struggle were crystallised, and there we later recognised the front line in the fight against oppression, dictatorship, poverty and unemployment, for a better, brighter world.

But during that hot spell of holiday weather in the summer vacation of 1936, very few people (even in the well-informed circles of the Book Club) noticed the thunder clouds or realised just what kind of a storm was going to break over the world.

It was a few days after my father and I got back from France, in the third week of July, that the news broke: there had been a military coup against the democratic Republican Government of Spain, by a group of insurgent generals. On the 18th, Francisco Franco, a military gentleman whom nobody here had ever heard of – though he was no doubt well known among his friends as an ultra – and a junta of high army officials (exiled by the Republican Government to the Canary Islands for refusing to take an oath of allegiance in the spring) had landed from Morocco in Southern Spain, we learned, with an army of Moors and mercenaries, supported by large numbers of Italian airman and aeroplanes. The rebels seized towns and villages in the extreme West and South West, and garrisons in one or two cities had joined them. They set up headquarters in Burgos and Salamanca, and under the title *los Nacionalistas* they were proclaiming themselves the rulers of the country in the name of España, the Holy Church, and Anti-Communism.

Two weeks after the uprising, reports began to come in of stiff resistance to the Fascists all over Western Spain, and of terrible reprisals and massacres. Although strictly censored, some idea of the atrocities was transmitted to British newspaper readers via Havas, Reuter and *The Times*: in Badajoz, for instance, 1200 militiamen had been shot immediately; mass executions were going on in the Bull Ring. On 19th August, *The Times* reporter referred to the dreadful process of 'cleaning up' at Badajoz, where 'further mass executions are reported to have brought the total up to 1500.' We read another *Times* report a few days later, from Irun: 'It seems only too likely that Irun will pass with Badajoz into the history of the civil war as a name for cold-blooded slaughter. The Foreign Legionaries and Moroccan troops are stated to be sparing not a single man, woman, or child who falls into their hands.' And this was happening, it appeared, wherever Franco's forces took over and found any opposition.

These reports from reliable sources left me stunned: was it possible such things could go on in a so-called civilised society? And would there be no move made to save the rest of Spain from such atrocities? From Madrid, mercifully, there came news that Caballero's government had declared Franco a traitor, and called on the Spanish people to defend the Republic; and that wherever the Fascists had not taken them by surprise, the population had responded to a man. We read that thousands of workers in the capital, in Barcelona and other towns were flocking to enlist. They were straight away mobilised into a People's army, their uniform the blue boiler suits (*monos*) in which they had volunteered, their only weapons a fearless faith in the rightness of their cause and whatever out-of-date guns and pistols a peaceful regime could supply. The Republic had no tanks, no planes worth speaking of, no heavy artillery; Franco had the well-equipped arsenals and the trained regular military force, and as it soon turned out, generous supplies of aeroplanes and war material from Mussolini, tens of thousands of Italian troops, and hundreds of Nazi technicians.

There was enough evidence of Fascist foreign backing for the rebels to horrify English opinion, even in the early days of the war, and Liberals and Left-wingers called for British support for the legal Spanish government, while strong protests against the Nationalists' atrocities came from all sorts of humanitarian organisations. Committees sprang up in many parts of Britain with the object of putting pressure on our Conservative government to send arms and supplies to the Republican Loyalists before Franco overran the country – for it looked as if that might happen in a matter of days; Caballero and Azaña were appealing urgently to the apparently deaf democracies for immediate help, above all to be allowed to buy the war material which they so desperately needed.

But the Aid Spain committees were as yet uncoordinated and by no means ubiquitous, and in Cambridge, dozing in the semi-stupor of the Long Vacation, there seemed to be no prospect of anything happening, nothing one could do – and I read the reports from 'our correspondent in Burgos' with an anger and dismay that seemed literally to choke me.

However, about the middle of August I was parking my Baby Austin at the Great Gate of Trinity (a privilege allowed by the porters occasionally to daughters of dons) under the disapproving stare of King Henry VIII, when I spotted a scientist friend whom I knew to be sympathetic to the Spanish Republicans. 'Why isn't anybody doing anything?' I asked him; 'is everyone in Cambridge fast asleep?' He told me that on the contrary a number of Long Vacation students were wide awake, but so far only the Communist Party members had organised anything. They had already held several meetings in the district, with speakers on Spain, and were planning to go into villages in Cambridgeshire and even farther afield if they could find transport. 'I don't suppose you would lend your car?' he added, eyeing the Austin 7 doubtfully. I said, 'why not, I'd be only too glad.'

'What would your father say?' – I explained that my father, even if he did happen to be the Dean of Chapel, was extremely broad-minded, and anyway would not consider it his business to interfere.

So we fixed a time, and the next afternoon the little car was loaded up with leaflets and pamphlets explaining the situation and calling on the British people to defend democracy and to hit back at the Fascists by sending help to Spain.

Two well-known young Cambridge communists climbed into the Austin and we set off on a hundred mile tour, through the flat quiet fen country, stopping at small villages and in the market places of little towns to talk to the people standing about there, and to distribute literature and leaflets.

The main objective was Hunstanton, at the height of the season crowded with holidaymakers with nothing much to do but sit around in the sunshine. On a grassy slope near the beach our speakers pitched a small platform and addressed the loi-terers with an impassioned appeal for support for the Spanish people. The audience listened politely if somewhat apathetically, and I marvelled at the perseverance and courage of the speakers; nothing would have induced me to start trying to sow seed on such apparently stony ground. But as I took round the tin for a collection, rattling it in front of the recumbent couples and Bank Holiday families, I was pleasantly surprised to find that many of them were prepared to drop in a few coppers, and that nobody sneered or jeered or suggested that we might be better employed. My Communist friends considered the expedition a great success, and I drove back to Cambridge feeling on top of the world, and reflecting that if it was actually possible to do something for Spain in what is surely one of the least politically conscious parts of the United Kingdom, there could be no limit to what could be done in more lively areas.

The thing was to be ready to work with anybody who was willing to do something positive in this Spanish business, which, as the days and weeks went by, appeared more and more clearly to be our concern. The then British Government showed that it was not prepared to lift a finger to help the Republicans, had refused to send arms, and had put pressure on the French government not to do so either. 'Non-intervention' was the order of the day, supported by the TUC and the Labour Party leaders. But most of us could see, even in the very early days of the Spanish war that, in the words of Joseph Stalin, 'the struggle in Spain is not the private affair of the Spaniards, but the common cause of all advanced and progressive mankind.' Whatever one thought of Stalin, these words were soon proved too true.

As I gathered together books and papers for my lecture courses in Yorkshire and packed my case, I thought sadly of the activity in the South of England – Cambridge, where the students would be organising and collecting funds, and stirring opinion, and London where already a dozen Aid Spain Committees had sprung into being, where anti-fascist meetings and pageants and plays were taking place every evening; but it struck me too, that provided one could find even a few like-minded people there was really no reason why something could not be started in the most unpromising place. And what was wrong with York, anyway? Nothing, except my fears of the Unfamiliar – which would automatically cease to exist, of course, the moment I got there.

Chapter 11 – Spanish Relief

He says 'My reign is peace' so slays
A thousand in the dead of night.
'Are you all happy now?' he says,
And those he leaves behind cry 'Quite.'
He swears he will have no contention,
And sets all nations by the ears;
He shouts aloud, 'No intervention!'
Invades, and drowns them all in tears.

W. S. Landor, *A Foreign Ruler*

York, serene and quiet in the dusk of that evening in mid-
September, seemed a very long way indeed from the turmoil and
troubles which were tormenting the rest of the world. The
cathedral towers, like twin guardians of the little city, brooded
over its ancient houses and narrow 'wynds' and 'gates', and when
you stood in the Close where the old dwellings clustered round
the great building, like chickens round a mother hen, it was easy
to imagine yourself a 15th century pilgrim, but for the distant
rumble of the railway, or the noises from the chocolate factory,
which established the fact that this was AD 1936.

To live in one of the narrow streets where the houses almost
rub noses across the paving, under the very shadow of the
cathedral on one side and two minutes' walk from the Shambles
on the other, gave one the feeling of living in the past and had its
special charm. The GFS Hostel where I was staying was thus
situated, and it was an experience in itself to live for a bit in such
surroundings, quite apart from the company, which consisted of
people with very different backgrounds and ideas from one's
own.

The other 'girls' in the establishment were quiet, kind,
sedate people, who thought me quite mad for being interested in
such far-off matters as German politics and the Spanish war.
They called me 'the MP', a most undeserved honour, probably

because I was the only one among them who had given a thought to such things.

I liked them and the house which was old and rambling, but clean and comfortable, with a regular routine and copious meals – huge breakfasts, and high tea, ideally arranged for someone who had to set off to take evening classes in remote villages, with hot cocoa when one got back from long foggy drives.

It was certainly a help not to have to look after oneself, during the first few weeks of a job which required fairly concentrated study and preparation during the day, and expeditions to distant moorland places every night. But when a friend later offered the first refusal of a self-contained room he was leaving, in a house by the river, the idea of independence and the possibility of a timetable of one's own, was too attractive to turn down. By then the classes were pretty well under control, some studying Shakespearean drama, others rehearsing modern Irish plays (what fun we had with *The Whiteheaded Boy* and with Lady Gregory's *Spreading the News!*) in Yorkshire dialect; and others taking a course on opera, illustrating it themselves with extracts from *Dido and Aeneas*, and Gluck's *Orpheus*. And I felt justified in spending some thought and energy on what was nearest my heart – the question of helping Spain.

By November 1936, things were extremely serious for the Republicans. France and Britain had not yet decided on non-intervention and although the Italian and German Fascists were intervening so blatantly as to render help to the Spanish Government an obvious necessity, no arms had been sent in spite of Azaña's repeated requests. By the middle of October, Moors and Francoist troops had arrived at the outskirts of Madrid, and were hammering at the gates, while the people of the city shouted '*No Pasarán*'[10] and built their barricades. On 24th October, in furious reprisals, the bombardment of the population had begun, with six Junker Bombers killing 209 civilians and maiming 300. For four weeks the bombings went on, destroying houses, churches, stations. 'On 10th November, many thousands of refugees spent the night in the open or in the shafts of the underground,' Arthur Koestler reported. From 17th November onwards, day and night incessantly, General Franco (in

Koestler's words), with the help of his foreign pilots, endeavoured to burn the city of Madrid with its million inhabitants to the ground... 'Sleepless, speechless, paralysed with terror, hundreds of thousands of *madrileños* spent the night in cellars, every moment expecting the building above their heads to collapse, and leaping tongues of flame to make their way down the stairs... On 18th November the bombardment reached its peak. The proudest buildings of the capital... fell a prey to the flames... The bombs were of the heaviest type... Over the centre of the town, round about the Puerta del Sol, the grim engines of modern warfare rained down death and destruction for sixteen hours on end...'

The bombing of Madrid ceased on 19th November. It had lasted four weeks, and at a cautious estimate had killed over 1000 people and severely wounded 3,000. And still Madrid had not given in; English visitors returning described with wonder in their faces, how the walls were plastered with *'¡No pasarán!'* and *'¡Madrid será el tumbo del fascismo!'*[11] The bombing, the first of its kind, with which Franco had hoped to break the Republic's spirit, and which was a useful exercise for Mussolini and Hitler's next war (we said, not realising how truthfully), had little effect on the people except to strengthen their resistance. It showed them the kind of salvation they could expect from Franco, should he prove victorious. It showed us in Britain the ferocious brutality of the friends of Franco, who himself had two months earlier in a newspaper interview declared *'Je ne bombarderai jamais Madrid... il y a des innocents.'*[12] (*Petit Parisien*, 17th August 1936.)

Public opinion began to show signs that England realised that a crime was being committed, and church people, Liberals, Labour, even some Conservatives raised their voices in protest. A campaign started on the Left, which drew in many non-political well-meaning people. Official Labour policy, as usual, was not to embarrass the Government (which was gradually deciding on non-intervention) but the Trade Unionists and the rank and file supported the demand for arms and relief. The Communist Party and many young writers and students, including my personal friends, John Cornford, Ralph Fox and David Guest, went out to fight in the first months of the war and were killed at Madrid or on the Sierra. A Medical Aid committee was formed in London, and sent out doctors, nurses, and ambulance drivers, many of them killed at the front. Clive Bell's son, Julian, lost his life driving an ambulance.

At home, reading of the deaths of friends, and of these tragedies, it seemed very much our war. Poet after poet wrote verses about Spain:

W.H. Auden's, *Spain:*

> Madrid is the heart. Our moments of tenderness blossom
> As the ambulance and the sandbag;
> Our hours of friendship into a people's army.

Rex Warner's, *The Tourist Looks at Spain*:

> In Spain is Europe. England also is in Spain.
> There the sea recedes and there the mirror is no longer blurred.

Jack Lindsay's *Map of Spain*:

> Oh watch the map of Spain
> And you can see the sodden earth of pain
> The least blood-trickle on the broken face
> And hear the clutter of the trucks that bring
> The Moorish firing-squad along the village street.

These were typical. Reporters wrote articles, public figures made speeches, musicians gave recitals, in every section of society people tried to do something to show their feelings and the martyrdom of Spain.

Those who could do nothing else joined in the campaign, as distributors of leaflets and secretaries of committees, and this was my role in the struggle for Spanish democracy. My landlady's front parlour soon became a committee room in which a number of people of extremely different views, but all firmly vowed to the principles of peace and freedom, met at weekends to discuss ways and means of raising money for Spanish Relief.

I had soon discovered that York was by no means as dead-alive as first impressions suggested, and that (although there was not as yet a Left Book Club group) there were many individuals both in the local Labour Party and in the Quaker community who were as keen as anybody, anywhere, to help. One very live wire was a lad in the Labour League of Youth (unfortunately all too soon to be disbanded) who knew everyone with progressive tendencies in the town, and gave every minute of his time out of school to producing and handing out circulars and leaflets.

We formed an ad hoc committee, with several leading Friends and Liberals, a couple of Communists, and a sprinkling of Labour supporters, and we decided to hold a meeting to raise some money for Medical Aid, at which the Archbishop, William Temple, was to be invited to preside. I approached him, in fear and trembling, hardly daring to hope that we should even get an answer to our letter to him, but I did not realise what an extremely generous and broad-minded man he was. His answer was unconditionally, 'Yes' he would take the chair at our inaugural meeting and we could count on him for support in any humanitarian action we undertook. I suspect that he would gladly have added 'political action', for he was well-informed and wise enough to know that only pressure on our government could be of real use to the Spanish anti-fascists. But the very fact that he went so far, marked him out as a quite exceptional man of the church – for the Church, both Anglican and Catholic, had so far committed itself either not at all, or firmly on Franco's side.

We fixed a date for the meeting, booked a hall, and invited a number of well-known local worthies, and representatives of organisations, as well as the general public, to come and hear the truth about Spain.

The room was packed, with a very attentive audience, and no wonder – our speakers were unusually eminent and interesting people, and the subject was one which was very much in the news, and at the same time one in which the issues were extremely involved and (often deliberately) confused. People wanted clarification and they certainly went home a good deal clearer than when they came, having heard a great many hard facts from two experts – Wilfrid Roberts, the young Liberal MP (from the Spanish Relief Committee in London) and Edith Pye (from the Society of Friends) a specialist in international refugee work – while the moral side of the case was expounded very forcefully and lucidly by the Archbishop.

Whoever was present must always remember the impression of that platform: the three figures, as unlike as they could be, Temple, large, rubicund and beaming; Roberts, weary-looking, gaunt and ascetic; and Miss Pye, tiny between them, but with a quiet compelling personality. Unlike in looks, presenting different aspects of the problem, but all hammering home the same conclusion: 'You have *got* to help Spain, if you have any respect for human rights, freedom, peace. Because all those ideals are being threatened today, and we in England have a great responsibility for saving them.'

After the speeches, a well-known and respected local Friend made an appeal for donations. He left it rather vague as to what fund would receive the money, but made it clear that it would be to a non-political relief organisation, for humanitarian purposes.

From Friends' House in London, the Quakers were already sending through the 'Save the Children' fund, and a 'National Joint Committee for Spanish Relief' was co-ordinating activities of the various bodies such as 'Youth Foodship Campaign' and the 'Milk for Spain' appeal, and 'Spanish Medical Aid'.

After discussing the question as to which of these committees we should send our money – what we had raised at the meeting, the ensuing collections, and the results of a printed appeal under the Archbishop's signature – we decided that the most urgent need was for medical supplies. And a month or so later, we handed about £100 over to our treasurer, a respectable employee in one of York's main banks. He carefully earmarked it 'For medicaments for Spain', and despatched it to London. But (whether intentionally, or through sheer ignorance we never could make out) he had not addressed it to Mr Roberts or Miss Pye's committees, and to our horror, we found on the receipt the stamp of the 'Nationalist' Spanish Relief Committee, which disseminated propaganda and collected money for Franco's friends and was sponsored by the Duke of Alba himself; our contribution was probably going straight into the pockets of some wounded Grandee or his family.

We rushed off a letter asking for our precious funds to be transferred immediately to the right quarter, and after a good deal of long-distance haggling, it apparently did reach its destination – the Spanish Medical Aid headquarters in London, and eventually (we hoped) some hospital in Republican Spain, in the shape of surgical instruments and drugs. But it was a very narrow escape.

We took care after that, and dealt with the National Joint Committee, which I must mention in some detail here as it later became so large a part of my existence. The organisation, by the beginning of 1937, was well-established and doing a remarkable job. Its success was mainly thanks to the untiring efforts of Wilfrid Roberts, its secretary, who though he appeared gentle and ascetic as a mediaeval monk, brimmed with restless energy and enthusiasm, and soon got to be known as 'the MP for Spain' rather than the Member for West Cumberland! He pushed the most ambitious schemes through for sending Foodships, setting up British Hospitals in Spain, raising money, receiving refugees, through the Committee, which was a highly respectable one and could certainly not have been labelled 'Red' except perhaps by the colour blind, or by those whose eyes were tightly closed by political prejudice, and who were endowed with the most fertile imaginations. The Chairman was the Duchess of Atholl, who had been Minister of Education in a Conservative government not very long before, and whose disapproval of Soviet Communism was well-known. She had realised the danger of Hitlerism to Britain, and from sheer straightforward patriotism had taken a stand against it in 1935; she realised too what Fascist control in Spain would mean, and after a visit to Barcelona and Madrid towards the end of 1936 was moved by what she saw of the devastation, the refugee problem, the situation of the homeless children, to come out, from humanitarian as well as political considerations, wholeheartedly on the side of the Republic.

She was risking her position and her career with the Tory Party, but was far too intelligent and honest to allow this to interfere with the declaration of her convictions. She wrote an excellent and comprehensive account of the Spanish situation in a Penguin 'Special', *Searchlight on Spain*, which sold 50,000 copies in a month, and was reprinted in two more editions.

When I could escape to London for a night or two I sometimes slipped into committee meetings of the National Joint Committee, at which she presided, and I was fascinated by her small frail presence. As someone said once, 'Not many inches, but every inch a Duchess.' She was always intensely concerned with the work of the Committee, and meticulous about details to the point of fussiness, but at the same time she had a firm grip on realities. Though she expected everybody on the committee to work extremely hard, she did not spare herself but attended every meeting, and spoke and wrote and travelled about indefatigably for the cause.

'Cambridge to Barcelona' collection for Spanish Relief.
Jessie Stewart, Frida's mother, on the far right.

The other 'officers' who sat beside her at the green baize table in the long panelled room in the House of Commons where committee meetings were held, were very different, but also extremely impressive people: Eleanor Rathbone, Independent MP with a strong handsome face and white hair tightly drawn back in a bun, the incarnation of the ardent feminist and internationalist woman; Geoffrey Garrett, a Quaker, four-square and efficient, in charge of the National Joint Committee refugee work and an expert on Spain; the two Grand Old Men of the movement, Sir Peter Chalmers Mitchell and Sir George Young would sometimes be there; white-haired and fine-featured democratic aristocrats, they had both of them lived in Spain for many years, and knew the full significance of the Fascist invasion. Though both were long past retiring age and might well have watched events regretfully but at a comfortable distance, they took a very active part in the campaign, speaking, writing, organising, to arouse others to the dangers of the Spanish war.

A great many distinguished people came in and out of the Committee premises, contributing their knowledge and influence – Lord Listowel (one of the Secretaries) J. B. S. Haldane, Gilbert Murray, the Dean of Canterbury, to name a very few, were always ready to speak or to sign letters or sponsor meetings. The office became famous and the work mounted, the staff grew, the results were impressive, but there was always more and more to be done, as the Spanish war continued and grew more bitter.

My sister, who was Wilfrid Roberts' secretary, was worked off her feet by her indefatigable employer, helping him to organise the Committee, and to bring pressure through Parliament on the Government and the Opposition. I heard of her activity with great envy, for I was still stuck away in a far-off county, and breaking my heart at being able to do so little, and only between my other jobs of work.

I was busy with classes in and near York, and in early 1937 had to give a short course of lectures in villages to the east of Hull. It was impossible to reach them from York, so I transferred to Hull itself, and lived there for the summer term of 1937. Some of the villages were right on the coast, an hour or more's drive through flat fenland, to within a mile of the North Sea; others were across the Humber, near Grimsby. I thoroughly enjoyed taking the classes of villagers, who, I think, looked forward to the music and acting as a change from the wireless and the local gossip which was all the entertainment available in their remote fastnesses. They sat packed tight in the little village hall or schoolroom to hear my attempts at dissertation on the history of opera, to listen to records of Verdi or Wagner, then to turn to the real business of the evening, singing and acting themselves.

There was remarkable talent among them, and some lovely voices, and in one village we rehearsed and eventually produced Purcell's *Dido and Aeneas* with a group of yokels and farmers' wives, to their great enjoyment and mine – and even though the standard was not as high as that of the Mermaid Theatre, we felt it well worth the effort.

In Hull itself there was plenty of scope for Spanish Relief work, and as hardly anyone there had so far raised a finger for it, I gave every moment available between classes to trying to organise a local committee. With the town's large industrial population and a lively University College, it was easy enough to get support. People in the Labour movement, among the Friends, and in the College joined to bring out an appeal for Spanish Relief, signed by a number of prominent people, and this eventually bore a fine crop of fruit.

I did not see the results of our early efforts in Hull, because towards the end of the summer term I got a letter from Sir George Young, who was running a transport service and two hospitals for refugees in Southern Spain, asking if I would take an ambulance out for them to Almeria. The little coastal town was, it appeared, fearfully overcrowded with refugees from Malaga, which had fallen into the hands of the Fascists in February, and strenuous efforts were being made to help the Spanish government to cope with the thousands of people fleeing from Franco's terror. I had read accounts of the machine-gunning of refugees on the road, and realised vaguely what this meant in terms of suffering, hunger and destitution – though it was not till actually confronted with it face to face that anyone could conceive the whole horror of it.

Although it was beginning to seem to me that charity, like sympathy, was not enough, and that arms for the soldiers was an even more urgent need than milk for the children, refugee relief was clearly something that had to be done, and this might be my only chance of doing it.

I had cherished ideas of volunteering for the International

Brigades, to help with nursing or bottle-washing or stretcher-bearing, but had never had enough confidence in my own efficiency or strength to offer my services. However, an assignment of driving an ambulance over and of helping in a refugee centre, where people after all would not be so very different from the simple folk of Ancoats or the Yorkshire villages, that I knew would be within my powers and I gladly accepted the offer.

The newly-formed Hull Committee grumbled good-humouredly and enviously at my going, and my professor (who was taking a rather dim view of my activities anyway) warned me severely that as I was going into a war zone and could not be counted on to return, my appointment should be considered as in abeyance – or something to that effect. I said I was sorry, but in truth this did not break my heart which was in the Spanish struggle, and while that continued I realised I would never feel enthusiastic enough about the classes to make a really good job of them. Having said this, I felt a real pang at saying goodbye to the inhabitants of Roos and other distant points who had so wholeheartedly thrown themselves into *Dido* and the staging of Bach's *Peasant Cantata*. For their part, most of them wrung my hand with a look of pity, obviously considering me slightly mad for hurling myself into the cockpit of somebody else's war. But one or two, to whom I had tried to explain the significance of the Spanish struggle over a cup of tea after a lecture, showed they understood why I was going, by their warm 'Well done, and good luck.' And 'come back to us when you've finished off Franco.'

There was only one hectic week between the end of term and the day we were due to leave with the ambulance, and I spent the time rushing round, being inoculated, getting passport and visas in order and saying goodbye to friends and family. The only things I regretted about going off were firstly, my parents' understandable anxiety (which I tried to appease by showing them on the map that Almeria was nowhere near the Front); and secondly the fact that the National Joint Committee were planning to bring over four thousand children from the Basque country, which was being mercilessly bombed and blockaded at that moment. After the destruction of Durango, and the appalling massacre of civilians at Guernica (the sacred city of the devout quiet Catholic Basques) by the German air force, public opinion was ready to support a large-scale gesture of sympathy and of protest against the iniquitous holding-up of our ships to Bilbao. Our committee felt that the least we could do was to rescue as many innocent boys and girls as possible, and it had ascertained that we should get a great deal of public support and that even the Conservative government would not prevent their entry into the country. A ship had been chartered to fetch them, and Dr Richard Ellis and Mrs Leah Manning had travelled to Bilbao to examine the children who were to come to England.

I went to a Committee meeting on the eve of our departure with the ambulance, and listened to Dr Ellis giving a report on his journey, and to the discussion of plans for the reception of the young Basques at a vast camp outside Southampton, which I was very sad to be missing. It was a great and brave undertaking, but the people who were responsible had complete faith that it was the right thing to do, and that the British people would support them. They were proved absolutely right, and the children were soon after welcomed on their arrival in England by representatives of almost every section of our population – from the Roman Catholic Church and Salvation Army to the Labour Party and Trades Unions, Co-operatives and Communists, all willing and anxious to make amends for the official hypocrisy and to express their feelings with regard to the murderous civil war.

Chapter 12 – Ambulance to Murcia

See Spain and see the world. Freedom extends
   or contracts in all hearts.
Near Bilbao are buried the vanguard of our army,
It is us too they defended who defended Madrid.

Rex Warner, *The Tourist Looks at Spain*

The day of our departure arrived, and I foregathered with my fellow traveller, an elderly nurse with a rosy face and white hair who despite her advanced years had volunteered to help at the children's hospital, at the garage where our ambulance was waiting, all loaded up with medicaments and tins of milk and chocolate.

It was an impressive sight, our White Elephant (as someone had disrespectfully called it) with its dazzling coat of snow white paint, and its inscription in big red letters 'From the Miners of Cambuslang to the Frente Popular.' I was sorry that it was not going to the front line of Popular Front Spain, but that might have been asking too much of it, as in spite of its new paint it was obviously not in its first youth, nor fit for much rough work.

We scrambled on board, and I drove it off among cheers from a small party of sympathetic onlookers, through the London streets where people gazed and goggled and even clapped, in spite of the rival attraction of the bunting and flags going up all over the place in preparation for the coronation of King George VI.

That, I thought, was something it was best to be missing. Some remarks from a pamphlet I had recently been reading came back to my mind: 'The Tory government is economising on the young, the sick, and the helpless as well as on the homeless. It attacks the standards of the working people. The Government says it cannot build the schools, houses and hospitals, because they have not got the money, materials or manpower. Now if that is the case, why are they spending so much money and utilising so many million feet of timber, steel tubing etc., etc., as well as manpower, on the coronation?'

Thinking of Manchester, and South Wales and Germany and Spain, I felt hot with anger at the ballyhoo, that was being staged to distract people from the important issues and tragedies of the world, and give them the impression that as long as the sun didn't set on the British monarchy and the Empire, we were all right.

Personally, I couldn't see how anyone who realised what issues were being fought out on the continent could take an interest in the goings-on at Buckingham Palace. My one thought was to get to the scene of real events as quickly as possible, and I drove the old ambulance as if she were a racing car down to the port at Newhaven, where she was hoisted on board and whence we crossed the Channel. After getting used to right-hand driving, I did my best to emulate Sir Malcolm Campbell in a race southward through France.

The poor old bus was more like a lame snow goose than a 'Blue Bird'[13] but she rattled valiantly along the endlessly straight dusty French roads, and only let us down two or three times with tyre trouble, which was easily put right. Wherever we stopped, people examined the ambulance with inquisitive interest and congratulated us on being *en route pour l'Espagne*. It was evidently quite a surprise for them to see that anyone should dare go from perfidious Albion to help the Spanish Republic, but we assured them that we were more representative of the British people than Stanley Baldwin – at which one garage mechanic said '*Tant mieux!*' and refused to accept payment for his services, sending us on our way with a '*Bonne chance et bon retour, Mesdames!*'[14]

At Perpignan we picked up another passenger, a young doctor who was joining the hospital staff at Almeria, and he took over most of the driving. It was something of a relief to have a rest from the wheel, and also a change of conversation en route, for dear old Nurse had one topic only, consisting of a long drawn out grumble over foreign food – aroused mainly by a meal of frogs which we had in a restaurant in Rouen, to her great disgust.

I remember the day we spent at Perpignan chiefly as the

one on which I first met volunteers for the International Brigade. They were three or four Americans, sitting over Pernods in a small café, and somehow we got into conversation. The sight of our ambulance inspired them with confidence in us, and they told us the exciting story of their group of volunteers. They themselves had just been released from Perpignan prison where they had been held for six months; when I condoled with them on this, one said, 'Oh, but we were the lucky ones, getting across the Atlantic. And now we've gotten this far, nothing's going to stop us getting into Spain.' Thousands of American boys would have given anything to come over, they said. As for the Canadians – didn't we hear about the thousand unemployed men in Winnipeg who had petitioned the authorities for permission to leave for Spain? They had written that they were idle men, and that they did not want history to record that they remained idle, while international Fascism struck at the very roots of civilisation. Of course, their petition had been refused, but nonetheless a good number of Canadians had managed to get to Spain, and were enrolled in the Mackenzie-Papineau Battalion.

Our American friends said they had heard it would be easy to enter Spain; but after the Non-Intervention Agreement it was in fact very difficult. They had arrived just after the agreement, two hundred and fifty of them, and had been threatened on landing in France, with deportation or jail. Determined to go on, they escaped the port authorities, and made their way through France in small groups of less than ten men. 'We acted like tourists, and tried not to talk or sing too Red!' Some of them had succeeded in reaching the Pyrenees, but our friends were unlucky. The police picked them up and bundled them into jail.

However, the rest of the groups got through; later, I heard a graphic account of their adventures: how they proceeded up into the mountains, falling over rocks, pitfalls, irrigation ditches, never daring to use a torch or strike a match for fear of the police behind them. 'Night grew cold,' wrote one, 'and the peak that meant Spain was as far off as ever. Slipping, cursing, bruised and footsore we struggled on, through blackness and in the teeth of a strong wind, stumbling into snowdrifts, our clothes almost torn from our bodies.' The gale was so fierce that they often lay down for 15 minutes till it abated. They reached Spain not so much through physical stamina as through their dogged determination to join the Republican army.

The volunteers in Perpignan knew from the guides what the journey meant, but in spite of it, and of six months in jail, they were proposing to start off that night themselves. I wished we could have taken them on board the ambulance and smuggled them out of France to save them the weary trek over the Pyrenees, but it was impossibly risky and might have ended in us all being sent back home ignominiously without ever reaching Spain.

So we said goodbye and wished them well, and set out ourselves for Port Bou. The little frontier town, normally sleepy and quiet, was swarming with officials and militia men with alert brown faces and wearing the universal blue overalls. At the customs barrier a bevy of them set on the ambulance and started to catechise us, in rapid Catalan which we found very difficult to follow, my Spanish being in the elementary stage and my companions having none at all. Mercifully, suddenly and out of nowhere, Sir George Young appeared – a superb figure in a flowing white cloak, white corduroy breeches and a broad-brimmed white hat – and, after introducing himself, took over the business of formalities. He was well-known at the frontier, as he often travelled to and from Almeria organising supplies for his hospital and meeting new members of his staff. The *milicianos* looked upon him evidently with a mixture of respect and amusement – referring to him as '*el hidalgo inglés*'[15] – and made no further difficulties.

Before we set off again, Sir George told us that he had decided that the ambulance should go to Almeria to replenish his stocks there, but that the personnel should stop off at Murcia, some 200 miles to the north of Almeria, where the situation was extremely critical. The Fascists were advancing from Malaga, and might reach it any day; they were shelling the coast towns and roads, and refugees were streaming north to Murcia, where help was now urgently needed. We did not demur at this; to be in Spain was enough, and all I wanted was to get to the interior of this most exciting of countries and as near the front line as possible. So we got into the ambulance, Sir George sitting beside the doctor driver, and Nurse and I squashed in among the crates and parcels at the back, and we rattled forward into Spain.

The road from Port Bou to Barcelona, like most Spanish highways at that time, was something of a nightmare for the driver – dazzling white dust rising in clouds, and thousands of pot holes caused by the convoys of very heavy military lorries. Then there were the breathtaking hairpin bends along the coast, at any of which you might meet an army vehicle or an ox-drawn wagon, which it was quite impossible to get past without one of you backing over the edge of the cliff and falling down the precipice into the Mediterranean, peacock blue, hungrily lapping at the rocks hundreds of feet below.

I was glad not to be at the wheel along that over-exciting route; being a passenger was nearly as bad, but one could at least look at the beautiful view over the sea to the left, and towards the mountains on the right; and when the road turned inland, one could enjoy the olive groves and the rolling fields where the corn was yellow and the flowers purple and scarlet – the colours of the Spanish Republic. I wondered whether the flag that hung from the balconies and waved over the roofs of every village we came to was inspired by the brightness of those wayside flowers or was it that the very fields were demonstrating their loyalty?

There was little sign of military activity along the road, until we reached Barcelona, where we saw a great many militiamen and officers in a variety of uniforms, army cars and lorries parked everywhere, and flags all over the place – the black and red of the FAI (*Federación Anarquista Ibérica*)[16] alongside the gay Popular Front banners. It was only a few days after the POUM (*Partido Obrero de Unificación Marxista*)[17] rising, which had caused a great deal of trouble, and some said had been organised by fascist or semi-fascist Fifth Columnists, who had played upon the anarchists' hostility to the central Government to split the Popular Front ranks.

Sir George, who knew everything there was to know about Spanish politics, gave us a dissertation on the history of the anarchist movement, and the role of the Catalan separatists; they had joined the government side in the war because Franco was out to suppress any independent nationalist grouping, and the survival of Catalonia as an entity was at stake.

The Anarchists were fine people and brave fighters, but their political differences with Madrid had caused some dangerous splits and one result had been the nearly disastrous counter-revolutionary coup of early May, which had been suppressed in the nick of time.

When we passed through there were still signs of the recent troubles, and we had to make detours to get past the remains of the barricades which had been raised during that fratricidal week. All seemed to be under control, but we noticed that the *milicianos* on the road posts near Barcelona were very jumpy, and for the first time on the journey we were unceremoniously held up while they examined papers and passes. However, Sir George was not having any nonsense, and after he had explained how very important his mission was, we were respectfully waved on.

I believe the soldiers, who were simple and friendly folk, imagined he was some high-up diplomat on whose goodwill Foreign Help to the Republic depended. He certainly looked and behaved the impressive part.

We eventually arrived in Valencia, and spent the night there in a villa occupied by a Quaker Committee which was engaged in supplying food to needy families. I was surprised to hear the lady in charge (a Swiss) say that they distributed provisions to Francoists as well as to Republicans. It struck me that when relief was in such short supply it should have been reserved for Franco's victims and not his admirers (who in any case were in the main better-off financially). The Friends were determined to be 'impartial', but the question 'which side are you on?' is one which cannot be avoided in these situations, and it is one which pacifists and Quakers, however humanitarian and worthy (perhaps because of their very virtues) too often do not answer.

By acting as though the question did not exist, they inevitably fail to be impartial, and give unwitting support to the wrong side. I didn't care for the atmosphere of the Quaker villa, which was like a competently organised welfare centre and lacked any sort of enthusiasm or awareness of the issues being fought out in Spain. But it was a beautiful place, with a garden of orange and lemon trees in full flower and fruit; looking out of the window into that cool grove was like seeing the bottom of the sea – a glimmering green underwater scene lit by golden and orange lamps.

I would have liked to stay on in the villa (having first found its inhabitants another home) if Valencia itself had seemed a 'sympathetic' town; but it was somehow uncongenial and had a sort of neutral smell which was surprising when one thought how Madrid, with whose fate it was so closely bound up, was at that very moment engaged in its life and death struggle, not so very far away.

I ventured to mention this impression to Sir George, who agreed that Valencia seemed to think itself a long way from the front. It was, like too many of the towns in the *retaguardia* (rear) a bit of a problem with its influx of evacuees from the war zone, many of whom only wanted a quiet, comfortable life, and some of them actively supporting Franco in a quiet way – sabotaging here, sending information there, keeping in touch with enemies of the Republic abroad.

I couldn't help asking the *Hidalgo* why the government allowed this, and he replied that Azaña and Largo Caballero had wanted to avoid antagonising British and French opinion by taking strong measures, and had tolerated and compromised with reactionary elements. 'This is partly why the Caballero cabinet is out,' he said. 'The left-wing parties and public opinion accused them of being half-hearted about the war. There's been a lot of inefficiency in organising the army and in production. The Communists are calling for a strong line, and are backing Prieto and Negrín; and whatever government is running the war it can't do without the Communists.'

'Why not?' I asked innocently. 'Because, whether you like them or not, they are the most energetic and determined people in the country at the moment,' said Sir George, who was no revolutionary, but knew his Spain.

This view was echoed by a NJR lorry driver, staying the night at the villa after a journey to Madrid with provisions, and back with a load of refugees. 'They don't know there's a war on, here,' he said. 'Place is run by a lot of incompetent noodles who let all sorts of fascist agents come and go and get on with no end of dirty work.'

I hoped he was exaggerating the danger. It seemed not to worry the rank and file Spanish soldiers we met in Valencia, who talked and behaved in a free and easy way that would hardly have been tolerated in any other country in the throes of civil war. Their native courtesy and kindness, and perhaps laziness, inclined them to treat everyone as friends. I was amazed at the way *milicianos* would talk to strange foreigners and give away all sorts of information in the course of conversation; usually nothing of any importance, but who knew when an enemy might not pick up just what he wanted to find out?

Chapter 13 – Hunger and Hospitals

There's a valley in Spain called Jarama,
That's a place that we all know so well,
For 'tis there that we wasted our manhood
And most of our old age as well.

Alec McDade, *There's A Valley in Spain*

In Valencia, the war seemed far away even though it was only two hundred miles off; and as we went south towards Murcia it seemed to recede further and further. We drove through orange groves, and plantations of olives, where peasants were labouring without any apparent concern (they didn't even look up at our rumbling old ambulance); then out into open hill country, where human activity tapered away completely in an arid grey rocky landscape, with the sun blazing down out of a velvety deep blue sky, for mile upon mile.

At last we reached our destination – a somnolent little white town, lying among red sandstone hills in an almost African heat and vegetation (one almost expected to see monkeys up the palm trees), with a flamboyant Baroque cathedral and picturesque market place, the centre of commerce, where the people from the province brought their fruit and vegetables. Apart from the church ceremonies and agricultural commercial transactions, Murcia normally slept peacefully in the sun. But one fine day early in 1937 it had woken up to find itself invaded by a vast flood of refugees, who had poured into it after two nights of terror on the southern roads.

They had fled from their homes in Malaga and other coastal towns and villages when the Fascists arrived, and had been shelled by warships, and machine-gunned by enemy aeroplanes as they stumbled along the coast road. They had not been able to stay in Almeria, which was itself sporadically shelled and chronically overcrowded, and had pushed on to Murcia, where many of them arrived fainting with hunger and exhaustion.

The little city's normal population was almost doubled when we got there on 30th May 1937. On top of the refugees from the south there were exiles from central Spain and a large number of wounded soldiers, besides the big hospital for International Brigaders which was full to capacity.

Frida working at the Children's Hospital in Murcia

By some miracle, almost comparable with that of the loaves and fishes, Murcia had managed to cope, at first almost unaided, with the influx. I wrote home that 'offices are working seven days a week, all round the clock, for the refugees. 12,000 were distributed among families in the town and district, and 11,000 quartered in large buildings in the town. One vast block of flats was commandeered, in a half-built state, to house some four thousand, and barracks, factories, etc., have been taken over as centres, and named after heroes of the war, Pablo Iglesias, Acasio, etc. Money was collected to provide mattresses (sacks filled with straw) and tables and benches and one meal a day. The Malagans have been living herded together like animals, with only the barest necessaries of life, in conditions of the utmost misery and dirt (they are notoriously messy people and have no idea of hygiene) for nearly six months now...'

They became hungrier and hungrier while food got shorter and shorter. The Committee in charge was in despair, 'at their wits' ends for supplies.' The miracle had worked but if disaster were to be averted, another miracle was needed; the situation was saved – temporarily again, by the arrival of an English lady, Miss Francesca Wilson, who was travelling in eastern Spain investigating conditions among refugees on behalf of the Society of Friends.

With extraordinary efficiency, and through her irresistible personality, Miss Wilson had managed to arrange for food to be sent almost overnight from Valencia, and crates of chocolate, tinned milk and soap were now arriving regularly and being handed over to the centres.

When Sir George's contingent arrived at the British Relief headquarters in the hotel Victoria, Francesca (looking as if she had just come from a garden party in a Sussex village, tall and slim and so very English in a light cotton frock, in contrast to the universal black of the Spanish women) welcomed us with open arms. She desperately needed help with supervision of the supplies, which could easily get into the wrong hands; and she had all kinds of other plans, which she unfolded as we sat in the hotel lounge that sweltering afternoon. Five of us – a stage army for the Relief of Mafeking! Francesca, however, had no doubts that her plans could be put into operation.

Two or three of us were deputed to take over the distribution of food and soap in each large centre; one of us was to organise classes for the children who were then running wild in the *refugios*; another was to supervise a women's sewing group capable, Francesca said, of turning out twenty garments a day – very necessary this, for, as my report goes, 'most of the women have only one dress, the one they wore on the flight from their village... and there are no facilities for washing clothes, even if there was enough soap.'

The last and most ambitious 'Wilson Plan' was to start a children's hospital, for which the need was perhaps the most crying of all: 'Lots of the children arrived exhausted and fell ill in the *refugios* which are not a fit place for any invalid,' I wrote. 'Several died, perhaps mercifully, as they could hardly have survived under such conditions for long; and quite a number were born and are now struggling for existence, tiny wizened things whom their underfed mothers can't adequately feed. There are a great many small children with huge bellies and scraggy arms and legs with skin diseases and diseased eyes, which would certainly get worse and spread among the others if not attended to soon.'

But the hospital scheme had to wait till the others were safely launched, Francesca said, as she took her helpers, Kathleen McColgan, a beautiful blonde Irish girl whose fair hair always produced calls of '*guapa!*' ('hey, beautiful!') and hisses of admiration from the local youths and me to the biggest centre, 'Pablo Iglesias', a huge dismantled factory where about a thousand were housed.

The first impression of the centre was quite unforgettable – the stench that assailed you as you approached the entrance, the sight of the muck heaps and piles of rusty rubbish and refuse, and of the ragged people sitting and leaning in the doorway, the filthy bony little children crawling about in the semi-darkness of the interior.

It was all like something out of Dickens at his most sordid, and hardly believable that it could exist in 1937. We went all over the building; some parts were not quite so depressing; in one room by a window a group of old men were sitting listening to a young lad spelling out the headlines of the newspaper. In other corners too, people were sitting trying to read – following words with a finger, and forming them with their lips – or talking, endlessly in the rapid soft Malagan dialect, or playing some sort of card games with filthy tattered old packs. But the overall picture was appalling, and the dirt and degradation made me feel quite sick with anger. Why were these people here? What had they done to deserve the suffering, the uprooting, the crowding like cattle in a strange stable far from their homes?

Nothing, except to have wanted to live a quiet life under a government of their own choice.

We were still more horrified and shocked when news came through an ambulance driver from the south, of the attack on Almeria by Franco's warships. The little defenceless town had been mercilessly shelled, scores of houses destroyed, and hundreds of people wounded and made homeless. It was almost more shocking than the bombing of Madrid in that Almeria was in no sense a military centre or even a post of resistance – merely a tiny place crowded with terrified refugees.

In the *refugios* at Murcia we discussed the news, and wondered gloomily whether it meant another influx of evacuees. The supplies were already quite insufficient to feed the children adequately, and several times ran perilously low.

I wrote home describing how painful it was 'watching the long line of mothers and infants to see that nobody slipped back for a second helping until everyone had had a first. Poor things, they needed third and fourth helpings, but 2,000 could only be provided once a day... poor darlings, they are terribly pathetic and clutch their biscuits and gulp their cocoa with such fervour. It takes two hours to queue them up and feed them and even then it seems very little achieved when there's so much waiting to be done.'

The idea of a possible new influx was almost too nightmarish to contemplate. Already supplies were getting low, and on more than one occasion there was a near-crisis. One day I wrote that 'this morning we arrived to give the children breakfast at eight and found the canteen had run out of *cioccolada* – so we spent two hours keeping them quiet while someone rushed off to interview a committee and extract some cocoa. They got it in the end, but I hope we shan't have the experience again of trying to amuse 600 hungry infants who had not fed for 16 hours!'

Mercifully, the central International Committee of Quakers had now heard of the need in Murcia, and extra supplies began to arrive. Less welcome was the arrival of American and Swiss personnel, into what we rather considered our territory: 'A sudden invasion of Swisso-Yanks yesterday,' I wrote ungraciously. 'they all arrived unexpectedly, proposing to start Infant Welfares and Children's Colonies and Heaven knows what else.'

In fact the well-meaning welfare workers vanished almost as suddenly as they had appeared – they may have gone on to Almeria, or they may just have kept out of our way. My prejudice against them was secretly based on a notion that they were Francoist observers – probably most unjustly – but after Valencia I tended to be as suspicious as the Spaniards were trustful!

Francesca, having launched her feeding schemes and the sewing room, turned her attention to setting up a children's hospital, and made a tour of the offices of all the local VIP's, from the *alcalde* (mayor) down. She succeeded in wheedling out of them a magnificent villa, (very modern, beautifully equipped with two bathrooms, two kitchens, all black and white tiled floors and marble stairs), in a garden on the outskirts of the town. We worked day and night to get it ready. Francesca had some anxious moments: 'After the first grand conference with the doctors I felt like fleeing back to England... They said there would be a hundred people a day coming with their sick children, and a very heavy bill for medicines. Then there was all the apparatus...'

But she refused to be daunted, and a few days later wrote that 'we went round to the *refugios* with a huge hotel bus and collected all the sick children from their straw and flies and brought them along for examination. We found ourselves landed with not only the babies but with mothers attached... and it looked like a maternity home. Then the typhoids began to pour in, in all stages of fever, delirium and sickness. It was a terrific business for one Sister to tackle, but Nurse S. was wonderful and Frida a perfect brick. Nurse S. kept reminding us that the proper quota for typhoids was one nurse to three patients. By that time we had thirteen for her alone...'

We certainly had our work cut out, and were hard at it, day and night, during the first week. But the saving of those babies was the greatest challenge of all time, I felt, as I ran to and fro for the doctors with drugs and disinfectants and bedpans and bottles, and sterilised instruments and scrubbed clothing till I was blue in the face. And what pride and joy to know that every one of the thirteen was in fact saved – they even survived the ruthless treatment of innumerable injections (which must have made them feel like pin cushions) to which they were subjected. We felt rewarded a thousand times over.

Between rush hours at the hospital, later on, I got permission to attend the local school to improve my Spanish, and sat with small girls of eight to eleven years, through their history and composition lessons. 'It reminds me of Vence school in a lot of ways,' I wrote home, 'except that they learn the *Internationale* as a school song.'

The *Internationale* was of course the adopted anthem of the rank and file Republicans, and sung on every public occasion – not because they were orthodox Marxists, or members of the Communist Party, but because the song represented to them the idea of resistance to oppression and expressed their own living experience. '*Agrupémonos todos en la lucha final, el género humano es la internacional*'[18] sang the little schoolgirls, and the old refugees, and the young soldiers, exalted by their sense of mission in '*el frente de la Libertad*'.[19]

This occurred to me very strongly at a local *Frente Popular* demonstration which I happened to attend in Murcia, and described in a letter home: 'The *grandioso mitin* was most exciting; I never saw such enthusiasm or heard such cannonades of clapping and shouting. The speakers were fairly easy to follow as their theme was what the press has been preaching all the week – *Unidad* and international solidarity. You should have heard the *Internationale*! It was much appreciated by the International Brigade soldiers who were present... they are thick on the ground here and very greatly honoured.'

Just as the song was a symbol, so were the Brigades. Ever since their arrival in the early days of the war – first as individuals, later in units which grew to be companies and battalions – their presence had warmed the hearts and steadied the nerves of the Spanish people. They were the representatives of the world's workers, and though there were never more than a few thousand of them, even at the height of the war, their fame was enormous and their deeds almost legendary.[20] It was well known that among them were the bravest and toughest of Europe's manhood: people who had suffered torture and hell in concentration camps, Italian anti-fascists who had survived the death cells on Stromboli, German Socialists and Communists who had fought in the First World War and came to put their experience at the Republic's service; Poles, Austrians, Hungarians who had suffered for their politics under reactionary governments. There were contingents from France, working-class almost entirely, and from Great Britain, including many students and writers, and from America, white and coloured, of all classes.

There were of course quite a few adventurers and vagrants, people who had been unemployed and joined the Brigades for no special conviction or ideal, but they soon dropped out of the fighting, leaving a hard core which earned a reputation in history that cannot be underestimated.

Something of what these men had risked and suffered was brought home to me at Murcia, when several of us from the Children's Unit went to a 'Big Dance' – *un Gran Baile* – organised by some local committee for the benefit of the International Brigaders, with whom the party was packed. Most of them were invalids or wounded, and I got the same sort of shock as when the wounded soldiers of the First World War were pushed in their wheeled chairs into my grandfather's garden in the summer of 1917. 'How can one be gay even at a *Gran Baile*, if your partners have an arm missing, or bandaged heads and limbs, as so many have,' I wrote miserably home. 'There are a terrible number of *mutilados* here from the International Brigade. Splendid people and marvellously brave and of course, anti-fascist to the bone. They are all champing to get back to the Front...' That was the difference between 1917 and 1937: these men had chosen to fight, accepted their wounds, and – impossible as it might seem – were even ready for more.

It was an effort to face the sight of pain and suffering, but we were asked and felt bound to go as often as possible to the International Brigade hospital and visit the severely wounded in the wards. As far as the situation allowed, they were well looked after, and amazingly cheerful as they lay in the close-packed wards, bearing the heat and the pain and the boredom stoically, patiently, even with serenity; they made me feel ashamed to be well and unscathed by the war which had treated them so harshly.

Most of these men were victims of the slaughter at Jarama, a battle for the Madrid-Valencia road when the Fascists had threatened to cut it (and sever the capital's lifeline) in February 1937. Here, the Brigade had been in action continuously for eighteen days, outnumbered by the enemy, driven back and re-forming several times, to attack over and over again, and finally after very intensive fighting to drive the Francoists back in a defeated rout.

One wounded soldier gave me his version of the battle: 'There were over six hundred of us went into action at Jarama on 10th February; a week later, there were a hundred and forty of us left not dead or wounded. Trouble was we hadn't enough modern arms: at first only museum pieces, Steer rifles forty or fifty years old; you couldn't load the clips into the magazine barrels, only one at a time. Then we got some new Russian rifles and machine guns, but only a very few tanks against all the fascists' heavy motorised stuff. Planes? We had a few small Soviet fighters, flown by Spanish pilots, against the whole German and Italian aviation!' No wonder the Soviet Union was popular among the Spanish people, I thought. And no wonder the Murcia hospital was so crowded.

The most impressive person in the whole hospital was one quite young man lying against the hard pillow, his face as white as the sheets and drawn with pain, who always grinned broadly when one of us came into the ward, and kept up a flow of wisecracks in a broad Scottish-Canadian accent while we were by his bedside.

The effort must have been very considerable for him, and we never stayed long, for it was obvious that he was in no fit state to keep up his social act. His name was Jack Brent. He had been shot through the pelvis while rescuing a wounded comrade in the field, and was paralysed in both legs. I often saw him in London later on, badly disabled but always miraculously cheerful. He lived in constant pain for five years after that, in and out of clinics; wherever he happened to be, he was laughing, joking, arguing, organising. And he died at least, undefeated till the very end.

Our impressions of the Brigade were, however, not by any means all sad. Life was made as bright as possible for the convalescents and less seriously wounded men, and parties and outings were constantly being organised by the *responsables*. We got to know several of these officers, who used to visit the villa and enjoyed Francesca's English teas, telling us long stories about their lives and experiences back home and at the front. They invited us to their socials and occasional expeditions, one of which I remember very vividly for its dramatic and nearly tragic ending.

We were taken on a bus to a beautiful place in the hills, along with some sixty Brigaders, and spent the day in a clearing in an olive grove, playing games, resting, talking, eating picnic meals and generally relaxing. A fair amount of wine had been brought, and as everybody was thirsty, more was drunk than perhaps altogether wise. It was very hot, and some people became argumentative, others amorous, some cheerful, others irritable. In the bus coming home a discussion arose, quite amicably at first, about nothing in particular; everyone joined in and made a lot of noise. I had not followed what was being said, being fully occupied in coping with the advances of some tipsy hero, but suddenly found the argument had developed almost into a free fight. Men had leapt to their feet, were abusing each other; somebody called out 'You're a b—— fascist!' This was the worst of all possible insults, and fists were brandished, blows exchanged, two Brigaders locked in a life and death tussle swayed nearer and nearer the open end of the bus, which was going at breakneck speed along the bumpy Spanish road, and one or other of the combatants was being slowly but surely pushed out. Their comrades grabbed at them without effect, and I was expecting to see the insulted party give his opponent a fatal push, when an enormous American negro caught his arm and – just in time – pulled them both back. 'Comrades, you ought to be ashamed of yourselves!' he roared, in a Robesonian bass – 'I'll shoot the next one who starts an argument!' He looked and sounded as though he seriously meant it, and everyone subsided into shocked silence. He apologised to the girls in the party. These things would happen. The lads' nerves were all to pieces, with this hell of a life...

We could well understand it. Everyone was edgy with the great heat, and the monotony of life and endless waiting in Murcia. Even when we had plenty to do we felt the tension, and when the work eased off I felt the atmosphere of the place oppressive, and longed to go somewhere that I could be of more practical use in the war effort.

Kathleen and I discussed going to the International Brigade headquarters at Albacete and volunteering for jobs at the front. But our friends in Murcia discouraged us, saying brutally 'They don't need camp followers. If you were trained nurses there would be some point, but there are plenty of Spanish girls to do the odd jobs. You'd be better off by half to go back to England and do propaganda for Spain – tell 'em the truth, make 'em wake up, and send us arms.'

We realised there was some truth in this and gave up our ideas of joining the army. I resigned myself to leaving Spain, but was determined to see Madrid first. A poisoned thumb prevented my being much use in the hospital, but would not interfere with a few days' sight-seeing in the capital. All I had to do was to wait patiently for one of the British Committee's lorries which occasionally visited Murcia with supplies, and returned to Valencia to pick up provisions for the Relief Unit in Madrid.

Eventually a van arrived. While Jack, a hefty Cockney, unloaded his cargo into the garage of the villa, I asked him to take me back with him on the return journey. He scratched his head and puckered his brow, looking me up and down as if to assess whether I'd be a liability. 'No pass? Wot abaht if they stopped the van?' It was obviously irregular, and I might get us both into trouble if the proper documents weren't produced when required. Luckily, I suddenly remembered a covering letter for all just such emergencies, from the National Joint Committee in London – testifying to my loyalty to the Republic, and to my worthy character and political soundness. At the worst, they could only turn me back – at the best, all I wanted was to set foot in Madrid, – absurdly like a pilgrim seeking inspiration at a shrine...

Chapter 14 – *¡No pasarán!*

So that men might remain slaves [...]
These machine-guns were dispatched from Italy
So that the drunken general and the Christian millionaire
might continue blindly to rule in complete darkness,
that on rape and ruin order might be founded firm
these guns were sent to save civilisation.

Rex Warner, *Arms for Spain*

We set off from Murcia very early one Sunday morning at the
end of June. Jack had to collect a load of tinned milk and
foodstuffs for Madrid, which was waiting to go to Valencia. This
meant staying the night there, although I would willingly have
travelled all day and night non-stop, just to get to the heroic and
almost legendary capital.

We rattled and bumped over the moon-cratered country –
more arid than ever in the middle of summer – reaching the
pleasant green suburbs of Valencia in the afternoon. *Los
quakeros* were kind and offered us beds; this was a godsend as
every corner of every hotel and lodging in the town was crammed
with its swollen population of refugees and an inflated military
and civil administration.

I was struck once more by the lack of urgency in the
atmosphere of the town; there were almost as many advertisements of *bailes* (dances) and concerts as war posters, and among
them we saw a *Gran Corrida de Toros* (Grand Bull Fight)
announced for that very day. Valencia was one of the few towns
in Republican Spain where bullfights were still permitted, and
Jack suggested going to see it: 'I don't care for them myself, but
it's something you oughter 'ave a look at once.' I wasn't keen –
was it the shadow cast by my animal loving Aunt Edith? But,
overcome by curiosity, I agreed, and we went along and took our
places in the crowded arena.

Apart from the enthusiasm, near idolatry, of the crowd for

the *toreador*, what struck me most was the primitive paganism of the ceremonial side, the trappings of the bull, the dance-like performance of the gorgeously attired *picadores* (the cruellest part, I thought), the inevitable final combat between *matador* and *toro*. The slaying of the bull made me feel sick, but I joined faintly in acclaiming the brave and graceful *matador*.

A comic bullfight followed, and very funny it was. The mock bull (a donkey, with huge horns attached to its head) was led in by a band of woodwind and brass, and a couple of trumpeters pranced about in place of *picadores*, trying to excite him with their tootling. The *matador* entertained the crowd vastly by his acrobatics, turning somersaults off the bull's back, and finally, instead of killing it, mounted it and rode off to the jubilant strains of the band.

In the evening, after loading up the lorry, we went out again, to a concert of flamenco music in a café, 'Might as well make the most of the joys of the *retaguardia*,' said Jack. The singing struck me as crude but exciting, one had to be a connoisseur to enjoy flamenco – the *valencianos* couldn't have enough of it, but it all went on much too long for my liking.

I could not sleep much that night, from excitement and the pain of my thumb, and was glad when it was time to get up next morning for our start to Madrid. We left before dawn and jolted along in the dark for an hour or two. My arm ached and throbbed, and when we came to an International Brigade hospital I begged Jack to stop so that I could get it dressed there.

He was quite glad of the break, and we stopped for nearly an hour after the orderly had attended to me, chatting and exchanging news with some of the soldiers – most of the slightly wounded cases who were keen to go back into action. They were envious of us going to Madrid, a city with some fight in it, even though nothing much was happening there at that moment.

Madrid had in fact been comparatively quiet since early in 1937 when the Fascists found that they were not going to be able to take it by direct assault, nor break its spirit by bombardment. It had had a terrible plastering during the first months of the war, and the centre had been badly damaged by bombs; the west side had been reduced to ruins by shelling from the Fascists on the University front.

Franco had announced that he would make a triumphal entry into the city at the end of September; the people of Madrid had answered with a defiant '*¡No pasarán!*' They built barricades, armed themselves with whatever ancient weapons they could lay hands on, turned the town into a stronghold, disregarding danger and death.

The Fascists were halted. Then Franco, who had declared that he would not bombard his fellow countrymen, let loose hell on Madrid. German and Italian planes rained bombs on the civilian population for six weeks on end. This did not break their spirit, and the attacks were called off (or rather, transferred to other centres of civilisation, Barcelona and the Basque country). There were Moorish troops entrenched within 500 yards of the Republican lines, but apart from desultory sniping and machine gunning, the front here was quiet now, and the city lived as normal a life as could be expected under the circumstances.

Madrid's chief anxiety in the summer of 1937 was food. Rationing had been imposed early on, and everyone got a basic minimum; but even with drastic restrictions, and the evacuation of the children, old people and others who could not help in the war effort, the remaining population faced a hungry autumn and winter if the democracies did not send large quantities of milk and meat and corn.

In fact, the Soviet Union supplied many shiploads of wheat, and Britain sent considerable quantities of milk and chocolate and sugar, for which (if the foodships arrived and were not sunk by Franco's torpedoes) the Spaniards were duly grateful – though I heard it said more than once, that they would really rather have had arms.

Over and over again in Spain people expressed astonishment and bewilderment that the British and French would not sell the legal Spanish government the weapons it so desperately needed, and for which it was willing to pay cash down. Non-intervention meant in fact that while the so-called democracies refused to supply arms, Italy and Germany were pouring in everything Franco needed: 100,000 troops, and hundreds of technicians; warships, planes, guns unlimited.

Nobody could deny the presence of Mussolini's army since the rout of Guadalajara, where hundreds of Italians had been captured, since the destruction of Guernica by Stukas and Messerschmidts, or since the many boastful speeches by Hitler and Mussolini in support of Franco. They were guilty of atrocious crimes; but surely the British Government's crime was as bad – of allowing the criminal to go ahead while refusing to condemn him or to help the innocent victims?

As for the leaders of the British Labour Party, they knew the full extent of the evil, and spoke fair words about helping Spain, but did next to nothing. 'We hold out our hands to the brave Spanish people,' as I heard Herbert Morrison say at Friends' Meeting House – Yes, but empty hands, Mr Morrison, which you would hardly expect the Spanish people to grasp in heart-felt gratitude, would you?

I wished some of the British statesmen who refused to help the Republic could have been on our lorry as we rattled into Madrid that lovely early summer morning. High up in the sky a formation of aeroplanes, small black dots, circled two or three times, then moved up higher still. 'Ours?' I asked the driver, who had been here many times and knew the look of them. 'Wot an 'ope,' he grunted. 'Ours 'as something better to do than waste juice 'anging about up there. No, they're Franco's all right. But they aint droppin' nothing much these days.'

Two or three grunts from an ack-ack gun followed by some little white puffs in the blue sky sent the black dots away westwards, and for several weeks after that I saw no planes over Madrid.

Where I stayed, in the villa requisitioned by the authorities for our committee workers and lorry drivers, we saw and heard very little in the way of aerial wars. I wrote home that 'Archie, as the AA gun is called, is extremely efficient, and there have been no bombs in Madrid now for months. Their planes can't come low enough to aim. They shell the centre of the town sporadically and ineffectually. Nobody takes any notice and one has the feeling of being as safe or safer than in Valencia or Murcia where they've never seen a shell, but are digging up the whole town to make underground *refugios*. Here there are none.' People of course used the metro when necessary, but had not done so since the winter. (They were forced underground in 1938, when the worst of all the bombardments preceded the end of the war.)

I'd come to Madrid in the hope of being able to do some humble job, but as my hand was out of action I had to wait, staying in the villa and rather guiltily sharing the rations of bully beef and chickpeas. However, I did a lot of sight-seeing which came in useful to the propaganda department later.

I was horrified by the desolation of the streets in the quarters which had been bombed in the raids of 1936, or consistently shelled, where every house had a gaping wound in its side or roof, or was gutted by incendiary bombs; the authorities always took immediate measure to clear away the debris and fill in the shell holes, but the destruction was appalling, and although even greater havoc was wrought all over Europe by the explosives of World War II, I still think of the damage in Madrid – involved in a war through no fault of her people or government – as more shocking than almost anything I have seen or heard of since.

I wrote for a broadcast later of 'the way they were preserving what they could of ancient buildings and monuments – bricking-in fountains which have fine sculptures and statues, for instance, so as to protect them. They have shut up all the museums and art galleries and have moved the Prado pictures to Valencia for safety – disappointing for a visitor but necessary for posterity.' I also mentioned that 'churches are still standing, hundreds of them all over Madrid, only a very few, apart from the ones bombed by Franco, were burned or destroyed at the beginning of the war when it was found that the enemy was using them as arsenals. As for anti-religious propaganda, on the hundreds of posters that paper the walls of the town there is not one that can be called anti-religious. The feeling is anti-clerical, not anti-religious.' I certainly had expected to see much more 'desecration' after the outcry in England against the Republican treatment of the Spanish clergy. The latter had won a harvest of hatred by their power and wealth and privilege, their leech-like hold over education, their support of reaction, and their resistance to any progressive measures.

I myself only heard one first-hand story of violence, about a whole village which demonstrated against a particularly unpopular priest. The church had been set on fire for the simple reason that machine guns had been found installed in the tower. This happened in many cases during the first weeks of the war, but was later prevented by the authorities as far as possible.[21]

Churches were not wilfully damaged, as Cromwell's men damaged English churches, but were emptied of valuable ornaments and statues and pictures, which horny-handed *milicianos* carried to safety. Occasionally the empty buildings were used as stores or even garages by the Republicans – it gave me quite a shock one day to see an army lorry driving out of the door of a church! – but a notice '*Monumento Nacional*' could be seen on most of them, beside, as often as not, a rough inscription in white paint to the effect that '*Jesu Cristo fue Socialista.*'[22]

As for the monasteries and convents, most of their inhabitants made their way to Franco, or were evacuated; some even joined the Republicans. The available buildings were converted into schools for refugee children or into military hospitals. I visited two of these during my time in Madrid, and wrote home on 2nd July that I had been 'all over a very interesting military hospital, once a vast convent, where they treat war prisoners, and talked to several Italians who looked well and cheerful. They were treated absolutely like brothers by the Spaniards, and were playing games and reading and resting. They can even go out for walks as long as they don't walk back to the other side, which they are hardly likely to do...'

I visited another hospital for prisoners later on, and interpreted for a visiting journalist; one or two of the questions and answers which I took down verbatim are perhaps worth quoting for the light they shed on conditions on the other side:[23] The first prisoner was a boy of thirteen!

'How did you happen to get drawn into the war?' he was asked.

'From hunger. *Es la verdad.* In our village the Fascists killed my parents. I was running away to Seville, as I heard that the workers were resisting there. But it wasn't true, they were shooting all the workers they found who had a card or who were even suspected. They said they would feed me if I joined the Falangists, so what was I to do?'

'Are there many of your age fighting?'

'Not many as young as I am, but there are quite a lot of 15 and 16 year olds over there.'

Turning to another boy, the journalist asked 'And how old are you?'

'Just 17.'

This lad had worked in Morón, 'sowing and looking after melons, mostly. When the Fascists came to our province and they murdered thousands of people. I ran away to Malaga, meaning to enlist with the Loyalists. I entered the Battalion Pi i Margal, lying about my age, as they wouldn't admit me otherwise. I fought at Malaga up to the last minute, and was taken prisoner... I was just going to be shot when my uncle saved me – he came with the Falangists – and made me enlist with them instead.'

'Did they make you attend Mass?'

'You bet. I don't know a single word of prayers but I didn't say so, not to get into trouble with the priest. And when they wanted us to pray out loud in church we said 'Ba ba ba' over and over again and got out of it like that.'

'How much did they pay you?'

'All that talk about paying needs explaining. They promised us 75 *céntimos* a day. But after owing us the money for several months, when they did pay they began to take off subscriptions of all sorts – for the Wounded Fund, for the Church, for some memorial or other, and a thousand other things... and left us with about 10 *céntimos* each. *¡Qué va!* Hunger and misery all the time.'

A third converted monastery housed refugee children who, I wrote, 'were all drawing war pictures. It was so pathetic that their minds were so full of bombs and warplanes. I asked them to draw some pictures for '*los niños ingleses*'[24] and they were thrilled and set to work right away...'

Besides wandering about Madrid, I concentrated on getting my hand cured, and certainly succeeded, if by somewhat drastic means. The Military Hospital near the villa took me as an outpatient, and the Director himself, Dr Pérez Dueño, one of the best surgeons in Spain (who incidentally turned out to know our old Cambridge friend, Professor J. B. Trend – so small is the world), lanced the abscess, which was by then pretty deep and far-reaching.

I had to go to have the hand dressed every day, which was no fun, but one could only treat it as a joke compared to the major operations which were being done in the hospital theatre daily.

There was a little open-air booth for drinks just outside the hospital, and after treatment I used to go and sit and anaesthetise myself with cheap Malaga wine, and talk to the *madrileños* off-duty. They were always friendly and polite, and would ask what people in England thought about the war.

The third or fourth day after I began going to the hospital, a big offensive was launched on the Brunete sector of the front. The first indication of this was the arrival of dozens of ambulances packed with badly wounded men who were disgorged into the hospital in their bloodstained overalls. Every inch of space, wards, waiting rooms, passages, was crowded with them, grey-faced, tight-lipped, hunched up with pain, silent except for the occasional groans and a very few of the wounded exchanging experiences, while they waited with immense patience for their turn for treatment.

That day the orderly who bound up my hand did so in a great hurry. 'You needn't come again, *camarada*,' he said. 'It will be all right – let's hope.' I thanked him and cleared off. Even if it had not been more or less 'all right' it would have seemed almost indecent to come again till all those desperate cases had been attended to – and that must have been a matter of many weeks.

As soon as I could manage to type with eight fingers, I went to the Press Department to offer to do any donkey work – translating, typing, bulletins – that was going, and was sent to the censor's office, which I described in a letter home as 'the back room of a sculpture museum, and full of strange statues and even stranger human beings. All the journalists congregate there – Pitcairn etc., and any great swells who come to Madrid usually turn up there.'

The new offensive had just begun, and the foreign journalists were hanging about waiting to send their wires back to England, France or America. Sefton Delmer of the *Daily Express* was looking through the morning hand-out and groaning, 'My God! When are we going to get a human story!' (I really couldn't help wondering what more he wanted than a look round Madrid.) Others were speculating what the offensive would bring, some of them arranging to make an expedition to the Brunete front. Among these was a very pretty slim fair-haired young woman with a camera over her shoulder. Gerda Taro was the photographer Robert Capa's close companion and she was no mean camera-woman herself.[25] She had come to Madrid mainly to attend the Writers International Congress which was taking place that week. There were two Scandinavian writers with her: Lundt, a Danish poet, and Nordhal Grieg, grandson of the composer, who later was in London with the 'Free Norwegians' and lost his life in a bomber shot down over Berlin.

Someone pointed out the Austrian journalist in charge, and feeling frightfully shy, I approached him and asked whether I could do any secretarial work for anyone. There were, it transpires, some jobs for the radio people, and also for two journalists who needed help with typing and translating, Georges Soria of *L'Humanité* and Ted Allan, of a Canadian paper; so I went off with an armful of work, very happy at last to be doing something which might remotely be considered useful.

Soria left after a few days, but I worked with Ted for several weeks in the office, to the clatter of typewriters and rush of ticker-tape news. He was small with dark shining eyes, a shock of jet black hair and a very Canadian turn of speech. He was immensely energetic and cheerful, always on top of the world. But one terrible day Ted came into the room where I was working, almost in tears.

He was just back from the expedition to Brunete, where there had been a bad accident in the confusion of a sudden retreat. Lorries and armoured cars had come hurtling back along the road, and the journalists' party had barely escaped being knocked down. Gerda Taro had been in front of them, taking photographs, and had not realised the danger. She had been knocked off the running board of a car and run over by a tank. She died in hospital the following morning.

It was almost incredible that it could have happened to that lovely little figure, and we none of us could really take it in. The effect on the whole office was shattering. It was a personal tragedy for every one of us, and it somehow summed up the hateful chaotic waste of life in wartime.

The Writers' Congress paid a tribute to Gerda and her courage at their next meeting. Tributes are not of much use to the dead, but one felt that Gerda would have been glad to be remembered by this gathering of progressive writers and poets, some of them the leading literary men in the Western world. Pablo Neruda was there, and Ilya Ehrenburg, Heinrich Mann, Martin Anderson Nexo, and Ludwig Renn (who was also a Captain in the International Brigades). André Chamson and André Malraux were among the French delegates, and Sylvia Townsend, Rex Warner and Stephen Spender among the British.

I wrote enthusiastically home that 'the whole thing was rather exciting and I was awfully glad to get in. It was disappointing that Strachey and John Lehmann and Auden weren't there, but England was quite well represented. Each representative spoke for about ten minutes, so it was as well that they didn't all come...' A flippant p.s. to the letter commented on the great heat: 'Today everyone was going about in shirtsleeves at the Writers' Congress. It was funny to see old Alexis Tolstoi shedding one garment after another. The ones in uniform – Bates and Renn who are officers in the International Brigade – could not shed, poor things. Malraux and the other Frenchmen looked fairly cool but everyone got excited and hot with all the ceremony and processions and leaping up at very short intervals to salute extra-special comrades, and sing the Internationale.'

Stephen Spender wrote about the Congress that 'its significance was not in any sense purely literary... in fact it was as emphatic an assertion as could be made of our conviction that the creation of literature today is inseparable from the struggle for a world in which the standards of culture are not destroyed by Fascism...'[26]

He was thinking, as were all present, of the drunken general

Queipo de Llano's words, 'When I hear the word "culture" I reach for my gun,' and of the murder of the poet, Lorca, by Franco's Civil Guards; and of the Nazis' proclaimed doctrine 'Science is a product of Blood,' and 'We do not know science but only that science which is valid for us Nazis,' and the persecution of German Nobel Prize winners, Einstein and Franck, and of Freud, Wellecz, Thomas Mann; and of Mussolini's victimisation of such figures as Salvemini and Silone – the burning of books, the crushing of art and of thought, the fascist regimentation of the young.

In an account written in 1942, Stephen Spender gave a curiously incomplete and biased picture of the Congress: 'I was a member of the International Writers' Congress which met in... besieged Madrid. At this Congress the French writers, when making their speeches, had (with the notable exception of André Malraux) always one gambit: to attack André Gide... These intellectuals, playing furiously the game of political necessity, declared that any criticism "outside the Party" of the Soviet Union was pro-fascist propaganda. Their querulous trembling of criticism and truth did in fact encourage their opponents.'

Not a word to describe the fervour and the faith and the passion of those speakers, or the inspiring impression of the Congress as a whole. And in the following four pages of the account, only three lines of praise for the Spanish Republicans' 'exultant faith' to 128 lines of criticism of the anti-fascists' 'mistakes' and their 'deception or stupidity and blindness.'

Although Spender insists in his autobiography that 'the pink thirties' were all a youthful illusion, what he said in June 1937 was the closer to the truth and basic reality than his later comments – and much of what he said applies equally to world conditions today. However that may be, the Congress of 1937 had great symbolic value; it did the people in Madrid immeasurable good to know that so many great and eminent men had come from all over the world in spite of dangers and difficulty, to pay homage to Spanish heroism, along with their own Bergamín, Machado, Juan Ramón Jiménez and other leading Spanish writers, who wholeheartedly supported the Republican cause.

Chapter 15 – A Visit to the Trenches

Spain is not Spain, it is an immense trench
A vast cemetery red and bombarded
The barbarians have willed it thus.
The earth will be a dense heart desolated
If you nations, men, worlds [...]
Do not break the ferocious fangs.

Miguel Hernández, *Recoged esta voz – Gather this voice*
Translated by Inez Pearn and Stephen Spender

One day I heard that some of the British drivers were going to visit the trenches in the University City, and I implored them to let me go with them. My good friend Jack agreed, provided I could get my pass fixed up. For this I needed a recommendation from somebody in a position of authority, and Jack suggested that Ralph Bates, who was in charge of the information service of the International Brigades, might be able to help.

We went along and confronted him in his office, full of maps and papers and blueprints, with Brigaders of all nationalities running in and out. He was friendly but as he had never seen me before, he hummed and hawed and made out that it wouldn't be so very easy. While I was waiting anxiously for his answer, in blew – the only word, for it was the advance of a whirlwind – Anna Louise Strong, the famous woman journalist who had travelled all over the world covering revolutionary events (or so I seemed to remember). She was one of the most impressive people I'd ever seen, large, open-faced, big innocent blue eyes, close cropped white hair. She obviously knew exactly what she wanted and had made up her mind to get it.

She descended on Comrade Bates like a typhoon on a cardboard village, and knocked him flat with her demands: she wanted a pass for the front, where the fighting was heaviest of course, it must be tomorrow at the latest, she wanted to go with so and so, and she must have a good interpreter, and would he arrange the transport and *salvo conductos* right now? Well, Ralph had only enough breath left after the assault to murmur, 'Sure, Comrade Strong,' and she swept out of the room as fast as she had come in. Later I got to know Anna Louise well, when compiling a phrase book for the International Brigade and in preparing news summaries for her.

It may have been relief at her departure, or the feeling that having acceded to all her demands, he could hardly say no to a humble request like mine. At any rate he signed and handed over a card which was the first step to being allowed to go to the trenches.

There were several other steps to be taken before one had the requisite permission, including a visit to the *Ministerio de la Guerra* and several of its sub-departments. We got my final *salvo conducto* from the *jefe* of the section for the University City front, whose office, swarming with militiamen in every sort of uniform, was the top room of a high house which overlooked the whole front from the University City away over rolling fields and hills to the Sierra – a marvellous view, green meadows and blue mountains bathed in a gold afternoon haze. It seemed impossible that there among the dips and hollows were machine guns and men whose one idea was to kill.

Against the blue distance the buildings of the University City rose, their square lines and yellow and russet tones making them look like the Greek temples at Paestum or Girgenti. And so they were – temples of learning and culture and science, and like Girgenti, ruined now but still beautiful.

The University had been planned as a group of buildings, one for each faculty, with a specially fine one for Medicine, and a great hospital, '*el Clínico*', for treatment and practice. So far only a few buildings had been completed but the Spaniards were immensely proud of the 'city', and it was a major tragedy for them that so much of it had been destroyed. The worst damage was done to the *Clínico*, which for months had been fought over and remained for some time partly occupied by rebels, partly by Republican troops.

Only a short time before I saw it, the Government had decided to blow it up, and loyal troops were secretly withdrawn from it. Asturian miners, experts in the art of dynamiting, tunnelled under the building to lay mines. And up it went, with five hundred fascists inside it. The young officer who told us this added a bitter comment on Franco's contribution to culture and science.

Armed with our safe conducts we went down into the street and set out towards the front. It was a beautiful afternoon, and in the brilliant sunshine the destruction in the war-torn street seemed even more sinister. It got more and more desolate as we went on. Every one of the houses facing the Casa de Campo had been shelled, and stood with disembowelled rooms, ceilings hanging down in ribbons, piled-up rubble, bedding, picture frames, fireplaces in a strange surrealist muddle. The street itself was ploughed up, the tramlines shooting into the air, the lamp-posts twisted and bent, the trees leafless skeletons. Not a soul in sight on the very long road, and the silence of death all round – it was all very extraordinary when one thought of the Puerta del Sol with its cheerful people and its cafés, less than two miles away.

After about a kilometre we reached the entrance to the trenches – a courtyard where a group of *milicianos* were enjoying their midday meal. The cook was dishing out helpings of fried sparrows and onions from a huge pan; he pressed us to taste, and I was dying to sample the dish, but time was short and we had to push on.

We went into the entrance hall of the Medical School, once a beautiful room of marble and stucco, but now a waste of rubble and plaster; then through into the lecture hall, with its blackboards shattered and benches turned upside down, broken, in heaps, or scattered by shells through the roof. Our guide, who had been a student here, hurried us through – he obviously hated the sight. We went on to the refectory where soldiers lived and slept. The walls were covered with frescoes they had painted depicting the glories of the Republic, and with suitable slogans as captions. They were crude daubs, but simply shouted out the vitality and gaiety of the artists.

Next we proceeded, bent nearly double, along narrow trenches leading toward the *Clínico*, while shells went screaming overhead, soaring across and landing with a thud in the distance.

The communication trench led downwards into what seemed like the bowels of the earth. At any rate, we were feeling our way in pitch darkness – then up to daylight again and into the semi-permanent dugouts where the troops had been living for several months.

I had half expected the horrors of 1917 – mud, lice, rats – but was quite wrong: these trenches were clean and dry, and had been converted by their inhabitants into charming little dwellings with doors and windows, panelling and furniture, brought from the university classrooms, and with ingenious devices for hanging up clothes and airing them. Some had planted flowers outside the doors; others had carved their names or slogans over the entrances.

Every little compartment had a name – Casa Florida, Hotel Victoria, Hotel Rusia, Villa Pasionaria, and so on – and each competed for a prize for comfort or *cultura*. As we went past the doors we could hear flamenco and guitars, and when we came to one labelled Casa Lenin, where the commanding officer lodged, we were invited to step in and listen to the gramophone, of which they were fearfully proud. We sat down and heard a record, husky and trench-worn (it was the only one they possessed), while they clapped their hands and tapped with their feet – except for one, a young soldier who was sitting bent over a piece of wood which he was carving into a tray. He told us that he was from Cordoba, 'where they do a lot of carving,' and he hoped to win a competition for the most beautiful article produced in the trenches.

Next door to this was the company's office, full of people working and reading by electric light, and they asked us to look round the *biblioteca* (library); they had carpentered shelves to hold their books, a collection ranging from arithmetic texts to economics, thrillers and picture books, over which someone had pinned up a portrait of Goethe! Surely, I thought to myself, this must be the first time war has been such a breeding ground for culture and education.

We proceeded for about a kilometre, right up to the points where occasional firing took place. There were militiamen beside their guns, waiting for a chance to pot at a Moor ensconced in the remains of the *Clínico*, five hundred yards away. 'Just let one put his head up and see what happens!' said a cheerful little Andalusian. I said he was lucky to be doing something for the final victory – or something to that effect – and he offered me his post, made me sit down by the gun, showed me which lever to lift and where to push – Hey presto! – I had fired a shot for freedom.

The thought that I might conceivably have killed someone, even a Francoist Moor, gave me the shudders, but I thanked him heartily and wished him success and peace as we said goodbye. I often wonder what happened to him, and to the guitarist and the wood carver from Cordoba. Were they among the more fortunate ones who got out of Spain in 1939? Any other supposition did not bear thinking about.

I spoke about that trip to the trenches very briefly on the radio a few nights later. The British commentator had been taken ill with jaundice (and poor thing, put on a diet which it was impossible to obtain in half-starving Madrid), and he asked me to stand in for him till he recovered. It was the beginning of many nights' vigil in the dark little room high up in the Telefónica building, where two or three of us sat waiting to read the news or give a talk on the situation, beginning, *'¡Aquí la voz de España!'*[27]

It was some slight satisfaction to do the talks and to feel one was meeting General Queipo de Llano on his own ground – the air. Even if one could not emulate his atrocity stories, or present the facts in quite such a horrifically picturesque way as he presented his fictions, one could at least contradict some of the wild statements he was making about the 'Marxist beasts' with a few home truths about the goings on of the Fascists, beside which the behaviour of the Republicans, decent by any standards, was the height of civilisation.

Apart from broadcasting and odd jobs (such as editing a Spanish Grammar for the English-speaking International Brigaders, which I did for Anna Louise Strong, and which contained a section of phrases not usually found in such books, useful to anti-fascists in wartime – pass the ammo quick! My gunlock is rusty etc.), there was not much for me to do in Madrid; and though it was like being torn up at the roots, it seemed better to go home and try to tell something to our own people rather than to stay doing jobs I could do less well, and consuming precious Spanish rations.

I remember the journey back very clearly, in a train packed with *milicianos* singing and strumming their guitars, the hours between trains at Barcelona (where there were no more barricades – the POUM had been disbanded and an uneasy coalition reigned between the FAI and Republicans), visiting an International Brigade hospital at Port Bou, where I had to sleep on the pebbles of the beach, so crowded was the little town; and the return to the world this side of the Pyrenees – a quite different, only half-awake world. But in Paris I found something of Spanish awareness again – the movement for Spanish Relief and the demand for arms for Spain was tremendous, and it was impossible not to see that it was only the attitude of the British Government which prevented all the help necessary going from France to Spain. In the World Exhibition, housed in palaces along the Seine from the Trocadero to the Pont Neuf there was a corner of Spain itself: photographs and handicrafts and posters from Republican territory. In charge of it was a couple of typical *milicianos*, dark, bright-eyed, intelligent, and both of them, alas, typical in another way of too many of the Spanish army – short of a limb.

On one side of the pavilion hung Picasso's *Guernica* – a background symbolic of all Spain's suffering. Two thoughts crossed my mind, I remember: one was that Mr Chamberlain ought to be made to live with that picture for a year; the other, that Picasso's painting of the final triumph of the Republic, as exuberant as Guernica is tragic, would be something to look forward to indeed.

Chapter 16 – Basque Children

Tell the workers of England
This was not a war of our own making

John Cornford, *A Letter from Aragón*

It was a very curious feeling being back in England in August 1937 – as if one had been given a pair of spectacles which enabled one to see things which other people could not. Of course, thousands of people in England had the same glasses – all those who had been to Spain, or had read the reports of honest journalists, or had radical instincts – but those thousands were not a high proportion of the millions of British people who had to feel strongly about Spain if she were to be saved. If only public opinion could force the British Government to give up the sordid farce of non-intervention there was no doubt at all that the Republicans could sweep Franco out of Spain – as everyone who knew the country, from Sir George Young to the humblest *miliciano*, could see.

Organisation there was better than it had ever been, since Negrín had taken over from Prieto and formed a government of national unity with a programme of energetic measures, designed to draw the whole of Republican Spain into the country's defence; even Murcia and Valencia had been galvanised! Morale was excellent, three-fifths of the country was under government control and the refugee problem was pretty well solved; though the need for food supplies was extremely urgent, at least everyone had a roof over his head.

Behind Franco's lines, the population, though decimated and terrorised, was in silent revolt, pinning its hopes on the government's victory. That victory would have been a certainty if the Republicans had been able to get arms from France and England. But as it was, they were hopelessly handicapped. They could hold out for a long time but they had not the means to advance and break through.

A horrible feeling was beginning to haunt their friends that time was getting very short. If victory was to be theirs, it was vital that the British people should be roused from their apathy – and quickly. The latter had got to understand the issue which was in three words, War or Peace; for defeat of the Spanish Republicans meant, in the end, Hitler and Mussolini's conquest of Spain, their acquisition of valuable raw material for their war industry, and of a military base of great strategic importance controlled by their puppet; there could be no doubt that a Fascist success in Spain would encourage the dictators in their drive to world domination, and that we might very well be forced into war to prevent this, and under very unfavourable conditions.

This all seemed crystal clear to Left-wingers, and even to many Conservatives who supported the demand of arms for Spain on purely patriotic grounds. It must have been equally clear to the Labour Party leaders, who could have rallied the whole working-class movement in a campaign to save Spanish democracy had they wanted to. But no; they preferred not to embarrass Neville Chamberlain's government. So the launching of a mass movement which might have swept the country and turned non-intervention into positive help for the Republic, was never attempted.

Apart from the Communist Party and the Left Book Club and other leftist groups, the whole question of 'Aid for Spain', the job of rousing public opinion and spreading information, was left to the relatively small group of enthusiasts who ran the National Joint Committee and its affiliated organisations. Their tasks were colossal: they had four thousand Basque children on their hands, refugee hospitals to support, food ships to pay for and load with provisions, medical supplies, clothing, etc. Money-raising was the most urgent job, and a steady flow of leaflets and appeals poured from the office in Marsham Street to the literature stalls at meetings and demonstrations. There were pamphlets, reports, books by the score, both the Spanish Government's own material (beautifully produced and illustrated) and our own writers' – the Duchess of Atholl's *Searchlight on Spain*, Koestler's *Spanish Testament*, Frank Pitcairn's *Reporter in Spain*, Sir Peter Chalmers Mitchell's *My House in Malaga*, George Steer's *Tree of*

Gernika, to name only a few; besides these were the day to day hand-outs by Charles Duff's Spanish News Agency, and the feature articles in the *News Chronicle* and the *Manchester Guardian* and the *Daily Worker*.

There was no excuse for anybody not *knowing*, all that was needed was a slight push by the Labour Party in the right direction. But that push never came.

From the autumn of 1937 onwards one could not work for Spanish Relief in England without a feeling of great bitterness about politicians who had it in their power to save the situation, but did nothing.

Still, that was not a reason for not throwing oneself heart and soul into the work of trying to make people understand, through whatever ways lay open to us. There were plenty of ways: to bring the Spanish war home to the British, one had only to introduce to them the Basque children living in their locality. By this time there were forty-odd Spanish Children's 'colonies' housed in private mansions, Salvation Army hostels, Convents, work houses, up and down the country. Wherever there was a group of children needing a home, local sympathisers had helped, formed a committee, found a house, and undertaken to look after them. And wherever there was a colony, in spite of hostile propaganda and some few minor misdemeanours by wild boys and girls uprooted and far from home, they made their way to people's hearts and were adopted and loved.

They had arrived straight from starvation and bombing in Bilbao, dirty and ragged, with skin diseases and trachoma, they had been received and cleaned up in Southampton Camp (beautifully described in Yvonne Cloud's book, *The Basque Children in England*)[28] sorted out and divided roughly into groups of Basque Catholic Nationalists and 'reds', and then distributed all over the country.

By the time I got back to England, the homes were more or less organised and staffed, and were running partly on a subsidy from headquarters, partly on money raised locally. When I went to Cambridge to see my parents after my Spanish expedition (which had caused them far more worry than it had me) I found my mother busy helping to organise a hostel where thirty children were housed, with the support of my father, who had become strongly pro-Republican and a great democrat – he had even persuaded the Combination Room of Trinity College to take the *Daily Worker*, for its Spanish news. In Cambridge, an appeal for funds had been published, under the signatures of several eminent dons, including Canon Raven, Professor J. B. Trend, Dr Plumb, and Mr F. L. Lucas, and a model home had been provided for the children, who were treated to the best that Cambridge could offer them in the way of education – Rosita Bal, a pupil of de Falla's, taught them music, Mrs Youngman art, and they went to concerts and plays and exhibitions to their hearts' content.

The supporters and friends of the Basque Home were rewarded by an extraordinary flowering of talent among these children, who decorated their hostel with brilliant and original paintings, made furniture and ornaments, danced and sang and acted with a gaiety and vitality that was as touching as it was unexpected in these war orphans – many of the Cambridge contingent had lost one or both parents. The girls made clothes and knitted, and the boys excelled in gymnastics and football and later many of them found places in leading teams. They were without exception intelligent and attractive children, and an excellent advertisement for Spanish Republican Youth – though it can fairly be said that the Cambridge Committee did not exploit them for political ends as some supporters were occasionally accused of doing. (And after all, why not? The children themselves were only too glad to do propaganda for their cause, and their drawings were full of socialist slogans, and gallant anti-fascist fighters!')

The National Joint Committee was not averse to combining propaganda with child welfare, and gave me a dual job which covered both aspects of the Committee's work; on the one hand, I had to visit the Basque homes and to report to London on their welfare and needs, after talking to staff, children and *señoritas* (that I spoke Spanish was my chief, perhaps my only, qualification); on the other hand, I had to try to raise money by organising meetings, with speakers on the Spanish question, and concerts at which the children themselves could perform.

THE BASQUE CHILDREN

will perform in

FOXTON VILLAGE HALL

on

Tuesday, October 25th, 7.30 p.m.

SPANISH NATIONAL DANCES

SPANISH FOLK SONGS

FILMS OF SPAIN

Entrance Free   **Collection for Spanish Relief**

*Flyer for a performance by the Basque Children at Foxton Hall,
illustrated by the well-known Cambridge artist, Gwen Raverat.*

There was no difficulty at all in arranging concerts, for every home had its quota of star singers and dancers among the children, while practically all of them were able to join in a chorus, or a Basque *jota* or spinning dance. The exceptions were the youngsters housed in the convents, where they were not encouraged to sing and dance, and where life, I found on visiting their bare and gloomy quarters, was far from gay. Jollity in any form was (to put it mildly) a secondary consideration with the Catholics who had taken the children in with the object of saving their souls; it would however have been churlish of our Committee to complain of the austerity of the young Basque lives, for in fact their bodies as well as their souls had been saved by the humanitarian action of the Catholics, and they were treated with genuine kindness.

SPANISH SMILES

Photo]   [*Cambridge Daily News*
Basque children from the Cambridge hostel are giving daily performances at the Spanish Shop, 33, Bridge Street, where an exhibition is in progress in connection with the Central Spanish Relief Committee.

'Spanish Smiles', Basque children performing in Cambridge.

156

The Salvation Army also showed a spirit of true Christianity by temporarily adopting about a hundred of the non-Catholic children, and in their hostel at Brixton a certain amount of religious observation was introduced into their routine. These children were a tougher proposition than the little Basque Nationalists, most of them coming from socialist or communist homes where prayers and hymns were unheard of. However, the officers of the Salvation Army in charge succeeded in teaching them enough English to learn some of their songs. They brought the house down with their rendering of *Jesus Wants Me for a Sunbeam* and *The Bells of Hell Go Ting-A-Ling-Aa-Ling* at a concert in London, given before they left the Brixton hostel and were dispersed to other homes.

They Embraced Our Cameraman.

Appearing for the first time on any stage in dresses and dances of their own devising, a party of eight Basque children delighted a large audience at the Kettering Central Hall on Wednesday evening. Here are are six of the girls in one of their characteristically Spanish dances. The children speak little English, but with Southern vivacity they clustered round our photographer (whom they called the "Photo Man") after this picture had been taken and warmly embraced him.

'They Embraced Our Cameraman':
Basque children dancing in Kettering

I travelled hundreds of miles during that autumn and winter, in a valiant Baby Austin, and must have visited almost every sizeable town in the country. Wherever committees existed they had to be looked up and shown how keenly interested the central office was in what was going on, while one had to urge them to make even a little more effort to raise money, and to explain the ever-growing need to help the children and Spain.

It was like being a commercial traveller in some kind of invisible goods which one offered on credit. One had not many customers, but those that were interested in the particular line were marvellous clients who welcomed the traveller and took all there was to offer. Unlike most *commi-voyageurs* (commercial travellers) I found it a most heartening and stimulating experience, and the results most rewarding.

Liverpool and Preston, Blackpool, Coventry, Hull, Newcastle, Leeds, Durham and many other towns started new groups; Leeds, Manchester and Warrington promised to redouble their efforts and arranged great Town Hall concerts with a group of Basque Children, Consuelo Carmona the dancer, Isabel Alonso the singer or other public-spirited professional artists; Scotland was roused into starting a regional organisation to support a Basque colony at Montrose, a cold rather bleak spot where Kathleen McColgan was holding the fort and keeping up the children's spirits and temperatures by teaching them Scottish dancing and games.

Kathleen's own spirits were flagging somewhat, and she suffered considerably from the attentions of a Wee Free Minister who visited the hostel constantly, ostensibly to supervise the moral welfare of the children, but actually to enjoy the company of their superintendent. We plotted together to get her transferred, and a few weeks later she was off to a more congenial if equally difficult job, organising a Spanish Aid committee in Northern Ireland. This would certainly have defeated me but she had enough charm and blarney to break through even the defences of the bourgeoisie of Belfast.

After Aberdeen and Dundee and Perth, which were as friendly and helpful as they looked grey and forbidding, I drove to Stirling, not with any hopes of winning support for Spain, but to revisit my aunt Edith and my boy scout uncle. Pillars of the Conservative Party, they both obviously thought me rather mad or hopelessly misled, but I knew I should not come away empty handed from such kind and public-spirited people. 'Waste of time to wear yourself out for the little Dagoes,' commented Uncle Maurice, and my aunt sighed and murmured something about bull fights, and the cruel way the Spaniards treated their donkeys. But they listened with patient pity to my plea for the Republicans, and gave me a generous donation to the Montrose children's funds. I felt guilty at imposing on their kindness, but loved them for it.

After giving my uncle a contribution towards his slum boys' summer camp, I said goodbye and went on to Glasgow, where one could appeal without trading on personal relationships, for Left-wing, Liberal and Labour support for the children. Before leaving the grim dark hard-working city I had the promise of a rousing campaign for the cause and of a strong all-Scottish committee; and the result after a few months was a fine flourishing movement which proved the best possible reward for the 'commercial traveller.'

I was beginning to get letters from the head office suggesting that my stay in bonny Scotland had lasted long enough and that there were other parts of the British Isles to attend to. I wrote back to the effect that I had struck gold and could not leave it untapped, but would return soon, visiting a number of North-Western towns on the way, and soon started south across the Grampians, feeling sorry to leave Scotland but looking forward to revisiting Lancashire, which for all the poverty of the depression seemed to me one of the warmest-hearted and most welcoming parts of the world.

On the way south I stayed at Wilfrid Roberts' home in Cumberland to report to him, and to see the hostel nearby – eighty-odd children housed in an old, rather bare, but spacious work house, their welfare assured by being under the wing of Lady Cecilia Roberts, Wilfrid's imposing and splendid mother.

I stayed the night in the great Liberal house, where even the soap in the bathroom was stamped 'The country needs Liberalism.' As I thought of what the Roberts had done for the anti-fascist cause, of Wilfrid's untiring work for Spanish and British democracy and his family's generosity and broadmindedness, I felt inclined to agree with the soap. At the same time I remember thinking, 'If only they were socialists!' Even the older generation, Lady Cecilia and Lady Mary Murray, her sister, would have been leading the left-wing movement in England if they had been a few years younger; they were far more radical than a great many so-called socialists in the Labour Party.

I drove south by Preston, Manchester, Blackpool and Warrington, visiting Left Book Club groups in each place, and trying to revive a somnolent committee or start a new one in each.

In Manchester, of course, Spanish Relief was a really live issue, and people were very wide awake; contingents of International Brigaders had gone from the area and come back to tell about Spain and stir working-class feelings of solidarity; the Liberal traditions ensured strong middle-class support. Somehow, however, the Basque children were out of the picture, owing probably to the fact they were housed in a Roman Catholic Convent and kept mainly under close supervision by the nuns. Not many people knew of their existence, and hardly any visitors had been to see them. I arranged to take them out for an afternoon, and we visited a Spanish Republican ship harboured in the Manchester Ship Canal, manned of course by their compatriots. When the children, escorted by two nice looking *señoritas* and the priest in charge (Spanish priests had been sent by the Basque Government to keep an eye on each Catholic group) arrived at the ship they got a tremendous welcome from the crew, who entertained them with songs, accompanied by a guitarist, and provided a sumptuous Spanish meal. Later on, I introduced the children to some members of the Manchester Co-op, and from then on, I believe they never lacked for visitors or English friends.

But it was from the little towns to the north and north east of Manchester that the best response came – from unemployed Colne and Nelson, and hard-hit Rawtenstall, where everything appeared to be half-dead except the spirit of the local people. I called on the Labour Party secretary and was referred to a certain

160

John J——, a tailor, who was one of the few men in the area working on his own job; I found him sitting cross-legged on a table, sewing away and talking to a couple of out-of-work mates. He made me sit down, gave us all tea, and we sat for two hours discussing what could be done in Rawtenstall for the Spanish Republicans.

I don't remember what resulted – perhaps they collectively 'adopted' a child (for 10 shillings a week a Basque became a 'foster child'), perhaps they guaranteed 5 shillings a month to the Medical Aid funds; whatever it may have been was worth infinitely more, from the spirit in which it was promised, and from the fact that these people realised what was at stake and were prepared to make what amounted to a very substantial sacrifice to help. I left them with feelings of the greatest warmth and admiration, wishing there were millions more like them.

While the North was the most fertile ground for our endeavours, the South was by no means barren; even in the holiday resorts, help and sympathy were forthcoming after some exploratory expeditions. The number of Free Church Ministers (more understanding than those of other denominations), Town Councillors and local VIP's whom I called on must have run into scores. Many of them became sponsors of local committees which, with the Left Book Club groups, Co-operative Societies, Communists and Liberals (the usual backbone of the campaign) we managed to start in such unlikely places as Worthing and Brighton and Folkestone.

One bright Saturday morning on the South Coast, I found the urge to cross the Channel irresistible, and boarded a boat from Folkestone bound for a day trip across to Boulogne. It turned out to be a busman's holiday, for when I called at the local *Front Populaire* headquarters, they told me that much of their activity was directed to helping Spain, and they suggested a visit to a large centre for refugee children not far along the coast. This had not been my idea, but after all why not?

In the first café I came to, the *proprietaire*, himself not much interested in politics told me where the local Aid Spain committee met, who the secretary was, and how to find him. (In some notes jotted down that day I 'wondered how many shopkeepers in an English town could tell one straight off where to find the Spanish Relief Committee!') I ran the secretary to earth in the *mairie* (town hall), where he held an important official post, and heard about Boulogne's efforts which (I scribbled) 'make ours seem very small indeed.' Our collections and meetings paled beside the *manifestation*, held in the biggest hall in the town month after month, and their outdoor demonstrations 'where helpers go round with flags held out like a sheet into which the audience drop their notes and coins.' 'They have sent load upon load of food and clothing, and every month a caravan of lorries passes collecting *vivres*. They send 3,000 kilos of goods and 5,000 francs to Paris every time. Fifty local volunteers have gone out to Spain to fight, and the committee provides for their dependants, some twenty families. And yet they don't consider they have done enough.'

M. Bonne, the secretary, explained apologetically that 'Boulogne is a difficult place – very bourgeois.' The Roman Catholic Church which had great influence there was very sympathetic to Franco, and tried to prevent help going to the Republicans. But the committee he said, was going to make even greater efforts; they were covering the town systematically with leaflets, and following these up with house to house collections, and there would be a series of *fêtes champêtres* (garden parties) in the country around, during the summer.

'Boulogne is not a rich town,' I commented in my notes. 'In spite of the recent wage reforms, some of the fishermen are not earning more than 38 francs a day, and the dockers get an average weekly wage of 200 francs (about £2). Compared with the inhabitants of Folkestone opposite, those of Boulogne are very poor, but they can give generously and make sacrifices in a cause which they realise is their own... if only British dockers and fishermen realised it as well!'

I decided to miss the ship home that night, and go instead along the coast to the big Trade Union rest home which had been turned over to house refugee Spanish children. This was an ideal home indeed – the hundred children were living in a superb old chateau, having the time of their lives. The TUC secretary who was responsible asked me anxiously how it compared with homes in England: 'They are not dressed like little milords, we know,' he admitted, 'but they are happy, *n'est-ce-pas?*' I assured him that we'd be proud to do what he had done, in any of our Basque hostels, and that we especially envied the solid Trade Unionist support that they had.

He agreed that our Labour Party leadership had a bad name with the French workers. Perhaps he had heard Sir Samuel Hoare's congratulations to the TUC for their 'wise attitude over the Spanish crisis.' Maybe he knew, too, of Mr Bevin's speech in 1937 when Spanish delegates had appealed for action, and the British spokesman had refused to budge – in a speech described by M. Vanderveld, the by no means red Belgian Trade Union leader, as 'a cold douche.'

'*Tous les laboristes britanniques ne sont pas comme ça, nous savons,*'[29] he added. 'They'll surely change their line if the friends of Spain work hard enough.'

I went back to England cheered by this typically French attitude, and praying for the long life of the Popular Front – and for the advent of a similar movement in Britain. Because if this could be realised, Europe could still be saved from fascism – if not, the chances for democracy were none too good.

Chapter 17 – Falling Bastions

1st Lunatic:
Madmen of Westland! In this hour of supreme crisis
I feel called upon to say a few words... Let us never forget
that we are Westlanders first and madmen second.
As Westlanders we have a great tradition to uphold.
Westland has always produced 10% more lunatics
than any other country in Europe.
And are we going to show ourselves inferior to our forefathers?
Never!

W. H. Auden & Christopher Isherwood, *The Dog Beneath the Skin*

The outlook for 1938 was black indeed. While the storm in Spain continued unabated, dark and threatening clouds were piling up in Central Europe. The Nazis obviously needed to divert their population from their economic problems ('guns before butter' was not a popular slogan or one they would accept indefinitely without some results).

They had been checked by the Spanish Republicans in what might have been a great propaganda victory and was in fact, more of a defeat; so they turned to what seemed an easier prey, and began to bring acute pressure on Austria (which Hitler had always declared to be a part of greater Germany) to submit to Nazification from within. Chancellor von Schuschnigg had always, in spite of his Clerical Fascist regime, proclaimed himself a firm supporter of Austrian independence. He had kept the Austrian Nazis under control, had refused to have pro-Germans in his Cabinet, and had always tried to play Mussolini off against Hitler.

But he signed a pact with Hitler in 1936; one of the clauses committed Austria 'to conduct its general policy... in accordance with the fact that Austria recognises herself to be a German state.' This of course was tantamount to accepting Germany's suzerainty. Ever since 1936 the Nazis had been secretly

164

infiltrating the Austrian government, its police, the civil service; by January 1938 the country was ripe for a German coup. The workers' organisations had been suppressed since 1934, and though they were very active indeed underground, the only legal instrument for defending Austria's independence was the Fatherland Front, an organisation consisting mainly of Schuschnigg's middle-class Catholic supporters.

One of the best-informed writers on Austria, G. E. R. Gedye, deplored what he called 'the hopelessness of Schuschnigg trying to fight Nazism with this unreal business of the Front. There was a brightly glowing faith among the Communists. Among the Socialists there was a steady certainty of final victory... based on the sheer logic of where the interests of the great majority of the population lay, on a deep sense of rightness amidst a wrong-headed world.'

Schuschnigg's tragedy was that 'blinded by his Catholic hatred of the reds' he left unutilised 'this passionate desire of the masses to keep Austria free of the Brown horror from Germany... wasting all his talents on trying to infuse life into this meaningless Fatherland Front.'[30]

On 12th February Hitler summoned Chancellor Schuschnigg to Berchtesgaden, and there delivered his ultimatum, which was in fact Austria's death sentence. Schuschnigg stood up in a dignified manner to Hitler's insolence, to being vilified as a 'dwarf' and 'Jesuit's spawn' etc., and he refused to accept eight of Hitler's points. But he gave way on three of the most important, one of which was the installing of Seyss-Inquahart (a known Nazi but pretended supporter of Austrian independence, who later became Hitler's Governor General of Austria).

It is perhaps worth quoting Mr Gedye's account (from a first-hand source) of the interview, for the benefit of those who harbour any illusions about Hitler's sanity:

He shouted at him, 'How have you dared all these years to oppress and torture my people – my German people in Austria? Now your hour has come. God has made me Führer and ruler of every man and woman of German blood in every country on earth. You shall bow to my will as all the rest of the world shall bow, or I will break you... You will accept and sign here at once or I give the order to march into Austria immediately.'

In turn, Hitler bullied, shouted, burst into tears... and shook his fist in the face of the Austrian Chancellor who looked at him with a cool aloofness which only increased the other's frenzy. Again and again he shouted, 'Listen to me... I am the greatest of all Germans – the greatest German who has ever lived!... My people in Austria are starving, Herr Schuschnigg... I am going to march in... There is not one country which will lift a finger to save you, and I have three divisions ready to march.'[31]

This uncontrollable frenzy of Hitler's was typical. A pro-Nazi British diplomat remarked after one such display that he felt that 75 million Germans were now controlled by a madman. He drew the strange inference that Britain ought to humour the madman by yielding to him on every point!

There was alas, one truth – and one truth only – in Hitler's diatribe: that nobody would lift a finger to save Austria. When Schuschnigg at the eleventh hour raised the ban on the underground Left, and called for a plebiscite for the country's independence while the Nazis massed for invasion on its borders, the British government showed through Neville Chamberlain's silence, that it intended to do nothing to prevent invasion.

Two hours before Schuschnigg's plebiscite was due to begin, Hitler ordered his army to march in to Austria. The local Nazis emerged from their holes to give them a big welcome, and by the end of the day the reign of terror had begun.

At the time, many British people did not realise the full horror of the Austrian story following the Nazi takeover. But soon anyone reading between the lines of the laconic newspaper reports shuddered to think what was going on there, largely due to our Government's inaction. It was too late to make amends, even if it had been possible, when we got details of the frightfulness of the occupation: the suicides (several hundred a day in Vienna alone), the murders, the torture, degradation and ruin inflicted on innocent Jews. I thought, miserably, of the Lowensteins, our doctor hosts of 1933, and knew they could not have escaped – for the most terrible thing about the Austrian tragedy was that there was no way out for the victims. Some Germans had been able to escape Hitler; but to the Austrian fugitives, all frontiers were closed, and the proportion of massacres and suicides and concentration camp deaths was higher than at any time in the horrible history of fascism.

Austria's neighbour, Czechoslovakia might naturally have been intimidated by the aggressive and brutal attitude of the Nazis, now in Vienna and making rude and threatening gestures in the direction of Prague; but the Czechs were 'not frightened but hardened like Bessemer steel by the fate of Austria.'

In the meetings which were rapidly organised in London to explain the events in central Europe, I heard a speaker insist on the Czechs' will to resist, and their belief in their well-organised army and modern arsenals; and of course their trust in Britain, Russia and France to carry out international obligations and to stand up to any further nonsense of Hitler's. Unfortunately, the USSR, though ready and willing, was geographically ill-placed to help; France was in the throes of a political crisis, the pro-Fascist Laval only too anxious to appease the Nazis; while Chamberlain and Lord Halifax, in spite of pressure from the Left, continued their policy of turning a blind eye to German aggression.

Demands from Czechoslovakia's Nazi leader, Henlein, for full independence for the Sudeten Germans within the Czech borders, were recognised by anyone *au fait* with the situation as being the thin end of the Nazi wedge. Meetings, protests, representations to Mr Chamberlain made no difference; anti-fascists in London still hoped and clamoured for a stand. Instead we got an announcement that the Prime Minister was going to Berchtesgaden to meet Herr Hitler. On 14th September, the word went out for all who could manage it to go and give him a worthy send off: and the crowd, hoping to make it clear that Hitler must be warned off any adventures in Czechoslovakian genocide, shouted out with one voice, 'Stand by Czecho!' Instead, Edvard Benes, the Czechoslovakian Prime Minister, was warned that he would be left to his own devices, as far as Britain was concerned.

On 28th September, Chamberlain announced his second meeting with Hitler; this time he was going to Munich, by the

Führer's request. Not many people realised just what Chamberlain's visit to Munich at Hitler's request would mean. In the House of Commons, Members of Parliament, appalled at the thought of Nazi bombers over London and knowing all too little about either Neville or the Nazis, cheered him and wished him God Speed. Only William Gallacher, the solitary Communist, refused to join in, and was considered very sour for saying, during the debate, that he 'would not countenance the cutting up and destruction of a small state.'

When Chamberlain returned from Munich, waving his umbrella and announcing 'peace in our time', he was greeted again with cheers of relief. It was only after some days that thinking people began to realise what 'peace' meant, both to ourselves and to the Czechs: the handing over to the murderer of a victim, gagged and bound, the presentation to the gangster of a stock of guns and ammunition and a position which enabled him to command a continent. Anyone could see now, however wishful their thinking, that Hitler, after devouring Czechoslovakia, would be in an admirable position to demand more and more. And that we had betrayed a brave would-be ally for the sake of a quiet life – for a few, a very few short months.

As refugees from Prague, Brno, Bohemia, arrived in London, with the all-too-familiar pitiful tales of terror and persecution, it was difficult for us to hold up our heads. Every progressive person in England must have felt the shame bitterly, and every left-winger must have joined in some form of protest. It was terrible not to be able to do something effective – but there was nothing to be done – except to carry on with anti-fascist activity in Britain to the best of one's ability.

One way of fighting Hitler was still open to us and that was to win support for his victims in Spain. There was plenty to do at any rate on that front, where surrender was not for a moment considered, hard-pressed though the defenders were. That year the National Joint Committee ran dozens of meetings, and organised scores of concerts with the children, at which somebody spoke about the situation and the fascist danger to the world (the rape of Austria and the Czech crisis added to the urgency of these speeches), and appealed for money and help for the Spanish refugees.

Our chairman, the Duchess of Atholl, gave a spirited example of how to combine propaganda for the Spanish children with exposure of the Nazi danger in Europe and the possible disaster of the Munich policy. She flew, that September, to the United States, and spoke at big meetings in New York, Boston, Chicago, and met Adlai Stevenson and Roosevelt, whom she did her best to interest in Spain. 'I am afraid I did not succeed, or at least he would not commit himself,' she wrote, ruefully, later. 'On the general European situation, I may perhaps have made an impression,' she added, with the comment that 'the President did not seem as alive as he might have been to the danger of Hitler, but there was no doubt he was anxious about Europe.'[32]

On her return, the Duchess found she had put the cat among the Conservative pigeons by her remarks in the USA. She was accused of 'having blackened the country,' in spite of the fact that she had gone out of her way to defend Mr Chamberlain as far as she could; but she was asked to resign her seat as Tory MP for West Perth.

This was the culmination of many months' Tory disapproval of her anti-fascist activities. Although her work for the Spanish Republicans and her pamphlets and books were inspired by the most patriotic motives, and though nobody could have been less of a 'fellow traveller', she had been severely reprimanded several times. And although she realised the possible consequences, she had bravely appeared several times on platforms with well known 'reds', and had even been seen beside Harry Pollitt himself at one meeting. Worse still, she was accused of having joined in the singing of *The Red Flag* on one occasion, and in spite of her subsequent protestations that she did not know the tune and had no idea what it was (indeed that she 'had been rushed out of the hall by the friend who brought her,' at the opening bars) the mud stuck. She applied for the Chiltern Hundreds, and the by-election took place in West Perthshire early in December.

A little-known local farmer was put up as official Tory candidate against her. The Duchess was so familiar a figure, and her standing so high in the area, that her supporters were very hopeful of her success. And her supporters included, besides all her anti-fascist pro-Spanish friends, many distinguished figures, who wrote or spoke or otherwise helped in the campaign: Captain Liddell Hart, Professor Gilbert Murray, Lady Violet Bonham-Carter, J. M. Keynes, to mention only a few. Winston Churchill, who rang up most evenings to ask how she was getting on, wrote that 'your victory as an Independent member... can only have an invigorating effect upon the whole impulse of Britain's policy and Britain's defence.'

Many of the younger generation travelled up to Scotland to help in the Duchess's campaign. It seemed to us terribly important that she should win the election, and it was a fine opportunity to tell the country some home truths and to show the world that people here wanted a new and progressive line in foreign policy.

The contest was exciting and the issues at stake significant enough for it to attract a lot of attention; and the spotlight of publicity turned sharply on the damp, sleepy corner of central Scotland, suddenly invaded by all sorts of prominent political personalities. Press and radio reporters gathered in dozens in the local pubs, which were delighted to find business so good, and their usually quiet corner of northern Britain so much in the limelight. The pubs resembled the 'local' near Marsham Street, owing to the presence of so many of our Committee, who had left Spain to look after itself in this emergency, and had evacuated the office in order to canvass and campaign and act as chauffeurs for the 'Republican Duchess'. Everyone who could drive or lend a car was welcome at Blair Atholl, and I drove the Austin Seven all over the grey-green country, bumping along hilly roads through Scotch mist and driving rain, visiting remote hamlets with election addresses, and piloting speakers to meetings.

Her Grace was very calm and dignified under the strain, which must have been considerable; she had never been seriously opposed before in this feudal area, and the challenge was for her as much personal as political. In fact it was not. The challenge was one of principle against a whole party political machine; and the Tories were determined that they were not going to be put in their place by one dissident individual, whatever her title.

The Perthshire Conservatives rallied as never before to the true blue flag, and made sure their labourers and employees did the same. Their cars were everywhere, taking farm workers to the polls, with the hidden implication that they must vote the conformist ticket or else... The Duchess had relatively few cars, a slender purse compared to that of her opponents, and only her conscience to speak against the great myth, backed by wishful thinking, of Mr Chamberlain as the Saviour of Peace. 'To query the Munich settlement was to be a warmonger, and my opponents only too often claimed on their platforms that my policy meant war,' wrote the Duchess in her post-mortem on the election: 'I believe I lost many women's votes on this account.' When the result was declared, she had lost the seat by 1,313 votes.

We all returned to London or to our various homes, feeling disappointed, but having fought a good fight. The thousands of votes that the Duchess herself had won represented after all a great many supporters for her policy. But the results showed that we still had a great deal of work to do to convince people of the dangers of the situation.

I went back to organising Basque concerts with an even greater sense of urgency than before; a long-term programme of events was waiting to be put into effect, and there seemed never to be enough time for all there was to do.

We had found during the spring and summer that the best and most economical way of arranging concerts was for a group of children to tour given areas, driving in a bus or cars, or on occasion in a van lent by the International Brigade Association or in a Spanish Medical Aid committee ambulance (which was always very effective) from town to town, staying the night in private houses where the little Basques made many new and firm friendships.

We had a lot of these tours, in Yorkshire, Northamptonshire, the South of England, East Anglia and elsewhere, all of them pretty successful financially and in arousing interest in the children and, through them, in the Spanish war. The tours I remember best were in the Lake Country, where we stayed in Youth Hostels, and walked, climbed and picnicked in beautiful spring sunshine during the days before the evening perform-ances; and one in the Isle of Wight, where we went round the Holiday Camps and had a wonderful reception from ready-made audiences of two or three hundred strong every night.

But the most exciting of all these ventures was our journey to Switzerland, with a small group of highly trained and very talented children from the home at Guisborough in North-East Yorkshire. Ruth Pennyman, who had organised the home, had also used her considerable talents to produce a highly professional little show, with a family of four children (one of whom, seven year old Juanita, had a delicious voice and an extraordinary stage sense), a Basque Nationalist lad, Joseba, who was an expert on the pipe and tabor, and two other small boys.

The Swiss winter-sports centres seemed ideal places for money-raising, and the hotels would obviously provide large audiences of wealthy people (whether they would be sympathetic to the Republican cause was problematical, but they could not fail to be moved by the children). There is nothing like reaching for the highest possible star, and I got in touch with the manager of Suvrettahaus, the great St Moritz hotel, who happened to be in London in November. To my delight, he was friendly and quite sympathetic, and agreed to have the seven children and two or three helpers to stay for two nights and for them to give two cabaret shows at the hotel.

With a written agreement to this effect, I was able to approach all the other resorts with pre-ordained success. We got fixed up at Pontresina, Davos, Gmund, not to mention Zurich and Wintertur; and Swiss Air flew us out, free of charge, from London to Zurich in the middle of December.

The whole expedition seems like a dream now: the Bilbao dockers' children were wildly excited by everything, the flight, the snow mountains, the skiing on the nursery slopes, the Bergbahn, and most of all, of course, by the luxury of the hotels in which we performed, ate and slept. To be waited on by digni-fied gentlemen in tail coats was the height of bliss for the little Basques; they rose to the occasion and sang and danced admirably, raising over £300 for the cause.

BASQUE CHILDREN FLY ON CONCERT TOUR

Basque children boarding an airplane at Croydon yesterday to fly to Zurich. They will give concerts in Switzerland to raise funds for their maintenance in England. Before they made their first flight the pilot showed them round, and explained what makes the wings go up.

'Basque Children Fly on Concert Tour'. Frida in the foreground.

There was only one shadow over the whole adventure. This was that things were going very badly in Spain. The Republicans had been driven back on every front, Catalonia was on the point of falling (the International Brigades had been withdrawn by

173

Negrín's orders in October 1938, but some of them returned, unable to watch without helping in those tragic days). Worst of all, the government which had moved from Madrid, now had to move from Barcelona to Figueras, a little town in Girona. Unless a miracle happened – the impossible miracle of British or French intervention, defeat seemed almost inevitable.

The children didn't know how serious things were, and we kept it as dark as we could. Even when the news of the fall of Barcelona came through, a night when we were in Zurich, they did not hear about it.[33] But it was with heavy hearts that Kathleen McColgan, who was with us, and I, travelled homewards on the last day of the tour. We came through Paris, stopped in a hostel for one night, and gave a concert under the auspices of one of the Aid Spain committees to a crowd of Popular Fronters who were not as well off as the winter sportsmen, but whose enthusiastic welcome exceeded any of our previous audiences. In Paris, people were greatly depressed. It was the end of 1938, which had been a very bad year: the Blum government had fallen and given place to a reactionary clique who were destroying all that had been built by the Popular Front. The forty hour week had been repealed, wages were frozen, and any pretences of a democratic foreign policy had been abandoned. Everyone was terrified of what would happen in 1939. Other years we had jokingly wished each other, or rather, wished our enemies 'A Merry Crisis and a Happy New War!' That year, such jokes would have been in very bad taste indeed. With Hitler in control in Austria and Czechoslovakia; Franco in Spain; Daladier in France; Chamberlain in Britain, democracy was indeed on the run. How were we going to reverse the process and save the rest of the world from fascism?

Chapter 18 – A Nation in Retreat

The stars are dead. The animals will not look.
We are left alone with our day, and the time is short,
    and History to the defeated
May say Alas but cannot help nor pardon.

W. H. Auden, *Spain*

When it came, it seemed impossible, incredible, unthinkable. Though we had all dreaded it secretly for the past six months, though it had over and over again been averted by the marvel of Spanish tenacity and courage, till endurance seemed no longer humanly possible – when it came we simply could not take it in: the disaster of the Republicans' defeat in March 1939.

For nearly two and a half years they had stood out, almost alone, at the cost of overwhelming sacrifice. Now that all their heroism had proved lost, and evil triumphed, many of us were filled with a furious despair and a determination that somehow the Spanish people must be avenged, somehow the battle for peace and justice must be won, somehow the allies of the Jew-baiters and butchers must be kicked out of control of the world's destinies.

It was in this spirit that the youthful Left went into the activity at home for saving the Spanish refugee army, for rescuing the victims of Henlein and Hitler in Czechoslovakia, and for forming a Popular Front in England to force out the Chamberlain government. The latter was the most urgent task, for if we could get rid of the pro-Fascist cabinet, the rest would follow automatically.

Sir Stafford Cripps, representing a section of the Labour Party, Maxton of the Independent Labour Party and Harry Pollitt, had launched a campaign for unity at a great meeting in the Empire Hall in 1937, and the movement had gained impetus in the succeeding months. There were high hopes of its success; but the cool reception by the Labour leadership doomed it to failure.

I felt, as many of us must have, that with such a leadership there was little hope of a real change just then. And though it was clear that political work was the most important, it was also the most frustrating. The intrigues and gossip and hours and hours spent in meetings were so boring and so ineffectual – if only one could get to the spot, and help personally, practically, with the work of salvaging what was left of the Spanish army in France.

The stories which were arriving in the Joint Committee's office from Perpignan of the debacle and of the arrival from across the Pyrenees of vast numbers of old men, women and children, as well as of the bulk of the defeated Republican Army, were unbearably sad. The Spaniards hoped and expected to find sympathy and generosity from the French, but were confronted brutally by soldiers and police. Taken by surprise by the suddenness and size of the exodus, the French authorities had not provided medical services or rest centres. The exhausted refugees, many of them collapsing and dying, were herded at gun point to sites on the coast north of Cerbère, and left, without help or protection, surrounded by barbed wire, to fend for themselves until some friendly French or foreign agencies could come to their rescue.

To cope with this influx of 200,000 refugees was a superhuman problem, which could only be solved by international government action. The Governments, however, only too anxious to win the favour of the new Spanish rulers, showed no inclination to help. It was left to voluntary organisations to get on with the job.

The French Aid Spain Committee was quickly on the spot to rescue Spaniards and settle them in France, which was clearly the simplest and most desirable solution; then a number of sympathetic organisations from other countries set up offices in and round Perpignan through which relief from abroad could be sent into the camps, and refugees brought out and enabled to emigrate.

Our National Joint Committee sent out the nucleus of a staff, which took over a house to store supplies and act as headquarters for relief work. I heard that Spanish-speaking helpers were needed, and I moved heaven and earth – in other words, the heads of our Committee – to be sent out as a volunteer.

It was suggested that it might be more useful to help in the efforts to raise money in England, where a campaign had been launched to get as many Spaniards as possible out of the internment camps and bring them here or send them to South America. Hundreds of pounds were needed to charter and pay for a ship to convey two thousand to safety in a country where they could live and work. Chile, Mexico and the Dominican Republic had agreed to receive a limited number of chosen trades and professions, provided funds were raised for their transport.

I could see that money-raising in England was very important but I was in a fever to help on the spot, and being – luckily – qualified in being able to drive a car and to speak Spanish, I persuaded the authorities that I might be of some use in interviewing the refugees and in fetching them out of the camps.

It was strange to be in Perpignan again. The last time had been in 1937, when the movement was in the opposite direction, and soldiers of all nations were waiting impatiently to go into Spain to join the International Brigades, their hearts warm with faith and hope; and *Front Populaire France* had been gay and confident in the May sunshine.

In May 1939, the little town was just as sunny, the drinks just as potent, the flowers every bit as bright. But the whole atmosphere was, for me anyway, grim and sad and uncertain. Not many miles off, spread out along the Côte de Vermeil, were those plague spots, Barcarès, Argelès, Saint-Cyprien, each harbouring twenty to thirty thousand refugees in conditions of the utmost destitution and misery, behind high wire fences guarded by Senegalese and other African soldiers with fixed bayonets.

Nobody blamed the French Government for not providing grand hotels for the defeated army (even though that army had fought as valiantly as any in history for long months to keep war and fascism from France, and to keep Spain from falling into the hands of France's enemies). Nobody expected the Spaniards to be fed on the fat of the land when they arrived in their tens of thousands at two days' notice, and surged across the border uninvited. But one did expect a certain sympathy and respect to be shown to these heroic people; one could not but find it shocking that they were treated as dirt by the authorities, herded into waste tracts of sand on the arid windy coast, with no covering at all, and given a solitary meal of chickpeas, day after day after day. Nobody objected to the colour of the guards' skins, but it was, to say the least, tactless to post the camp entrances with steel-helmeted negroes who closely resembled the Moorish troops whom the Spaniards had been fighting for two years.

The first time I drove over to one of the camps – Argelès, I think – I was absolutely sickened by the immensity of the problem. For several miles off one could see the haze of smoke, and a little nearer, could smell the acrid fumes of the hundreds of little fires that had been lit by the men in the camp to cook their meagre rations, mingling with indescribable stinks of other natures.

On getting to the gate of the camp, one saw the lines of wooden huts that had been built, and the scores of little makeshift shanties which the refugees had erected out of old blankets and stick and bits of tin as protection against the bitter East wind.

That wind! It must have been first cousin to the 'mistral' which blasts the Midi, for it was like it in ferocity and persistence, and even more infuriating under these circumstances. It swept across the shore, stirring up the grey sand and flinging it in the refugees' faces, getting inside their poor ragged clothes, into the food and the blankets. 'Blow, blow thou winter wind,' said Shakespeare. I think man's ingratitude and the wind were about on a par in this case.

It was poor consolation, in view of the enormous scale of misery and desolation, to be able to bring a few things to comfort the prisoners – food, clothes, soap. But they received the small offerings with enthusiasm, and our vans which went over every day from Perpignan were welcomed as though we were providing unlimited luxuries for the whole camp. We got great numbers of special requests, presented by the leaders of groups of *barracas*, as they called the huts.

They organised themselves very efficiently from the start, and within a few weeks had set up committees of hygiene, of culture, of recreation and education. What we were most often asked for, after clothing, were books, writing things, and artists' materials. And of course, soap – not only for washing themselves and their clothing, but for sculpture! I still treasure the two small carvings made from blocks of coarse yellow soap – one, the figure of a refugee struggling against the wind, the other a 'Crucifixion' of a Republican soldier. (They have stood up well to the burden of the years, the only drawback being that the soap tends to dry and crumble in hot weather, and to sweat heavily on wet days.) The books and magazines and paintings produced in the camp were astonishingly professional and full of zest for life.

The greatest joy for the Spaniards and for the van driver was, of course, the odd occasion when we had to fetch someone out of the camp. That was indeed a fiesta for the happy man and for his friends, who saw in his departure a ray of hope for their own future. We drove out of the gates with cheers all round, and brought the *miliciano* to the committee's office, where he was given clean clothes and money and sent off to have a bath and a good meal.

The ones who came out of the camp were all too few, and they had to have a personal invitation to enter the United Kingdom, along with a guarantee that they would not become a charge on the tax payer. They often had to wait for these, and spend several weeks at the Committee's house at Narbonne, run by two very efficient girls who had been nurses with the International Brigade, and knew how to look after their charges and restore them to health after the appalling ordeal of the past months.

The committee did a great deal of work in sorting out applicants for visas to various South American countries and in finding jobs for them both inside and outside France. It reunited a lot of families and provided them with medical inspection and treatment, and, most important of all, some kind of passport. Peter Rodd, the son of Lord Rennell, who worked with the

Committee for a short time, had devised a sort of international paper for refugees (commonly known as the Rodd Passport) which enabled anybody to travel about in default of any other document.

The Hon. Peter was at Perpignan in person, seeing to the distribution of these 'passports' and though definitely no 'red', he earned the gratitude of many thousands of Republicans who might otherwise, through the inhumanity of bureaucracy, never have left the camps. Thanks to him and to Donald Darling, who was in charge of the office, and who had an enthusiasm for Catalonia which drove him to work tremendously hard particularly on behalf of the Catalans, a list was compiled and a contingent assembled for emigration to Mexico in June 1939. The London Joint Committee had done a fine job in raising the money for the voyage, and had chartered a ship, the *S.S. Sinaia*, which lay in the harbour at Sète ready to leave as soon as the passengers were aboard.

S.S. Sinaia

The sailing of the ship was the climax of many months' work, and it was certainly a most moving occasion. A galaxy of VIP's, which included the Duchess of Atholl, General Molesworth, Wilfrid Roberts, and Lady Hall, were there to see the Sinaia off. We had a hectic two days collecting the women and children who were due to sail and who were housed in some barracks in Perpignan where they went through their medical examination, and were vaccinated and registered. Lists had to be prepared and checked, of the names of the emigrating families. Nancy Mitford, Peter Rodd's then wife, was there during the last hectic week, and has described the turmoil and excitement, and given some of the names of those families' children in her novel *The Search for Love*. She found them quaint and amusing, but I thought it really rather touching that the children who would in the old days have been 'Trinidad', 'Concepción' and 'Jesús María' were now 'Independencia', 'Solidaridad' and 'Lenin'!

The Duchess of Atholl, right, with a Mexican diplomat and his wife on board the refugee ship the S.S. Sinai, 1939.

While we were compiling lists, a request came through from one of our secretaries in London for the names and trade unions of the refugees who would be sailing – in order, of course, to win support from the unions in England who might be prepared to contribute money for individuals who belonged to their own trades and professions. It seemed to me a reasonable and good idea, and I went down to Barcarès Camp where the men were being housed – in a section apart from the less fortunate non-migrants – and asked the head of each *barraca* to get details of the affiliations of the men who were to sail. They were glad to comply, and I went to collect the lists the next day. But when General Molesworth heard of this he flew into a rage and had the lists destroyed; whether he resented London's 'interference', or whether he just couldn't bear the words 'Trade Union' I never discovered, but to my great distress, he was terribly cross.

However, all small disagreements were forgotten in the great event of the day. At last we saw the fruit of our labours, the beginning of daylight for two thousand suffering people with the fears and horrors of war and imprisonment behind them. Several crowded trains carried the emigrants from Barcarès and Perpignan to Sète, and it was the most stimulating journey I ever made, packed in with the women and children, cheering and shouting and singing. They filed on board and everyone fore-gathered on deck, where speeches were made and the loud-speaker blared out the national anthems of Britain and Republican Spain. We all stood to attention, and I don't think there was one of us who had not got a very large lump in their throats.

And there were not a few surreptitious tears – not for the two thousand who were departing, but for the thousands who were left behind, and most of all for Spain herself, plunged into the darkness and desolation of fascist dictatorship and defeat.

Chapter 19 – The Phoney War

First, there is a war about to be declared.
Second – but who cares about the second?
Summer is a-comen in. If there is war,
What sort of summer will it be?

Will there be any green grass left at Lords?
Will there be any horses to run at Ascot?
Will there be any brass bands to meet the returning heroes
Supposing any return?

Louis MacNeice, *Out of the Picture*

It was a heavy, anxious summer, that last summer of peace; the sky was cloudlessly blue and serene, but there was precious little serenity in our hearts. The optimists still declared that war could be avoided if, at the eleventh hour the Labour movement would unite in a Popular Front, overthrow the Chamberlain government, sign a treaty with the USSR, and show Hitler that any further attempts at annexing other territories would lead to catastrophe for Germany. But the majority of people took the more pessimistic view that a complete change of heart of reactionary leaders, Labour or Conservative, was most unlikely – 'Can the Ethiopian Tory change his skin, or the Labour Leopard his spots?', it was asked. The gloomy question of not whether, but *when* Hitler would choose to plunge us into war, was predominant. For he was now in an exceptionally favourable position – controlling (with Mussolini and Franco) much of the Mediterranean, and vital stretches of the Danube, his war machine at a high pitch of training and preparedness; while we ourselves were relatively unprepared and did not want war, he both wanted further adventures and needed them as a diversion from his internal economic crisis.

Most of us knew that Hitler could still be stopped from plunging the world into war if the British government had wanted to stop him; he had won victory after victory piecemeal, because the democracies had surrendered at every point, hoping that he loved us so much that he would not attack us, but (strengthened by our kindness) he would turn his attention to the conquest of the Soviet Union. We knew, too, though we dared hardly hope, that we could prevent any major war by a firm agreement with the Soviets and with France, to resist any further German aggression by force of arms. France already had a treaty with the USSR; if we could sign a similar one, there was still a chance of peace for the world.

Our hopes were high (but not unduly high) when after much pressure on the government, Neville Chamberlain at last agreed to enter into negotiations with Moscow. It took weeks, however, for him to convey this decision to the Kremlin; and although the Soviet government expressed its desire to have an immediate meeting, another few weeks went by before Chamberlain sent his reply. After all the delay, this was to the effect that Mr Strang, a minor Foreign Office official, (not Lord Halifax who had been invited), would be sent to Russia for discussions at an unspecified date. This envoy set off not by plane or warship (as the Russians urged) but by cargo boat taking five days. He had no credentials, and no powers to take binding decisions without reference to London. The talks naturally came to nothing, and in June Mr Strang returned home empty-handed.

In England, by then, everybody was talking about war, civil defence, and Air Raid Precautions. Discussion raged around the questions of whether Anderson shelters would be of any use, whether the Underground stations would stand up to heavy bombing, whether poison gas would be used, and whether the gasmasks for babies could possibly be satisfactory – they were curious contraptions, like a miniature oxygen tent or goldfish bowl, in which a child could be bodily encased. J. B. S. Haldane brought out his book on ARP (published in a Left Book Club edition) in which he categorically and authoritatively stated that the Government's proposals for defending the civilian population were worse than useless. A group of scientists in Cambridge put forward a plan to protect Cambridge from air raids, which exposed all the existing arrangements as ludicrously inadequate.

The Spanish Relief activities had dwindled to next to nothing, though of course the Basque children still needed support, and occasional concerts and meetings took place. But in the bosom of the Committee there was more and more talk about sending the children back to Spain. This had been happening in driblets for some time; where the parents had asked for their offspring and things were quiet, it would have been unreasonable to refuse to let them go, though even then one couldn't know how much pressure had been put on parents to ask for their return. The Roman Catholic Church had been clamouring for it both in Spain and in England, and the London Committee which had Catholic representatives on it was split from top to bottom on the question. Those who ran the children's homes and had looked after them for two years naturally felt strongly that we should have some guarantee of their safety and wellbeing before sending them (particularly the older boys) back to the hungry, war-stricken areas ruled by Franco, who would certainly have no tender feelings for them.

One could well imagine José Luis, or Jesús Hernández, tall strong youths of avowed Republican sympathies, being pressed straight into some labour gang or even put in prison for the crime of having escaped to England through the help of our anti-fascist Relief Committee. Many of us would far rather have waited some months and sent somebody to investigate conditions in Spain before letting any child or youth go back. However, funds were drying up, it was by no means easy to raise money for Spain now that hostilities were over, and people in Britain pre-occupied with their own anxieties.

By the middle of the summer it was agreed that all the children, except orphans and special cases, should be sent back. Members of the office staff and friends from the local 'homes' and committees took turns in making the journey to the Spanish frontier with them.

I saw that I was out of a job again, and before trying to find another, went for a short visit to Cambridge, where the atmosphere had never altered, and I could relax and imagine that all was well with the world. A few hundred miles away, countries could be invaded by barbarians, cities razed to the ground, freedom stamped upon, culture destroyed, yet this seat of learning seemed unaware that anything was amiss.

The same old dons strolled across the velvet lawns, the same choirs sang the same anthems in the college chapels, the same or similar amateur groups sang or acted Elizabethan gems of music and literature. It was all very peaceful and beautiful, and I enjoyed being at home with my parents, who had become very much more involved with the Spanish Republic and sympathetic to my strong feelings. But I was too restless to stay long in retreat and ached to get back to London and to some sort of political activity. I didn't even feel like going to Pontigny, when Mme Desjardins wrote inviting me to attend a *décade – que vous interesserait sûrement*34 at which *les réfugiés* was the subject for discussion. I couldn't really believe that the Pontignassiens would get down to brass tacks, and there were so many practical problems which needed solving that to debate the philosophical implications seemed a waste of time. However I did go, impelled by the feeling that this might be the last *décade* at Pontigny (as it indeed proved to be), as the representative of the London Committee for Spanish Relief, thus giving myself some moral justification for an enjoyable fortnight in France.

The world situation had become so bad that it had at last penetrated the consciousness of those who gathered at Pontigny; this time the speakers were taking very seriously indeed their duties to society, and their responsibilities to the exiles and refugees with which France was teeming – Italian, German, Austrian, Czech, Spanish – who had escaped to the home of Liberty, Equality and Fraternity in vast numbers each time a European bastion had fallen.

Madame Desjardins had worked out a plan for land settlement, which she proposed to submit to various ministries, and she also had schemes for refugee hostels, health organisations, education and nurseries. These were discussed very fully, and the *décade* moved along harmoniously and profitably, everyone in general agreement, and enthusiastic about the proposals put forward by our hostess.

But all of a sudden a bombshell fell in the middle of the

gathering, shattering the peace of the Abbaye, destroying new-formed friendships and giving poor Madame Desjardins the job of calming the most agitated party Pontigny had ever witnessed. The big bomb was, of course, the Soviet-German pact, signed on 23rd August 1939, by which Hitler pledged himself not to attack the Soviet Union, and vice versa.

It was of course a very great shock, even, or perhaps most of all, to those who saw in Soviet Russia a bulwark for peace, and a tower of strength against Germany. Some of us refused to condemn Stalin's move out of hand, and we reserved judgment. But most of the visitors at Pontigny immediately dropped their tolerant attitude towards the Soviet Union: 'We should have known it would happen! You can't trust the Russians. *Stalin c'est un autre Hitler ou pire*,'35 they insisted. I spent a fruitless afternoon having a heated argument with young Claude Mauriac, son of the famous author, who said, '*Je savais qu'il y aurait quelque chose de louche!*'36 I argued that we ourselves ought to have signed such a pact with the Soviet Union long ago, when they constantly proposed it; but we had not done so. We should have known that Realpolitik would compel them to avoid war with Germany by some such measure.

Later, proof came that Coulondre, French ambassador in Berlin, had long been urging a Franco-Soviet and British-Soviet pact, and had informed his government and ours that the Soviet Union would feel compelled to sign a non-aggression pact with Germany if we did not.

Neither Mauriac nor the other young intellectuals at the house-party would see my point of view. I had, I'd thought, made some good friends there, but seeing their bitterly anti-Soviet attitude, their willingness to accept the dicta of *Le Matin* and *Gringoire*, out-and-out fascist papers, and to range themselves unquestioningly with the reactionaries, it was clear that there was too great a gulf between us to be bridged by discussion.

Although the Desjardins did their very best to smooth things down, everybody was so agitated that the party was obviously doomed. I made the legitimate excuse that it was essential to get home, in case of the outbreak of war, which was expected any minute.

News was coming through of German troops massing for the invasion of Poland; of Neville Chamberlain's appeal to Hitler not to advance; of British and French diplomats scurrying about to find face-saving formulae, but finally failing; and of the ultimatum which was delivered to Hitler when the Nazi troops goose-stepped across the Polish frontier on 1st September.

It was during the two day ultimatum period that I crossed Paris, a city tossing in a bad dream. The French had half expected a surprise attack by massed German bombers, and there was a general feeling of almost disappointed, semi-relieved suspense when no air raids occurred. However, the French Government, under Paul Reynaud, were behaving as though the war had already begun; they had called up several age groups and hundreds of reservists, and young men were everywhere making their way to barracks and registration offices.

There were long queues of women at shops, buying up sugar and coffee and tinned food; there were lines of schoolchildren, suddenly brought back from their 'colonies de vacances' (holiday camps), waiting at the stations for anxious parents to receive them. Worst of all, there were scores of people queuing up for gasmasks, a sight to send shivers down anyone's spine. And even though I did not for one minute believe that gas was on the agenda, this sight certainly made me keener to get back to London, where people, one hoped, would not be quite so jittery.

In fact, the government-inspired jitters in Britain were laid on just as in France, only a few days later. We all collected our gasmasks, in their little cubical cardboard boxes, and carried them round for several days. As there was no sign whatever of the Luftwaffe at that time, most of us soon abandoned the encumbrance, at least on country walks; but I did see several courting couples in Cambridge, with their cases solemnly slung over their shoulders, taking a Sunday afternoon stroll down the quiet Huntingdon road, well after most of us had realised the war was 'phoney'.

Just how phoney it was, dawned on us about three weeks after the German invasion of Poland. Hitler had paid no attention to Chamberlain's suggestion that he should not enter that country, and had gone through it like a knife through butter, (melted somewhat by prior air raids). Britain and France had been powerless to help the Polish government, and some of us wondered why they had ever proposed to do so.

Hitler's latest victim succumbed after a short, brave, but hopeless resistance. We took in a number of Polish airmen and near-fascist Generals, and left the rest of the population to its fate at the hands of the Nazis. Hitler immediately began operations of starvation, repression and plundering of the country, with the usual systemic persecution and pogroms for the two million Jews living there. Under the terms of the Russo-German pact, Hitler was at least deprived of about a million more Polish Jews who had passed into the part under Soviet rule. Appalling stories of the Nazi's mass transfers of Jews into concentration and labour camps, of the ghastly treatment of the Warsaw ghetto, came through and made us sick with shame and misery, but nothing could be done. Our help had been too little and too late.

After the rape of Poland came an uneasy pause, several months of suspended animation, while we wondered 'Can this be war? And if so, what sort of war?' The fact was, that the British Government's failure to stand by Poland, or to do anything effective about stirring people to a great war effort, or even clearly to present the issues for which we were supposed to be 'fighting', made it soon appear that the war was not 'on' in any real sense. Mobilisation had begun, of course, but the very songs the soldiers were singing showed that the British army had no deep convictions about the enemy or the cause, nor awareness of what was what. *Run Rabbit Run*, and *We're going to hang out the washing on the Siegfried Line*, expressed their whole attitude to the war.

The fact that operations were still directed by Neville Chamberlain (*J'aime Berlin*' as the French called him) and Lord Halifax, the architect of Munich, was enough to raise doubts as to their sincerity about defeating Fascism. They certainly showed no enthusiasm about using the services of the anti-fascist refugees in Britain, who might have been their most reliable and willing helpers. Some of the very best of these were interned as 'enemy aliens' early in the war, and large numbers of German and Austrian refugees were shipped off to Canada and Australia instead of being given the chance they were longing for, to join in fighting their former persecutors.

One sometimes really wondered who we were supposed to be at war with, so little sign was there of anti-Nazi propaganda. Far more effort was put in by the publicists to maligning the Russians for whatever they did, than to mentioning the Germans' crimes. Great indignation was expressed at the Soviet Union's request to Finland for some twenty miles of territory (with fair compensation) which would have placed Leningrad out of range of enemy guns, should the Nazis occupy Finland and threaten Russia's most important port from the nearby frontier. The reactionary and pro-German General Mannerheim, under British pressure, refused to consider it, and the Soviet Union gave an ultimatum that they would have the territory as a necessary measure of self-defence. The Finnish Government decided to resist, large quantities of supplies and arms were shipped to Finland from Britain, and our government attempted to send troops, but were refused passage through Sweden.

The Finnish soldiers struggled bravely but hopelessly to prevent the Red Army from coming in, and lost their lives uselessly in a campaign which lasted three months, and need not have happened had their government not been determined to support fascist interests. Mannerheim and his friends were forced to resign, and a government willing to accept the Soviet terms was installed in Helsinki early in 1940.

The whole tragic episode was made an excuse in England to whip up as much feeling as possible against the Soviet Union, and one could almost believe it when journalists told one, off the record, that our politicians would have liked nothing better than to send a full-scale expeditionary force to Finland, and 'switch the war' to an anti-Soviet crusade.

I saw a small indication of the official attitude when I happened at lunch-time one fine November day to pass by a meeting being held in a street in Clerkenwell, where a member of the British-Soviet Society was explaining the reasons for the Russo-German pact to a small but attentive crowd. I was always interested to hear a serious speaker on Russia, and stopped to listen. It was difficult to hear well, as there were one or two tiresome hecklers in the crowd who kept interrupting, and I wished the police who were hovering on the fringe of the gathering would ask them to move on. At last, the speaker lost patience with the very provocative tough, and told him a few home truths about civilised behaviour. The heckler somehow started a free-for-all, everybody began arguing and shouting either 'Shut 'im up', or 'Let's hear 'im!', and though there was no sign of violence, the police decided this was where they came in. They ignored the interrupter who had caused all the noise, pulled the speaker, Pat Sloan, down from his platform and arrested him, took the names and addresses of some of his supporters, asked for witnesses – which I volunteered to be – and bade us be at the Police Court without fail at 10 o'clock the next morning. When the case came up it was dismissed after a short hearing, and Sloan was bound over for a year, with a reprimand from the magistrate who suggested that he was indeed lucky not to be living in Soviet Russia, as there he would not have escaped so lightly.

In the strange lull after the fall of Poland, the war seemed curiously unreal; gasmasks, barrage balloons hovering over London like silver whales stranded in mid-air (whether for observation, defence or decoration, nobody quite knew), the blackout, all created a surrealist sort of background to the people of London hurrying hither and thither, armed with ration cards and identity papers to volunteer for ARP duty, or to help in canteens for fire-watchers and wardens, at first-aid posts or railway stations.

As things were very slack at the Spanish Relief Committee Office, prior to its complete closing down, I volunteered for various jobs which I thought might prove socially useful, if not of direct importance to the war effort. First I spent a good many evenings washing up in a canteen in the St Pancras area; but it was so quiet, there being no air raids nor immediate prospect of any, that it hardly seemed worth the sacrifice of precious hours.

Someone suggested that what was really needed was some entertainment in those various canteens and centres where people were eating their heads off with boredom, waiting for something to happen which clearly was not going to happen yet awhile.

'Why not organise a Basque Children's concert tour round the ARP stations?', chaffed my friend, adding, 'Be a change from the Grand Hotels, wouldn't it?' Not such a paying proposition, I thought, but still worth considering,

However it was not a feasible proposition; so many of the children had already gone back to Spain that it would have been difficult to collect a concert party, even if the Committee agreed to the idea, which was problematical. Nevertheless, the idea of entertaining the browned-off war workers appealed to me, and it was something which might not be hard to organise, if one could find enough volunteer artists to co-operate. There were not many Spanish children, but there were other refugee singers and musicians who would be glad to help, I discovered on approaching various committees – Free Czechs, Free Austrians, Free Poles. There were also various amateur dramatic companies, including the mobile group of Unity Theatre which was only too happy to have a chance of spreading its gospel in the outposts of Empire.

Someone working with ENSA (the recently formed body for entertaining the Services) told me that the organisation had had any number of offers of help from amateur and semi-professional artists, which had been turned down as ENSA was bound to employ only professionals. As canteens and clubs could not pay full Trade Union rates they would welcome amateurs; and as many amateurs were dying to perform to somebody, what could be better than to engage them for the clubs and canteens?

I was given a long list of names and addresses of conjurers, concert pianists no longer in the professional market, mouth-organists, Jew's Harpists, ladies with monologues, gents with one-man bands, parents with infant prodigies, etc., etc., and I soon had a fine selection to offer any languishing Fire Station or ARP post.

With this list I approached the authorities (I forget which) and offered to lay on short concerts anywhere in London, to suit any and every taste. To my surprise the offer was graciously accepted, and I set to work to organise the shows.

They went down well, on the whole, though there were some awkward moments, as for instance, when into a very small Fire-Watching Station in East London poured a Czech choir forty strong, till singers and audience were packed like sardines and could hardly breathe. On another occasion a WVS or other female organisation provided the audience, and were deeply shocked by the somewhat broad jokes of the visiting comedian. Another time, Unity Theatre group forgot to be non-political as requested, and hit out at Neville Chamberlain rather too hard for the officers' liking. The selections they gave were usually quite mild satire, such as hits from their current variety show, *What's Left*, and songs such as *The Crowned Heads of Europe are Vanishing One by One*, and *The Black Blackout*, which usually went down very well indeed.

Had anyone complained, which in fact they didn't, that would have been the end of the concerts. Sooner or later somebody probably would have decided one of the innocent numbers was subversive, but that was a risk we had to take. In any case, the series was short-lived, because after a few weeks I had to abandon them – regretfully, for they were on the whole great fun – to go abroad on one last sad assignment for the Basque Children's Committee.

Chapter 20 – *Drôle de Guerre* [37]

The shrill voices of surplus children
Shake up the frosty dust
Lamps are lit
And bleak shadows like bruises
Rise under their golden eyes.

Herbert Read, *Inbetweentimes*

Everyone who had worked for some time in the National Joint Committee office was given a turn at escorting the Basque children back to the Spanish frontier at Irun. In the ordinary way I would have declined this rather sad mission, for I felt very strongly about handing anybody – let alone a bunch of good little anti-fascists – over to Franco. But to cross the Channel again was in itself a great temptation, and so was the chance of seeing Paris and my many friends there on the way back; somebody was needed to deliver messages and parcels at the concentration camp of Gurs, in the Western Pyrenees, where many good International Brigaders and Republicans were interned with very little hope of release – but just a possibility if they could be personally contacted and told how to apply for a visa to England.

So we went off, with our flock of three hundred children, over a very rough sea, and down the length of France. As far as we could see there was not much to show the country to be in the throes of World War II. Life went on very much as usual; the mobilisation had been carried out, but many soldiers were hanging about the cafés and bistros in the little towns. The main difference between war and peace was, it seemed, that there were a lot of English troops and officers about. They were not a bit popular, in spite of the *Entente Cordiale* between Chamberlain and Daladier, owing to their much higher pay, and their ability to buy up the food and drink as they liked, and to take out the most expensive girls or to offer greater luxuries to the prettiest girls.

We unloaded our children at St Jean de Luz and took them to the bridge which leads over to Spain. I could hardly bear to walk across into fascist territory, but felt the children just must be accompanied to the bitter end. I delivered them and their papers and small bits of luggage over to a sour-faced Civil Guard. A bus was waiting to take them on to Bilbao, and there was no time for long goodbyes; we embraced – I think there were thirty in my group to hug and kiss on both cheeks – and said *adiós*. One dared not even say *salud*, I thought – apt comment on the sort of prison they had entered. I couldn't bear to look back at them; I'm sure we all felt secretly like traitors, but were thinking to console ourselves, 'it can't be for long.'

The next job was to deliver our parcels to Gurs. Molly, another girl from the Basque Children's Committee Office, and I decided to take a chance of a hotel in Pau, the nearest town to Gurs, that night, and to go over to the camp the next day.

Gurs is quite a way from Pau, some seven miles, and we got up early to walk it the next morning, in lovely misty late autumn sunshine. We had not got far when a glossy black car drew up, and a French military gentleman – we could not guess from his stars and his ribbons whether he was a colonel or major-general or what – offered us a lift. He turned out in fact to be a Super-intendent at the camp, and luckily for us, quite sympathetic (so he said) to the plight of the internees. We gathered from his remarks that the Commandant of the camp was pro-Franco and more than somewhat severe to his 'red' prisoners; we would have been unlikely to see any of them individually, said our driver, if we had not been fortunate enough to have met him. He personally, he said, would like to let them out, but '*Que voulez-vous, c'est la guerre!*'[38] This seemed to me no excuse for keeping them incarcerated, but it was often said to explain away all sorts of malpractices and injustices during the *drôle de guerre*, and the real war too.

By the time we reached the camp, this officer was quite ready to make things easier for us. He said he would have a word with the chief, and we waited in a hut outside the entrance, on tenterhooks lest our journey should prove in vain. From the hut we could see the double hedge of barbed wire surrounding long

195

rows of *barracas*, with hardly a yard between each, huts like those of Barcarès, about as cheerful and comfortable as cowsheds. That the cattle within were human seemed to make no difference to the keepers.

After a quarter of an hour, which seemed like a quarter of a century, our officer came back and said we could come through to the reception hut. We were to be allowed to see two International Brigaders for a few minutes. This was an exceptional indulgence, granted in view of the fact, we were told, that we had come from so far and from a non-political organisation. (As workers in the Basque Children's Committee we passed, but if we had confessed that our parcels were from the International Brigade Association we might have fared otherwise.)

Eventually two prisoners were brought along. One was a Czech, the other a German; both had fought in Spain for two years, and bore marks of great suffering and endurance on their strong, haggard faces. They were clearly much moved by having visitors, and told us that it was a very rare event for them. The majority of relief workers had been unable to obtain entry to the camp, and lack of contact with the outer world was one of the prisoners' worst privations. We asked them about conditions, and were told that things were *sehr schlecht* (very bad). Clothing was a great problem, said one of them, pointing to his summer uniform: 'This is eighteen months old – I wore it when we crossed the Ebro, and ever since!' The other displayed his feet, which were shod in the most pitiful remains of military boots. Food? 'Our ration is one loaf between four men; in the morning a drink of coffee made from burned barley; midday soup of *garbanzos* (chickpeas) or lentils; in the evening a drink of watery cocoa.' But, they said, 'we keep busy – that's the main thing.' The morale seemed to be extraordinarily high under those conditions: they had obtained books and with grammars and dictionaries, they held language classes, and with handiwork and carpentry manuals they made models and furniture.

The Czech asked us to try and get books for them ('as many as you can') more important than food and clothes he said, and he gave us some models and magazines produced in the camp.

Photographs from a small, handmade book, showing an exhibition organised by Spanish refugees in the camp at Gurs, given to Frida during her visit.

We handed over our parcels and messages. It seemed fearfully little to give them, and yet we could not have brought more. There were so many of them and they had next to nothing. I could have wept but it wouldn't have made things any better. We just hoped they understood how we felt, and that it might be some comfort for them at least to have the assurance that people outside were thinking about them and working for their freedom.

In view of what Koestler wrote about Vernet in *Scum of the Earth*, I very much fear that our friends were not released in time from Gurs, which was a similar type of camp for anti-fascist foreigners in France. But I still hope that these men did find a way of getting out before the German invasion – the thing they dreaded more than anything else.

Molly and I made our way sadly back to Pau, packed our bags and took the express to Paris – a Paris of darkness by night and nerves by day. I could only gather from whispers and rumours what was happening, but it seemed that a witch hunt was going on, to a degree almost unbelievable in the country of Liberty, Equality and Fraternity. At the beginning of the war (which President Lebrun had declared to be a way 'to guarantee the freedom of every nation and the liberty of every individual within the nation'), M. Daladier's small dictatorial cabinet suppressed 84 Trade Unions, for their attitude towards the Soviet Union, and dissolved five hundred TUC branches, for the same reason, imprisoning many well known leaders of the CGT, such as Delobelle, Garcia, Semard, Rink.

Daladier at one blow destroyed a generation of Trade Union gains and all the advances of the Popular Front; factories were placed virtually under military dictatorship, the working week was extended to include Saturday and Sunday (to seventy hours in some cases), workers forced to pay special taxes of up to 20% to the State, absenteeism became punishable by up to two years' imprisonment, and so on.

One measure which shocked working-class and progressive opinion particularly was the arrest and imprisonment of forty communist deputies, who had requested time in the Chamber for a discussion on the German-Soviet pact. 'Even if we don't like their opinions, they have a right to express them! We have not yet declared war on Russia, have we?', said a Socialist woman friend indignantly. It seemed that the deputies were treated as common criminals and taken off to La Santé jail in handcuffs, their ties and shoelaces removed, their personal possessions confiscated. They were not allowed books, documents or letters, which meant that it was almost impossible to prepare their defence. Their trial was due to take place in the New Year of 1940, but until then their constituents would not be represented in the Chamber; nor would the electors in over a hundred towns where Communist councils were dissolved by emergency decree, and where Commissioners appointed by the reactionary Minister of the Interior took over. Almost overnight, all left-wing opposition to the Daladier government was conveniently muzzled.

Most of this I learned at a party at a friend's house, the night before I left Paris. There were several left-wing people there, who had good reason to know only too well what was going on; one of them was an Italian anti-fascist exile, another a Trade Unionist threatened with arrest if he expressed his opinion on the Government; we joked and had a good evening, but it was all slightly macabre, as everyone knew that the police were after several of the party for the mere crime of holding and voicing strong views about Hitler and his friends in France.

I was told that though most of the anti-fascist committees, such as Romain Rolland's for the Victims of War and Fascism, had been closed down, two of the Spanish refugee organisations were still functioning. Just before leaving Paris, I called at the Children's Office and found them harassed and rushed; the need for help was greater than ever before but they were terribly short-staffed. On the spur of the moment I volunteered to come and work for them, if I could get a visa – for a few months at any rate. They fixed up a job for me within ten minutes, and I went off to the Gare du Nord feeling light-headed at the thought of returning to Paris for even a short time, and at the same time deeply anxious at what I'd seen and heard of the witch hunt and the unscrupulous treatment of decent progressive people. How could any of us who believed in the defeat of Fascism give whole-hearted, or even half-hearted, support to a war which was being run by such confirmed reactionaries and enemies of democracy?

Chapter 21 – French Police State

What we have feared
Assumes dimension and a name;
The long shadow emerges from the wall;
The smoke is flame.

M Jean Prussing, *September 2, 1939*

At the beginning of 1940 I said goodbye to my parents and friends in England, casually enough, (as I expected to be away only two or three months at most), and returned to France in a curiously empty train – civilian and holiday travel between our two countries having almost ceased.

Life in *drôle de guerre* Paris was even queerer than in phoney war London. Things went on in a superficially normal way, apart from ration cards, black-out, severe supervision of identity cards, and the call-up of several classes, some of whom went to sit in the blackest boredom along the Maginot Line and others no further off than Issy-les-Moulineaux or Noisy-le-Sec. My friend the Pontignassian philosopher, J—— was stationed in this latter, remote suburb. I went to visit him at the outpost of Empire he was supposedly guarding, a dreary straggle of small houses among grey wintry allotments, rather in the spirit of one visiting a friend in hospital or prison.

His resplendent new uniform and kepi contrasted strangely with his most unmilitary expression and bearing, which betrayed an intellectual's misery at being involved in war and, he thought, such an unnecessary war at that. We went into a tiny bistro, the only one in the village, and over a couple of Pernods I heard the reactions of a typical liberal progressive Parisian: the war was a gigantic and stupid mistake into which the French had allowed themselves to be muddled by unscrupulous politicians of the Right. The British were the most to blame, but the French were almost as bad. It was only anti-Communism that had prevented them carrying out their treaty obligations to Czechoslovakia. '*Ah!*

La Czechoslovaquie!' J—— was particularly scathing and bitter about the betrayal of a country he knew well and loved dearly. But of course, now, there was only one course – to go ahead and finish off Hitler. 'Do you trust your government and generals to do that?', I asked. He shrugged his shoulders. It was too late to ask the question now. Of course, if two years ago they had taken the advice of men like De Gaulle, with modern ideas, instead of sticking to the methods of Weygand and Pétain, there would be more confidence in the army. One could only hope that the Germans would be as badly equipped and organised as we were told they were...

I left him to his despondency and went back to Paris infected by the same depression. It was the same with many university people I met. Nobody believed in this war. As for the country's 'leaders' and the muddle they had landed France in, J's shrug vividly expressed the feeling among middle-class people. Workers would have found a more vigorous form of protest against the state of war, which as always bore more heavily on them than on anyone else. *Would have* found... because in fact no forms of effective protest were open to them.

As previously mentioned, the war was made an excuse for clamping down on freedom of expression, on liberty of the press, on meetings and demonstrations of any sort. Daladier and Bonnet, after declaring war on fascism abroad, had proceeded to declare it on anti-fascism at home, and in no uncertain manner.

'*Les Communistes seront mis a raison,*'[39] Bonnet had promised the German government, when trying to obtain peace terms some months earlier. He now seized on the pretext that the Communists were not supporting the war, as they had not denounced the Soviet-German Pact, but were trying to explain the reasons for it. They must therefore be traitors, said the Government. So twenty-four members of parliament were in prison, scores of Communists and Socialists under arrest, their newspapers suppressed, most of the anti-fascist organisations closed down after seizure of their archives and funds.

The Spanish Relief Committee for which I proposed to work part-time was still allowed to carry on in a hand-to-mouth way, as their work consisted almost entirely of supplying medicaments to the refugees and large quantities of layettes to expectant mothers. The camps of the Spanish Republican prisoners still dragged on, and the inhabitants wrote begging for elementary necessities, not only for themselves but for their wives and children who were living in the direst poverty in the French countryside. The reports of hunger and hardship were appalling. One letter described how a mother and her children were reduced to eating grass; another painted a lurid picture of sickness in a reception centre which should have been closed long before, but still persisted, with its population of bare-footed and ragged Spanish Republicans.

As for the camps on the Côte de Vermeil, they had been partly emptied by the enrolment of men into labour gangs for war construction work, but partly filled again by numbers of foreign anti-fascists.

The scandalous treatment of these people – in the typical case of Vernet camp – has been described very dramatically by Arthur Koestler in *Scum of the Earth*; the degradation and misery of the camps extended far beyond that one place, and the nightmare of arrest and imprisonment hung over anybody who could claim to have been a victim of Hitler or Mussolini in the thirties, wherever his present residence – in the provinces or in Paris.

France, therefore, in the early months of 1940 resembled any police state; if you had left or even liberal sympathies you would be wise to keep them to yourself, or you might quickly find you'd been mobilised to a remote corner of the 'front' or were suffering the indignity of being on a black list, your movements watched, your telephone tapped, your friends and activities investigated. If you were a known 'red' and suspected of doing propaganda against the government, you would soon find yourself in jail.

Of course, these were everyday happenings in a fascist country, but this was France – land of the 1789 revolutions and the *Droits de l'Homme*[40] – and a France engaged, so they said, in a crusade against oppression.

I could hardly believe my ears when I heard of some of the things reported – appalling beatings by the police, and *interrog-*

atoires accompanied by the refinements of mediaeval torture. I wondered dismally what was civilisation coming to, if even the French, with their great traditions, degraded themselves to such depths? They were redeemed only by the heroic attitude of the victims – who were far more patriotic than ever the members of the *Deuxième Bureau*,[41] who later collaborated hand in glove with the Gestapo.

I learned to be careful indeed – not for my own safety, for British nationals enjoyed a certain immunity from police interference (though my Spanish affiliations might have roused suspicion) – but for the sake of my friends. We never spoke about anything but the weather on the telephone, or indeed in any spot where one might be overheard by strangers however innocent they appeared.

Through the committee for Spanish children I got to know many anti-fascist foreigners in danger of imprisonment because of their backgrounds and views, and of course, wherever it was possible I did anything I could through British connections, to help them.

It was easier to take a room under an English name than if one was a stateless Czech; it was possible to get visas to other countries if you had introductions to British subjects; one could take messages if one was a young woman with a British passport, and with fewer questions asked than if one were an anti-fascist Italian (and until Mussolini came into the war, Bonnet behaved like a cat purring and rubbing against his legs!) One could also send material to the English press and hope that some of the awful stories of torture might reach the outer world.

As the time of the trial of the Communist deputies approached I sent off letters and reports on the accused and on the background of the case, using a sort of code which I hoped would get past the censor. One package of documents that was sent, firmly tied up and sealed, never got to its destination in London, the owner of the address having been locked up and evacuated, and after several months the parcel came back to me in Paris. It arrived after its perambulations in a state of decomposition, the string half off, the paper torn and the contents exposed to full view. To my horror, the photographs of youths who had been beaten up, with their signed depositions on their treatment, and the pictures of the accused deputies and other well-known people stared out at the world for every clerk in the censor's office to see. It was a miracle that I had not been abducted and that I was not in Fresnes prison as a result.

The highly explosive material on the trial was given me by a very striking and brave woman, the former secretary of Henri Barbusse. I used to go and see her in her tiny flat on the outskirts of Paris, where she lived surrounded by Barbusse relics – photographs, first editions, manuscripts – and where she would talk for hours about Barbusse whom she had known well and worked with for many years. She took me, on his birthday (or on the day of his death, perhaps) to lay flowers on his grave in Père Lachaise cemetery. After walking for what seemed miles through that city of tombstones and necromantic monuments, we reached the place. To Annette's horror the memorial stone, a slab of pink marble sent from the Soviet Union by Russian miners, had been overturned and was badly cracked and chipped.

She went down on her knees beside it, trying to pull it up: 'The brutes,' she said. 'The brutes! But if they think they can destroy him and what he believed in by destroying this they're making a big mistake.'

Besides supplying me with information on the deputies' trial for the British press, Annette asked me if I would care to go to the opening of the proceedings, saying that it might be the only chance of getting in, as very likely the trial would take place in *huis clos*.[42] I jumped at the suggestion, as I had never attended an important political trial, and we went along together, early on the morning of 11th February. We were huddled along with the relatives and close friends of the twenty-one accused, at the very back of the big room of the Palais de Justice. The rest of the room was occupied by large numbers of witnesses, and still larger numbers of police; I could not understand why, as there was no reason to expect rioting or hooliganism, but I supposed that it was important for the police to make out that these dangerous elements needed as strong a guard as possible.

When the accused filed in, they certainly gave a very different impression, and made the squads of strong-arm men look very silly. They were very pale, and evidently tired and none too well in health – naturally enough, after many weeks in gaol – but every one of them had an expression of patient endurance that one doesn't associate with the physiognomy of gangsters. The blind Pierre Duclos, and Bonte, and Michels, to mention only a few, were typical of the best type of French working man, and even their opponents would admit from their records that they were infinitely superior to their guards (and possibly to their prosecutors!) in character and intelligence.

The atmosphere of the first day of the trial was highly dramatic as all important trials I suppose are; on top of the usual suspense and emotional undertones there was a current of a different kind – the awareness of everyone in the court room that two sides of a world conflict were facing one another a few feet apart. The French Communists, rightly or wrongly, prided themselves on their patriotism, considered that they were the true heirs of the revolutions of 1789, of 1830, of the Commune, and invoked Diderot, Stendhal, Victor Hugo, Henri Barbusse with complete conviction, roundly turning the tables on the prosecution in speech after speech. The Chief Prosecutor, M. Gallimori, became purple with fury, and thumped the table in his attempts to quell the flow of oratory. There was nothing for it but to sit through twenty-one speeches of defiant accusation that *he* and his friends were the real traitors and conspirators against France!

Having had their say, the deputies sat down, while the judge in lengthy legal verbiage announced that on consideration of the serious nature of the charge he had decided that the rest of the trial should be held behind closed doors. This was to be expected, as it was quite clear that if the accused continued to make these eloquent and forceful speeches the public might be moved to support them and to hinder the course of justice in bringing them to reason. So thereafter everything went on in secret session. The wives and friends and relatives went the next day, and the following five days to the Palais, and waited patiently in the public room for hours, hoping for a glimpse of the prisoners. The only time they could see them was as the twenty-one filed in or out, and on the occasions when a request was made by one of the accused which for some reason had to be heard in public, by the rules of legal procedure. Then the doors were opened for a few minutes, and one could see through into the inner court, while a beagle or whatever the French equivalent is, came out and announced in stentorian tones that the accused, Philimond Bonte, or Jules Racamond, or whoever it happened to be, requested, *au nom de la République Française*,[43] a pen and writing paper, or a calendar, or a *cahier* (notebook)!

Everyone who could get there went along on the last day of the trial when the sentences were announced. Although nobody had expected leniency, the harshness of the punishments made everybody gasp: ten years for most of them; five years for the older and the less prominent. Five years, in the remote *Île d'Yeu* even for the sightless Duclos. The man who commented '*Ils exagèrent!*' was putting it mildly. Most of the waiting crowd murmured '*Assasins! – Tortionnaires!*' or '*Bonnet au Poteau!*'[44]

Whatever one's political opinions this certainly seemed a miscarriage of justice that would have been unimaginable a year earlier, and couldn't indeed have happened if France had not been ruled by a semi-fascist government. I thought to myself, the *état de guerre* (state of war) would have had to be invented by Bonnet if it had not artificially arisen, so that he could thus summarily dispose in one stroke of so many powerful political opponents. It would have been utterly impossible, under normal conditions, and with France unmuzzled and free.

There came, just once, a chance of helping a group of exiles, Italian anti-fascists, who had been living precariously in Paris since the fall of the Popular Front and Laval's rapprochement with Mussolini. These brave people were many of them trying to get back to Italy to do underground work against the Fascist regime; an essential requirement for them was to have an up-to-date passport, stamped with the permits to enter Italy and to pass through Switzerland. They had an efficient organisation for forging false papers, but needed the latest official customs stamps, which would of course be unobtainable for anti-fascist exiles.

What better way of getting these stamps than to procure them through a British subject who could still travel without let or hindrance across the frontiers to Italy? Some of the Italian exiles whom I had met through the Spanish Relief Office approached me with a request that I should make a journey to Florence or Milan, to see whatever sights I liked, and to bring back my passport with the appropriate visas and stamps for them to copy and use on their friends' papers.

The idea appealed to me enormously, and I soon managed to fix up my passage to Italy via Berne and Domodossola. I travelled at the expense of the underground committee and thoroughly enjoyed the trip, visiting Bologna, Milan, Florence and Leghorn without the slightest difficulty or any questions asked.

The towns were enchanting, and greatly improved by the almost complete absence of any foreigners. It was a poor season for the hotels and tourist trade, as the war in Europe had scared off the Americans, and few British and French visitors, nor even Germans, would have chosen that time to go sight-seeing. So I roamed around the streets, the palaces, the galleries, enjoying the paintings and monuments almost in solitude. I wished my Italian had been more adequate (only Spanish came out when I tried to make conversation) but even so, people in shops and hotels, and the bored keepers at the empty galleries were not averse to pouring out their complaints about the European war, the cost of living, and the high taxes, to a sympathetic ear.

Apart from odd jobs for the anti-fascists, most of whom were living practically 'underground' at that time, there was little I could do, as the Spanish Committee had been closed down by the authorities, and most of my friends on it were scattered to the winds. The obvious thing was to go back to England, but there still seemed to be time for me to finish the course at the Sorbonne, which was ostensibly one of the reasons for my being in France, and which included taking an examination for a diploma in the subject *La Civilisation Française* in June. (In retrospect, and considering what happened to French civilisation in that summer, there is something ironic about the thought.)

However, I worked very hard at the syllabus, reading Descartes and Diderot, skimming Corneille and Racine, and attending lectures by very ancient professors who, I discovered, had taken my brother through an identical course in the year 1928! It all seemed curiously unrealistic, but there would be plenty of time for realism after the exam, I thought.

News came suddenly which shocked even the septua-genarians at the Sorbonne: On 8th April, we heard, the Nazis had overrun Denmark; then came news of the attack on Norway. There had been little resistance except from Norwegian shore batteries which sank the cruiser Bluecher. The country seemed to have been taken by surprise, or if anyone was prepared for a Nazi invasion it was the Norwegian fascists, headed by one Quisling, who had the doubtful honour of giving his name to all future collaborators with Hitler.

Britain could, it seemed, do nothing except shell and bomb military installations in Norway. When, one wondered, would Britain do anything more than sit by and watch her allies, the free countries, going down like ninepins before Hitler's assaults? The answer came sooner than we dared hope: in May, Winston Churchill replaced Chamberlain, at the head of a genuinely National Government. 'What a leader, and oh! if he had been sooner,' Miss Rathbone exclaimed, voicing many people's feelings. Churchill's anti-Nazi record was good, and whether or not one would have chosen him for a peacetime leader, he was clearly the man for this moment. Britain was at last going to stand up to Fascism – perhaps after all, the struggles of the thirties had not been altogether in vain.

Chapter 22 – Internment

I shall not ever forget the flower gardens of France [...]
The roses all along the way we went,
Flowers that gave the lie to the soldiers passing
On wings of fear, a fear importunate as a breeze
And give the lie to the lunatic pushbikes and the manic
Guns and the sorry rig of the refugees...

Louis Aragon, *Le Crève-Coeur* (translation: Louis MacNeice)

The fact that Winston Churchill had taken over the direction of the British war effort gave new confidence to all who wanted Hitler's defeat. But there was no similar change in Paris to stimulate the French effort: the same old gang were misdirecting operations, no reorganisation had taken place, de Gaulle's advice on modernising the military machine had been rejected, and when the Wehrmacht, after invading the Netherlands in mid-May swept westwards into France it was too late to repair the damage of months and years of defeatism.

Anxiety and fear were rife in Paris, that beautiful early summer. When news came of the debacle at Dunkirk the city began to empty like one of the legendary plugless Russian baths, the well-to-do leaving in big cars, foreigners making tracks for home, sealed vans being sent off, stacked with documents and equipment from ministerial offices; factory machinery was packed into lorries and driven away to various destinations in the south of France, while the workers were ordered to follow on foot, to their natural disgust.

As the rumble of guns began to be heard, and news trickled in to the capital of the collapse of the French army, of the steady advance by the Germans' vast and well-organised divisions, of the refugees, machine-gunned and scattered in terror on the northern roads, panic set in. Notices appeared on the walls and in the Paris metro adjuring the population to keep calm, and commanding public servants to stay at their posts. Nothing was hinted as to what was being done to stop the Wehrmacht from entering the city.

The government, Reynaud, Mandel and company, gave no sign of preparing to stand firm, nor of evacuating Paris. Intolerable uncertainly and confusion prevailed. During the first few days of June, as might have been expected, most of the people who could possibly do so, packed up and cleared out. I could have gone, along with various wiser English friends and journalists. But curiosity and bravado compelled me to stay as long as possible, and when I finally accepted a share in a friend's car, due to leave on 14th June, it was very late in the day.

Frida, centre, in Paris with friends and a horse-drawn field kitchen in the background.

On the 13th, returning after a council of war at my friend's house I watched the evacuees leaving Paris, and felt considerable misgivings about joining them: the procession along the Boul'Mich looked like a modern version of the exodus out of Egypt. Thousands of people, with their children and their animals, bird cages, furniture, kitchen utensils, farm implements piled high on prams and handcarts, and in cars which could only move at walking speed, were pouring out of the city, away from the unknown unimaginable threat of the German army.

I thought of the Spanish refugees in a similar tragic exodus; their story need not have been repeated here if we had had our way. But it was too late for regrets, four years too late.

I went back to the flat and packed up. A telephone call came from my friend; she had seen the crowds on the road too, and decided it was impossible to take the children out by car. We agreed that as I had a bicycle I should leave on my own steam early next day.

Going out that evening, into almost deserted streets, I heard the guns alarmingly near, and saw a huge black cloud to the north. This was the smoke from petrol dumps, set on fire, I suppose, by the retreating French. Quite suddenly there were torrents of black rain, falling vertically and soaking everyone to the skin, so that when I got home my face and clothes looked like a chimney sweep's. It was the most sinister evening of all time; but I went to bed and slept soundly, having prepared everything for an early start.

To my horror it was broad daylight when I woke and there was an ominous silence – no booming or rumbling guns. Having dragged on some clothes I hurried downstairs and met a terrified old concierge who announced through chattering teeth, that the *Boches* had entered Paris at four that morning and were all over the town.

'We are caught like rats in a trap,' she moaned. I tried to comfort her and myself by the thought that we were unlikely to be hurt if we stayed indoors; but decided none the less to try and make a dash for the Porte des Lilas, by side streets, and bicycle out. Of course it was too late. As I got into the street there was a roar of machines and six or seven motorcyclists rushed by at a terrific pace, but not too fast for me to spot the grey helmets and olive-green uniforms of the Reichswehr. I could not resist venturing forth to see what was going on, and found the streets still very empty except for occasional small groups of Paris gendarmes, whose weapons had been removed, standing about and looking thoroughly deflated.

Riding past the *Chambre des Députés* I witnessed a melancholy scene: a group of fat French policemen were engaged in hauling down the tricolour flag; and by the time I reached the Champ de Mars, horror of horrors, on top of the Eiffel Tower waved the evil black and white in red circle and cross of the Swastika. Nothing, I decided, could shock me after that.

Later that day, there was a march-past of the Wehrmacht, along the Avenue de la *Grande Armée* (supreme irony) and past the Arc de Triomphe. On principle one should perhaps not have attempted to watch it; but it was certainly a sight worth seeing, if only for the proof it offered of the results of Hitler's seven years regime, and of the aid given him by our democratic governments.

The Rhineland, the Ruhr, Czechoslovakia, Austria, Spain, Poland, had all contributed to the equipment and weapons which we saw so lavishly displayed. The parade stretched for miles, writhing along like a monstrous grey-green serpent, an endless body of men, hundreds of thousands it seemed, faultlessly uniformed, from their steel helmets to their belts stamped with *Gott mit Uns*, goose-stepping, marching, riding bicycles and motorcycles, sitting bolt upright in cars, tanks, field kitchens – a modern model army, mechanised down to the least infantryman. There were guns, heavy and light, and radar equipment, and more horses than one could have imagined possible. A typical Prussian general (could it have been Speidel?) monocled and monolithic, took the salute, while bands played military march tunes, drowned every few minutes by the roar of aeroplanes in formation passing overhead.

The French who had ventured out stood gaping. They had expected the Germans to be a disorderly rabble, running wild and beating everybody up and they were secretly relieved at this display of military discipline. The Germans paid little attention to them and were on that occasion and indeed for several weeks after, relatively *korrekt*.

After a few days, life resumed its course – hardly a normal course, for how could one get used to the swastikas everywhere, the jack-booted field-grey squads tramping the Paris streets, the closed cafés (often bearing a large sign, *Jude*), the brown-shirted louts invading the stores and buying up large quantities of goods with worthless paper money. Although the Nazis did not visibly loot or pillage, their method of denuding the shops was quite as effective: within two weeks, silk stockings, clothes and cosmetics (of which the Germans had been deprived for so long) had vanished from the counters, or the prices had soared far out of the reach of the French. The Germans were soon nicknamed *les doryphores* after the potato bug which strips the fields and is public enemy number one to the farmer.

Apart from the occupying forces, whole battalions of troops on leave invaded Paris, brought standing upright close-packed in charabancs, as a special treat to see the Eiffel Tower (which they were told was built by a German) and to clear the shops of clothes, food, everything. It was amusing and somewhat revolting to see them in pâtisseries, where a soldier would buy a large family-size tart and consume it on the spot, or make a sandwich of two slabs of chocolate with half a pound of butter in between and 'swallow it like a pill!', (as one of my friends remarked).

Systematic plundering soon began in the markets, where eggs, meat and vegetables were loaded on to vans and driven off towards Germany.

The resistance movement was said to have begun in Les Halles, the Covent Garden of Paris, when a Nazi soldier was shot while removing a lorry-load of fruit; as a reprisal, no potatoes were on sale for a week – a considerable hardship for the hungry population, but mild compared with what was meted out for similar offences later on.

In the early days of occupation the Nazis were anxious to appear as the friends of the French and to show that the British were their real enemies: gruesome posters were soon displayed everywhere, depicting a bloated Churchill strangling Marianne, or a villainous Tommy threatening a group of starving French children, under the caption, *'C'est l'anglais qui vous a fait cela.'*[45]

All news was presented with a pro-Nazi slant, of course, by the French newspapers which were allowed to appear; we learned in great detail of German successes and of French humiliations – of the signing of the armistice by Pétain, the division of the country into two zones – the northern one occupied by the Nazis, the southern 'governed' by the Maréchal and his fellow collaborators, from Vichy. We read of Italy's entry into the war, and of Mussolini's advance into the Balkans and Greece; we didn't hear of the valiant resistance in those countries, how Tito, formerly a commander in the International Brigade, had rallied a guerrilla army in Yugoslavia, and how in Greece Manuel Glezos had torn the Swastika down from the Acropolis and was leading a people's army against the invaders. The papers did not tell us, either, of the failure of the Germans' attempts to invade England, nor the setbacks in Africa, nor of General de Gaulle's appeal and the foundation of the Free French Movement.

But every Parisian in possession of a wireless set heard these things over the radio from London, and spread the news and took courage from the knowledge, as de Gaulle put it *'La France a perdu une bataille – elle n'a pas perdu la guerre'*:[46] that the best and bravest of her men had decided to carry on the fight outside, and counted on those inside the country to ensure victory.

The movement began gradually to get organised, small individual groups linking up and networks being created, but the Germans did not consider the Gaullists a serious threat in the early stages; they did, however, from the very beginning of the occupation turn their attention to the Communists, who were already organised in underground cells and were bringing out news sheets, circulating leaflets and chalking slogans *À bas les Nazis, vive Thorez*[47] on walls at night.

Communists and Jews were arrested by dozens; other early victims were foreign anti-fascists, and British men of military age. For several months, to our surprise, British women were not troubled, apart from the tiresome business of registering daily at the nearest police station. We managed to live somehow, thanks to the kindness of French friends, and to the pittance we could draw from the American embassy (repayable on return to England), I supplemented this with the takings from a Punch and Judy show – *Guignol* to the French – which I got permission to put up in the *mairie* garden of Neuilly every Sunday. I had plenty to do, what with making and painting the puppets, queuing for necessities, and going the rounds of my friends to keep up with the news, till the end of the summer.

In November, the Sorbonne reopened and I signed on again as a student, realising that the standards would have fallen, but curious to see what the Nazis were doing to French education. In the schools they had already introduced a new curriculum with the accent heavily on compulsory gym for boys and domestic classes for girls, had replaced the standard textbooks by fascist manuals, had forced non-Aryan teachers to wear brassards labelling them *juif* (Jew); they had been unable to sack progressive teachers – of whom there were hundreds, and irreplaceable – but they warned them against teaching anything deviating from the official line (a warning that was, needless to say, completely ignored).

In the university there had been three different *recteurs* (rectors) in two months; many of the most brilliant professors had been dismissed on racial grounds, in spite of vigorous protests from their colleagues, and from the students whose spirit was splendid. The latter were perhaps the most active and vocal militants against *les Boches* at that time, and constantly staging small demonstrations. On 11th November they turned out in a body to march to the Arc de Triomphe proposing to lay a wreath on the Unknown Warrior's tomb. No official German objection was made, but there was quite obvious provocation that afternoon from the pro-German *Jeune France* organisation, and from a Nazi officer's car which drove at breakneck speed down the avenue scattering the procession. A certain amount of disorder naturally followed, and German troops appeared; shots were fired – one student wounded, people knocked down and injured, arrests made, the university closed till further notice, and its students forced to sign on daily at the *poste de police* (like me) or sent home to the provinces.

All this did not break their spirit; the Sorbonne remained a centre of resistance right through the war. That episode was the first trial of strength, and the chief thing it showed was just how jumpy the occupying forces had become. It was on that wave of jitters that they arrested the bulk of the remaining British civilians in Paris. The excuse given was that an English woman had been discovered using a secret transmitting set.

Be that as it might, on 5th December, a cold dreary morning, we were rounded up, hundreds of us in each arrondissement, taken to the local *poste* where our papers were examined, bundled into Black Maria vans and driven to the Gare de l'Est ('for all the world like a Mothers' Union outing' as my diary remarks). Here we sat for six hours in a stationary train, which eventually steamed off in an easterly direction, but whither nobody had the faintest idea.

I found myself in a carriage with two coloured girls, one very old lady who had to have drops put in her eyes every hour, a fat elderly barman, and two French women, widows of British subjects. They were all very indignant and upset, and greatly worried by not knowing their destination. We had nothing to eat, nothing to read, and not a hope of a wink of sleep, so that the night seemed endless.

When dawn eventually came we still appeared to be in France. The German sentries parading the corridor were quite affable, and gave us slices of a revolting purple sausage out of a tin, but no information. However, we were soon to find out: the train slowed down at Belfort, but instead of going east to Germany, to our immense relief it turned south and puffed on, snail's pace and constantly stopping, to Besançon. Here it stopped, and we were ordered to get out on to the platform where large numbers of German soldiers were waiting to marshal us into a crocodile and escort us though the outskirts of the town to the local barracks.

Caserne Vauban, as it was called, consisted of a number of large grim buildings and smaller offices, surrounding a typical barracks square. High walls festooned with barbed wire, and sentries with helmets and rifles guarding the gates, gave us to understand that we were well and truly in Hitler's clutches.

We filed in with sinking hearts, while army carts followed and our luggage was unloaded and strewn about the ground. To the left was a group of khaki-clad soldiers whom we recognised as allies – French prisoners left behind to work in the camp; on the right a number of German officers stood smiling patronisingly at the haul made by their authorities.

It was certainly an astonishing collection. There were about a thousand people, of all types, ages and nationalities, gathered together under the convenient nomenclature 'British'. It turned out that at least two thirds of them could not speak English, as their only claim to our nationality was that they happened to have some connection with some part of the British Empire. There were Italians, Russians, Turks, Poles, Scandinavians, whose parents had happened to be staying in Malta or Palestine at the time of their birth; there were French and Dutch and Portuguese women married to Englishmen (widows or divorcees, it made no difference); there were French Canadian nuns of eighteen orders, in variegated robes – blue, brown, grey, black and white; there were coloured women from Jamaica, Martinique, Nigeria, all indignant at being picked up, for most of them had no special love for the British. The most indignant of all, perhaps, was the couple from Southern Ireland.

There was an equally weird assortment of men, only homogeneous in that they were all well over sixty. Most of them were former jockeys from Longchamp, but there were a number of Polish peasants (heaven knows why) and some white Russians. The male population also included a few younger men, Dutch, Danish and Belgian, but they were fairly soon released. I noticed one striking figure, who turned out to be Gordon Craig the producer; I thought to myself, at least we may get some drama going – but I never saw him again. People of influence, and those with money, somehow did not stay for many days in the camp.

The motley crowd of internees to be was gradually sorted out and directed to rooms in the barrack buildings. I found a corner in an enormous dormitory, lined with palliasses, and with an ancient stove belching out smoke which a harassed *poilu* (private soldier) was struggling to get under control; he soon gave up with a shrug, and told us that smoke in the rooms would be the least of our troubles.

He apologised for the filthy state of the place, the litter, the bed bugs, the general confusion, explaining that until a few days ago, 22,000 prisoners of war had been housed in the barracks, and that there really hadn't been time enough to clear up the mess they had left. He pointed out of the window to a back yard strewn with muck heaps: 'a souvenir of their visit,' he said, adding that if we wanted any utensils, plates, spoons, or forks, we could find them down there.

The new inhabitants of the camp – elderly ladies in fur coats, nuns in their flying robes, little old men, children even, were hard at it, rummaging among the rubbish. I joined the party, and secured a fork, a tin cup, and a fine big can, which I proudly bore upstairs only to find it had a large hole in its side. The cup served for supper which we queued for at great length, and which consisted of thin greasy utterly tasteless soup. I was too tired to care, and only wanted to sleep; and in spite of the noise of thirty other wretched women, grumbling, cursing, weeping and snoring, I managed to get several hours dead to the world.

The first day and night of internment were by far the worst. To do the Germans justice they tried to clean up the place *fur die Frauen* and to this end they appointed a squad of *Schwester* German girls in uniform who were ardent Nazis and tried to convert us to their doctrine, made us drill, gave us check bedcovers, inspected our rooms daily, and generally saw to our welfare. The *Kommandant* of the camp, Herr Braun, was a rough cheerful type from the Black Forest, who was not a member of the Party, and did his best not to maltreat us. He agreed to the formation of a Camp Committee through which we could present complaints, suggest improvements, and organise concerts and sports among the internees. As a result we soon had quite a number of educational activities, keep fit classes, folk dancing, language courses, books and equipment being supplied by the Red Cross.

It was a great chance of improving one's knowledge of foreign languages, as apart from the classes that were started, there were unlimited opportunities for practice. Even, I found to my great joy, of Spanish, for there were in the barracks half a dozen Republican refugees; they had been brought in from Besançon to dig drains and other rough work in the camp, and when the sentries were well out of sight, we had long talks about the Spanish war and their hopes for the future. They were convinced that the democracies would win the war, that Franco would then collapse, that the Republic would be restored in

Spain and they would go home at long last to Madrid. I wished I could have felt as hopeful: it seemed to me more likely that they would be sent by the Germans to build fortifications, or back to Franco Spain much too soon.

One of my only regrets at leaving the barracks was that it was probably the last time I should ever see them, and the very nice French soldiers who brought us in sweets and fruit from the town, along with the latest news from London radio – not that the news was very cheerful – what with the blitz, the conquest of Greece, Rumania, Hungary, Bulgaria, by the Axis forces, we sometimes felt extremely depressed.

The Barracks Yard at Caserne Vauban – sketch by Frida

Chapter 23 – Escape

Having given all they had to give,
To save from blood and fire and dust
At least a hope that we can trust.
We must remember them – and live.

Aileen Palmer, *The Dead Have No Regrets*

The train crawled endlessly through the flat fields west of the Vosges but eventually reached the wooded undulating country which surrounds the small spa town of Vittel. From the carriage windows we could see glimpses of huge hotels between the trees of parks and gardens. They looked like mausoleums, shuttered, empty and dead – a typical spa out of season.

As we came out of the train, we were formed into a file and were marched, as usual, between soldiers towards our new home; the local inhabitants, mostly women and children and very old men, appeared from nowhere to stare at us suspiciously. (They thought we were a party of German women sent to take a cure here by the Nazi authorities.) The troops fell back as we reached the hotel gates, and we were greeted by some important looking German officers and two or three men in civilian clothes; these we discovered in the nick of time were movie men waiting to take a newsreel of our arrival at the hotel, thus proving the magnanimity of the Führer. But the word ran down our line like lightning down a rod, and every one of us automatically turned away her head. So much for photographic evidence of our gratitude to Herr Hitler!

We entered the hotel feeling like fishes very much out of water, for many of us were wearing the old blue army coats and boots issued to us at the barracks, and carrying our peculiar bundles, and we must have looked extremely odd against the setting of marble pillars, plush carpets and crystal candelabra.

The bedrooms were equally impressive, each with an enormous mirror, running water, and expensive furniture. We settled down ecstatically and incredulously to a life of clean sheets and hot baths, which seemed extraordinarily unreal after months of bristly blankets and cold water ablutions in washing troughs.

Another unexpected blessing of Vittel was the surrounding park, which was open to us all day till seven at night; and after the black cinders and grey walls of Besançon we felt we were in heaven. It was something out of the world, too, to eat sitting down in a civilised dining-room, after a hundred meals consumed out of tin plates balanced on our knees. Although the coffee was still burnt barley, and the quality of the food *ersatz* as before – *Kunstkäse* and *Kunstmarmelade* (artificial cheese and jam) were the staple supper – it tasted infinitely superior to what came out of the barracks 'pig bin'.

But although the physical conditions were much better than at Besançon the atmosphere of the camp was less friendly and congenial. People shared rooms in twos and threes, and withdrew into small cliques; the communal spirit evaporated, and it became an effort to meet other internees and organise combined activities.

Our committee sank, wrecked by a female torpedo who had the ear of the *Kommandant* and convinced him that it was communist controlled; it was replaced by a quisling committee chosen from among the pro-Nazi internees (of whom there were quite a few) by Herr B. and made responsible directly to him.

The German 'sisters' having been sent off to help in the war effort, the quislings did the work of taking the register and patrolling the hotel and grounds to prevent our misbehaving or trying to escape. There was something repulsive about British women collaborating with the Germans in this way, and the new organisation was very unpopular; but people were not conscious enough of the need for democratic representation to fight for it, and we became less and less active, and relied on our private ploys and personal friendships to make life tolerable.

I was lucky in having room-mates and neighbours of my own interests and views. Shula, a young Jewish painter, and Penelope, and Oxford students, and Pat, a lively and attractive Hampstead secretary, were all ardent anti-fascists who had helped in Spanish relief campaigns, and between us we soon converted several others to our way of thinking; we had discussions which went on late into the night, on every subject under the sun, and tried to combine theory and action by organising various affairs aimed at raising the political and cultural level of the camp, and at annoying the Germans. Whether we succeeded in the former is doubtful, but we certainly achieved the latter: on the day that news came of the Soviet resistance to the Nazi attack on Russia we made certain that the Germans realised our feelings by getting as many women as we could to mention, to any sentry or German official who happened to be about, their considered opinion that this was Hitler's suicide.

On another occasion we organised a protest against the unfair distribution of Red Cross parcels, and against the personnel of the camp 'committee'. On 14th July we got up a fête to celebrate France's national day; this took place in a clearing in the park and was a very festive affair. To brighten things up we asked the Germans to play a record for us over the camp loudspeaker; it was, we explained *The Two Grenadiers*, a song by Schumann, well-known, one hundred per cent Aryan German composer, but we omitted to mention that the song contains a section near the end where one of the Grenadiers bursts into the *Marseillaise*.

The officer in charge of the gramophone agreed to put on the record, and halfway through the party the French Republican hymn rang out over the camp, to the great surprise and delight of the assembled guests who joined in with the utmost gusto: '*Marchons, marchons, qu'un sang impur abreuve nos sillons!*'[48] – before our captors realised the trick played on them.

We occasionally managed to introduce pro-Ally sentiments into our plays and entertainments in the hotel concert hall which we were allowed to use every weekend. But we usually had to be satisfied with 'straight' music, and the Germans saw to it that nothing they considered unsuitable was performed. Jewish composers such as Mendelssohn were taboo, and modern music and jazz discouraged. Everything had a political flavour for the Nazis: this was apparent even when we performed the Bach D minor concerto for two violins. As we lowered our instruments and took the applause (the first and last of my life!) I heard a monocled officer in the nearby box say, very loud and clear, '*Deutschland, Deutschland über Alles – nicht wahr*?[49]' I couldn't help feeling that J. S. B., solid old Protestant, good through and through, was turning in his grave, not only at our appalling rendering of his work but at the thought of being associated with such godless ruffians as these!

Although we passed the time somehow, many of us were getting very restive towards the end of the summer of 1941. The war seemed no nearer coming to an end; there seemed to be deadlock in the West; France lay apparently prostrate, like the rest of occupied Europe, incapable of throwing out the invader for the time being; the war raged on the Eastern front and the Red Army held the Nazis at bay, but the struggle might last for years.

The Germans kept telling us that decisive victory (for them) was at hand, but it was obvious that they dreaded being sent off to Russia and were extremely worried about events there. From French soldiers who worked in the camp office on card indexing and other secretarial chores, we heard reports of how the *Boches* would bring in quantities of drink and get tight when bad news arrived; they were often in tears when their turn came to go off.

Most of those who were drafted to the East never came back to the camp, nor one may suppose to their homes. Now and again, however, an officer was drafted to the camp as a rest cure from the Eastern front, and they were reported as saying 'it was hell let loose.' In the occupied villages everything was burnt or destroyed by the partisans. 'They have secret arsenals everywhere,' one officer said. 'We can't trust a single Russian...' We realised that there was one country at least which had not got a Fifth Column to betray its people to the invaders.

News of the resistance by the Red Army and the guerrillas was a source of inspiration to the French, according to our soldier friends, who told us that the underground movement was rapidly becoming organised, and that all sorts of sabotage and secret activities were going on. It made one long to be doing something, not just sitting idly under German supervision...

I began to get thoroughly restive and, when it leaked out that two women had successfully escaped from the camp, it seemed absurd not to make any attempt to get away too.

I found that Pat, my room-mate, felt the same way, and we decided that as soon as we could get enough money and the necessary contacts we would make a dash for it. After endless discussions and sleepless nights we set to work organising our escape in earnest – dropping hints that we needed cash, in innocent letters to friends in Paris, sounding out the French workmen as to the best way of getting out, the times of trains, the papers that were needed to get past official checks. These men were absolutely trustworthy, loathed the Germans, and were willing to take considerable risks to help anyone do them a bad turn and us a good one. The camp plumber offered to show us a manhole by which we could drop into a drain and thus crawl in perfect safety for miles; another offered to lend us his bicycle; another, the camp electrician, who worked in the concert hall, offered us the best solution: he could, he said, leave a back door open in the hall, and if we spent the night in there we could escape in the small hours and catch the early train to Besançon, where we should certainly find friends to help us.

We agreed on this, and worked out a plan to the last detail. After weeks of waiting, two separate money orders arrived for us. Pat and I had a council of war with one trusted friend, who agreed to cover our retreat by locking the hall door after us, and to put the Germans off the scent by signing the morning register in our names – which would give us a few hours' start before awkward questions were asked.

We decided not to tell anyone else, though it nearly broke our hearts not to say goodbye to our other friends, and we made up our minds to leave within the next forty-eight hours.

The following day, our electrician came hurrying to our room, ostensibly to mend a plug, but actually to tell us that it was now or never. The Senegalese soldiers, who did the dirtiest work of the camp, were cutting a hole in the wire of the outer fence by the back opening of the hall, through which coal was to be shovelled into the cellar. We could escape by just moving a strand of wire, he said. It seemed too good to be true after anxious nights spent envisaging tunnel-digging, drain-crawling, wire-cutting and all the classical ordeals of making an escape.

There would never be such a chance again, and we made up our minds to take the plunge. Creeping into the hall from the park at dusk, we ensconced ourselves in the tiny room out of which we would take the first step to freedom at daybreak. It was a dark chilly night and seemed to go on for ever as we sat there cramped and cold, hardly daring to breathe, keeping each other awake by nudges and pinches for fear of missing the moment to get out.

At long last the first grey streaks of dawn appeared, and we nerved ourselves for the fatal move. '*C'est le premier pas qui coûte*,'[50] I thought, and opened the door a chink. There was no sign of any sentry cycling round the park on his patrol. But as we moved cautiously out a heavy thud resounded nearby and we retreated in alarm. Another thud, and another, followed, just like the tread of a soldier's boots – but no soldier in sight.

Then I realised that lumps of snow were falling off the branches of a nearby tree, giving a false alarm. Gathering courage, we slipped out. Five steps to the hole in the wire. Pat lifted the cut strand, I stuck my head down and dived through the gap. Pat followed. We pulled our bags through after us. Still no sentry. Ten steps to the main road, six across it, and we felt better.

We turned into the road and walked past the main gate of the camp, looking, we hoped, as unconcerned and innocent as two village women on their way to market. There were two sentries on duty. They paid no attention whatever to us, though if they had troubled to take one look they would have recognised that Pat's height and long legs were far from typical of a French peasant girl.

Just as we passed them one got on his bicycle and followed us down the road. 'We're done for,' I thought, my knees turning to jelly. But he turned up a side lane and we walked on unmolested to the railway station, where we bought tickets to Besançon – no questions asked – and waited on the platform for the train.

We had a nasty shock when two women strolled by speaking

German, and we recognised the *Kommandant's* secretary, who certainly knew us by sight. We shrank back into a dark corner and prayed that our luck would not turn against us. Mercifully, nobody spoke to us and we boarded the train unrecognised.

Several other bad moments were in store at Épinal, the next station, where we had to change trains; the camp doctor, a confirmed Nazi, was standing a few yards away. Later we got into a carriage occupied by two German officers, who eyed us (we thought) suspiciously. But perhaps we were mistaken – the Wehrmacht had a habit of eyeing females. We tried to be unconcerned and sat eating the cold potatoes and dry biscuits we had smuggled out of the camp, with as much sangfroid as we could muster.

Eventually we arrived at Nancy and found there was no train on to Besançon till the next morning. We got the name of a respectable hotel from a porter, and hurried away from the Germans who we were convinced were following us; when we reached the hotel there were forms to be filled in with names, ages and last destination.

Poker-faced, we wrote down the most unlikely details, and were relieved beyond expression when the *patronne* did not query them, nor ask for identity papers which we did not possess. I wasn't sure whether this was mere laziness on her part – it is more likely that she was being really helpful. To our horror, however, we found that the Germans from the train had chosen the same hotel, and their jackboots were standing outside the door next to ours; so we gave up the idea of the lie-in we had so longed for, and decided to leave by the earliest possible train the next day.

We reached Besançon at an unearthly hour the following morning, and realised to our despair that it was Sunday and that our only pro-British contact in the town would not be accessible: for he was the dentist who had treated one or two of the internees at *Caserne Vauban*, and had murmured, through the buzz of the drill, that if anyone ever wanted any help they could count on him...

Alas! The dental surgery would certainly not be open on Sunday, and a long day lay before us, miserable friendless fugitives without papers, food tickets or anywhere to lay our weary heads, in a town swarming with German soldiers, spies and police.

We spent the morning in various churches, and in the early afternoon sat in the cemetery (to which the Wehrmacht would be unlikely to resort) and there ate the last of our biscuits and some green pears which we had managed to buy without ration tickets. Later, we made our way to the local opera house and slumped into gallery seats for a performance of *La Traviata* by a visiting opera company. I would have enjoyed this in any other circumstances – though the singing was atrocious – however, that day my mind was not on the music but on the question of what we could eat next, and where we would spend the night.

By an extraordinary stroke of luck I suddenly spotted some familiar faces a few rows away from us. They belonged to the little Spanish workers who had worked in the camp at *Caserne Vauban*. I was at once certain they would prove heaven-sent friends, and at the interval I made my way to their seats and greeted them as inconspicuously as I could. They, on their part, had no inhibitions, and with a shout of '*Hombre!* How did you get here?' made us sit down with them and explain our presence. They then insisted on leaving the opera and taking us off to a restaurant where they gave us an enormous black market meal, complete with aperitifs and wine. By the time we had worked our way through five or six courses it was getting late, and we nervously looked at our watches. When we explained that we had nowhere to sleep, they held a rapid consultation and finally announced that there was only one solution – we must come to their lodgings and they would fix us up with a bed. Pat at first flatly refused to consider this proposal, in which she discerned the most sinister intentions. I hesitated, but then remembered the famous *honorabilidad* of the Spanish – it would be discourteous and wrong in the extreme to suspect them of anything but the highest motives; and persuading Pat that we had no other choice, I accepted the invitation. We went out and stumbled along through the blackout clinging to our hosts for fear of losing them, and with them, our one hope of salvation that night.

When we got to their lodgings it turned out that there were

two rooms, one filled entirely with a large double bed and four bicycles, the other with one large single bed. Usually, Pepe the leader of the party explained, the four of them shared the beds, two in each. But tonight they would all pack into the double bed, leaving Pat and me the single room.

This incident, and the fact that they were taking a great risk – themselves refugees, and liable to arrest on the slightest provocation – confirmed my opinion that the Spanish peasants are indeed the noblest of God's creatures. I was only sorry that they would not accept a centime in payment, and that, after they woke us next morning before going off to their work, we never saw them again. I can only hope that they escaped trouble, and are thriving and happy wherever they may be today.

That Monday morning we got in touch at last with the French underground organisation, which was based, as we had hardly dared to believe, in the dentist's room, and with members all over the town. From the surgery we were sent to a cycle shop in a side street, and conducted through a jumble of bicycles and mowing machines, to a back room where a courteous elderly salesman, who seemed to have no interest in life beyond selling his goods, welcomed us with 'We're glad to see you, *mesdemoiselles*; we hope you're the first of many!' We were conveyed by car to a house in the middle of the town, where we were introduced to another polite and charming businessman and his family, who we were told would look after us until it could be arranged for us to travel into the unoccupied zone.

Here, although we were unexpected and risky visitors, whose presence might have led to arrest or deportation for our hosts, we were treated like daughters, given far more than our share of the family's rations, and taken sightseeing by the teenage children who were obviously pleased and proud to have two British escapees boarded on them.

I was astonished at the open way in which were taken about the town; although there were a good many Germans about, the inhabitants simply ignored them. We had to have new faces for new papers and went to the hairdresser and to the photographer; and having decided on our new names, to the Town Hall, where the Mayor himself presented us with food tickets and the Town

Clerk gave us identity cards.

There was a party of *Anciens Combattants* on 11th November to which we were invited; it was a wonderful party, with toasts of *'La France Libre'*, *'L'entente cordiale'*, and 'Victory next year' in spite of the presence of Wehrmacht men at the other end of the café; and one could not help being convinced that this spirit of confidence in the cause, and contempt for the Nazis, would win the war in the end.

Nonetheless, I was often on tenterhooks for my hosts' safety and at any rate in the house, tried to keep out of sight when the doorbell rang: I knew enough about Nazi callers not to want to risk being discovered and tried to persuade the family to be careful.

After several weeks of this curious existence we were at last told that arrangements were complete for our transfer to safety in *la zone libre*. We said goodbye with tears, to our kind hosts, and promised to revisit them after the war, *'après la victoire'*, the father corrected us: *'après la victoire finale!'*

We were driven, in one of the town's police cars, by two policemen in uniform, to a small town on the frontier; when we asked them what would happen if we were stopped and questioned by the Germans, one of them answered, 'We'll say you are our wives'; at this, the other let out a guffaw, and I thought this really *was* looking-glass land.

As it happened we sailed past the guards posted along the road and were deposited without incident at a respectable house in the main square of Arbois, where a sympathetic lawyer and his wife welcomed us for the night. They were well-to-do middle class Gaullists, like our other saviours, far from left-wing, but anti-Nazi to the core; this harbouring of escaped prisoners was a normal event for them and, if they were eventually shot for it, well, it was just too bad, all part of the day's work...

The organisation of this underground *réseau* (network) was admirable. We felt like a parcel being sent in the post and just about as ignorant of our destination, and of how the postal service functioned, as any parcel. All we knew was that we were duly conveyed from one stage of our journey to the next, through some unseen, super-efficient agency.

We did not of course ask the politics or the nature of the agency; but it seemed clear that everyone in those days in occupied France could trust anyone else who was against the Germans and against Vichy – here at last was national unity, forged in disaster, the kind of unity that we needed in England and would all need after the war was over...

Thoughts like these ran through my head as we sat around the next day waiting for the arrival of the *passeur* (cross-border guide) who finally turned up at nightfall, to convey us through the 'frontier zone', a stretch of about seven miles, to unoccupied territory. 'Passing' was a regular occupation of the local lads, and our young guide obviously took it as a matter of course – showing not the slightest trepidation as he strode ahead of us in the dusk, over some very rough country where enemy sentries were on the constant lookout for such as him and his clients.

'If I hear a guard I shall run; just follow me,' he told us, and added consolingly, 'They don't often shoot, but you never know... the dogs are the worst.' It seemed that Alsatian dogs accompanied the Germans and had a great reputation for rounding up miscreants.

To my shame, I almost wished myself back in the camp as we struggled on in the dark, over ploughed fields, collecting kilos of clay on our feet, through boggy swamps, through bushes and briars catching at our clothes. I found my heart was thumping uncontrollably when we stopped for a moment to listen for guards and dogs. But as we drew near the demarcation line we hurried in spite of our exhaustion, spurred by the thought of how humiliating and distressing it would be to be caught in the last half mile.

At last we saw the narrow track along a stream regularly patrolled by sentries: the frontier. To our infinite relief there was no sign of a German and we stepped across the little bridge – into freedom. It was difficult to resist cheering, but the boy warned us that we were not safe until out of rifle range from the bridge; and we crept on as quietly as before till we reached a farmhouse and got safely within its doors.

Here, a whole family which looked like something out of a Giono novel, sat eating by lamplight, surrounded by farm implements, sheepdogs, cats and milk cans. They hardly looked at us; it was evidently a regular clearing point for illegal travellers, and they were not in the least interested, apart from one lad, who introduced himself as a friend of our guide, and said he was coming with us on the last lap of the journey.

We started out again with the boys, who this time had bicycles which they pushed through fields and lifted over fences, till we came to the main road to the village, a steady sloping stretch of about three miles. Here Pat and I were each planted on the crossbars of a bicycle, and we hurtled downhill at a terrifying speed, clutching our bags and the handlebars as best we could and pinning our faith to our good luck, as we rushed through the night. By some miracle we arrived safely at the bottom, outside a small inn where our guides said goodbye and handed us over to the landlord, a beady-eyed, rubicund man of the Jura, obviously yet another link in the *réseau*.

He welcomed us and said a room was ready: 'But take care as you go through the room leading into yours,' he added, 'The sister of the local gendarme is sleeping there, and if she heard you speak English she might report you to her brother.' This was somewhat bitter: we thought that here we could talk in safety and freedom at last, but whereas in the occupied zone it was a guarantee of welcome to be British, it seemed that in the German-free area of Vichy rule, one had to keep it dark!

The following few weeks which we spent in the unoccupied zone proved this to be partially true, and it was perhaps natural that the north, which had up to then suffered so much more from the invaders, should be much more actively anti-Nazi. Whereas (as we had witnessed) the police and officials were a hundred per cent on our side under occupation, the Pétain militia and gendarmes were promoted for their collaboration with the Germans. Another reason given me for the general attitude in the Vichy zone, was that many wealthy fascists had left the north, assuming that life would be easier in the south and *cette pourriture* (that scum) was all too much in evidence.

231

Chapter 24 – Free France

The battle rages with many a loud alarm and frequent advance and
    retreat,
The infidel triumphs or supposes he triumphs,
The prison, scaffold, garrotte, handcuffs, iron necklace and lead
    balls do their work,
The named and unnamed heroes pass to other spheres,
The great speakers and writers are exiled, they lie sick in distant
    lands,
...But for all this, Liberty has not gone out of the place
    nor the infidel entered into full possession.

Walt Whitman, *To A Foil'd European Revolutionnaire*

Lyons, to which, again we were conveyed by car, driven by
mysterious members of the *réseau* was a great disappointment to
us: we had hoped for a city where signs of resistance would be as
much in evidence at least as in Paris; instead, a spirit of defeat –
cultural, economic, spiritual – seemed to prevail; the cinemas
were showing only dreary sentimental films, the bookshops only
displayed the safest and most conformist of books (when we
asked for Voltaire and Diderot even, we were told they were out
of print); people seemed suspicious and unfriendly; factories
appeared to be closed; huge heads of the Maréchal stared at us
from Vichy posters boosting '*Le Travail*' and '*La Famille*', which
I found even more repulsive than those of the Nazis in Paris.

There was something peculiarly nauseating about the
Pétainist propaganda, the grandfatherly figure exploited to put
across fascist ideas, the smarmy appeals to French patriotism,
when everything truly French had gone underground, or abroad.
To call the Marshal's militia and *Jeunesse* the representatives of
France was a bad joke; organisations on the German and Italian
models, parading in green shirts bearing fasces on their pockets,
they stood for nothing but reaction and ruin and betrayal.

It was a relief to find on reaching Marseilles (through the
good offices of the American Embassy, who had promised to see

to our return to England), that the Vichy slogans and appeals had made very little impression on the population, and that the miserable rations due to Nazi economic plundering, and the British radio propaganda had been far more effective. We were assured that there *was* a resistance movement in the south, and that it was gathering momentum every day.

We learned a good deal about life in Marseilles from a young Australian woman, married to a local businessman, who befriended us, and gave us generous hospitality as she had already done to dozens of escaping British subjects; she took us round the town and would stand us drinks at the most expensive bars, after which she would march us down the Canebière, singing patriotic English songs, and calling out abuse at the cars of the German Commission. She had infinite vitality and complete disregard for convention or personal safety. It did not surprise me to hear, a year later, that she had crossed the Pyrenees on foot, joined the Free French secret mission, been parachuted into France, and won glorious victories at the head of a band of *maquis* (resistance fighters). Her name, which became almost a legend over a large area of France, was Nancy Wake.

Our other friends in Marseilles were mainly stateless refugees who had fled from the Nazis and were eking out a miserable existence by doing odd jobs while waiting for permits to emigrate to the United States or Latin America. The cafes were full of these people, most of the Austrians or Czechs, who had suffered terribly in concentration camps; their stories brought back all the horrors of the pre-war decade, and again and again made me feel deeply guilty of our governments who had brought them to this, and even now would not admit them in and allow them to fight as they so longed to do.

We spent three weeks sitting about in Marseilles, exploring the Vieux Port, and occasionally journeying out to visit friends in towns within reach, such as Avignon and Toulouse, where my old friend the Pontigny philosopher, J., had settled down for the duration with all his family. His military career, begun at Noisy-le-Sec, and continued in the retreat and debacle, had ended abruptly with a slight wound in his leg, which was as good an excuse as any to contract out of the army. In spite of his great academic distinction, as J—— was partly Jewish he was not allowed, officially, to teach in the university; members of the staff there were, however, so disgusted at this ruling that they arranged private classes of students for him, and he was thus able to live and to support his old parents. His brother-in-law, Jean Cassou, a famous art historian and Spanish scholar, was in the nearby jail, for his part in organising the local resistance group.

I went with J's sister to take books and extra food to him in prison, and thought 'so this is how *la Nouvelle France* treats the flower of its culture!' When I condoled with the family they said that though the conditions were *infecté*, the prisoners' spirits were splendid; they spent their time in studying and discussions and singing Republican and patriotic songs. Our friends declared that they had complete faith in ultimate victory; how, they asked, with Russia and all the free peoples of the world on our side, could there possibly be any doubt about it? All they longed for was a British landing in France, which they were convinced would bring the war quickly to an end, for the Germans were deeply involved on too many fronts, and the population – *les vrais français* (the true French) – would rise almost to a man to throw the hated invaders out.

We assured them that we would do all we could to spread the truth about the French when we got back to England. We had seen enough of the underground movement at close quarters to know the stuff it was made of. 'We'll try and make a broadcast on the BBC,' I said, meaning this as a feeble joke; but they took it seriously, and asked us only to keep out personal names – for there were informers and traitors about, alas, even in the Free French movement. They entrusted me with various instructions relating to the *maquis*, which I learned by heart, and with a Gauloise cigarette which contained a top-secret message rolled inside it, 'to be given to the General himself,' or, they conceded to his most trusted lieutenant. Slipping it inside a packet of *vertes*, I promised to try not to smoke it – and was on tenterhooks until it was safely delivered.

We eventually got our papers enabling us to leave Marseilles and to travel via Spain and Portugal to Great Britain.

We were the envy of all our friends, and at the sight of their longing faces, as we said goodbye, my feelings of elation were mixed with guilt and regret, and sorrow at leaving France, joy and excitement at the thought of home and freedom.

We crossed into Spain at Cerbère, and I thought nostalgically of the last time I'd entered the country by that route. Nostalgia turned to near nausea at the first sight of the 'new Spain.' The Republican flag that had hung so bravely over the customs barrier in 1937 had been replaced by Franco's red and yellow, and the *aduana* (customs' house) was plastered with enormous portraits of the Caudillo, and of José Antonio Primo de Rivera, and with posters of happy peasants, their arms raised in the Fascist salute, shouting in unison '*Arriba España*', while the caption underneath read '*¡Una! ¡Grande! ¡Libre!*'

Instead of the friendly *milicianos* in blue overalls, the place swarmed with grim-faced *Guardias Civiles* bedecked in multi-coloured cloaks and three-cornered hats. Inside was Spanish officialdom; outside the local Spanish population hung about, looking listless and hungry; a blind beggar held out a hat, and small children with huge black eyes in thin pinched faces sidled up to ask for *una perrita, señorita!*[51] and having extracted a copper, clung to our heels like a swarm of bees till a policeman raucously ordered them to be off.

A hotel porter, respectable and relatively well paid, asked if we had any bread from France? The ration was not nearly enough for his family, he said, and they were always hungry... This appeared to be the usual state of things in the 'One, Great, Free Spain.' The only really well-fed people we saw on our journey across to Lisbon were the fat prosperous priests in the streets of Madrid, and the German officers, who appeared to be as much in occupation of the country as they were in France.

I found the sight of Spain really painful, and the only consolation was that we were able to see the Prado pictures, and to visit Toledo, with its marvellous Grecos – and even here the ruins of the Alcázar were a gruesome reminder of a horrible episode.

One thing that cheered me slightly was the fact which stood out a mile, that almost every ordinary person was against Franco and the Germans. Considering British responsibility for their unhappy condition, I was amazed that they did not voice dislike of us. Perhaps they realised that Baldwin and Chamberlain were not England; perhaps they had heard that Lord Templewood, then in Madrid to negotiate for the passage of British personnel through Spain, was crossing swords with Franco. Perhaps it was just the native courtesy of the Spanish.

We travelled by neutral but spy-ridden Portugal and Ireland back to Portsmouth, where we had the worst shock of all our troubled two years. We had heard about the Blitz, but we had discounted German reports, and we had no idea of the effects of the bombing: the sight of Portsmouth's rubble and ruins simply took our breath away.

We felt real deserters not to have been through it, both then and when we got back to London, where the desolation and destruction in whole areas of the city was absolutely horrifying. Automatically, on seeing it, I thought 'nothing in France was as bad as that!' But gradually getting back to normal life – as far as wartime life could be called normal, with the blackout, the absence of friends, the rationing, restrictions and sirens – I realised that we did at least breathe fresh air, not the stifling poisoned atmosphere of Vichy, and that we were not haunted by the Nazi occupation, and that we were on the winning side in an active open struggle.

The tide was flowing with the Allies now: in Africa, Rommel was retreating; in Russia, the Soviet forces were holding Hitler and draining the lifeblood of his army, victories had been won on the economic front and our war factories were producing, and lend-lease supplying, arms and food and equipment in ever-growing quantities. Soon after our return home, the Japanese attack on Pearl Harbour brought America into the war, and a wave of optimism went across the country.

Whether or not the war was being won, however, it seemed to me after a week or two back in England that people here did not realise at all what it was costing in terms of terror and destruction on the continent. The general public had heard of the ghastly concentration camps and of the mass killings of Jews in Germany and Poland, and were shocked and horrified when news of new atrocities trickled through. But they did not know the full extent of the nightmare of occupation in other countries, or realise that the quisling governments did not represent their peoples, who were potential allies. This was particularly true of France, about which I often heard it said, 'They let us down badly in 1940', and 'can we really count on the French?' Not many prisoners had escaped, and we proposed to a friend in the BBC that what we had to say might perhaps be new and interesting. To my amazement and alarm, I found myself facing a microphone one Sunday evening, trying to tell the story of our escape and of the French underground who had so bravely helped us, and would risk anything to help an Allied victory.

Following that, I broadcast in French and German and Spanish on the Foreign Service, and hoped against hope that our friends in Besançon and Toulouse might be listening in.

Apart from broadcasting, there were endless requests for speakers on France, from factories, army units, women's institutes, universities; and wherever one went, it was the same thing: nobody realised the meaning of the word 'resistance', and I felt that, as in the days of the Spanish war, this was something that had to be put across if one killed oneself in the attempt!

I carried out the Toulouse mission, duly presented the cigarette, intact, undamaged, to the *Porte Parole* of the Free French (after de Gaulle, the best-known figure in the movement), Lieutenant Maurice Schumann, immensely tall and cadaverous, at his desk in Carlton Gardens. He was installed in a palatial office, the headquarters of de Gaulle's staff and *services d'information*. With him were several officers and civilians whom he introduced as colleagues; one of them was Pierre Mendès-France, dark and dapper in air-force uniform, another was Jacques Soustelle, bespectacled and swarthy; though he was obviously quite young, Soustelle's restless eyes had a middle-aged shrewdness, and he was clearly a person of authority in this outfit.

Later, on the strength of that cigarette, I suppose, I was offered a job in the Information Service, working under Soustelle and in the same room as Georgette, his wife – a charming woman anthropologist, with a great sense of humour and forcibly-proclaimed anti-fascist and anti-American views, who told me a great deal of gossip about the general, whom she adored, and the goings on in the world of VIP's. In those days, de Gaulle was extremely pro-Red Army, and rather contemptuous of the British; on one occasion, after a demonstration in the Albert Hall in honour of the Soviet Army he remarked, 'Nous, nous ferons mieux que ça!'[52] He was 'un vraiment grand homme,'[53] Georgette said, in spite of being a little difficult at times, as when he would lose his temper on the telephone with Winston Churchill, and slam down the receiver with the explosion, 'You peeg Eenglish!'

The General, in those days, was a genuine advocate of national unity, and prepared to work with socialists, communists, atheists, and any anti-Nazi, to defeat the Germans; he welcomed the communists who managed to escape to London, and presented Fernand Grenier, the former deputy of Saint-Denis, with a photograph of himself, inscribed, 'á mon cher camarade...',[54] and with a post in his government in exile.

Soustelle also appeared to be leftish, and was very helpful to me in an encounter I had with the Gaullist police. When the security men grilled me and threatened me with dismissal if I would not give them certain names and addresses in France, Soustelle lost no time in giving them a piece of his mind: 'I won't have Gestapo methods in my department,' said he – and for the first time I realised that he was in charge of the Gaullist Deuxième Bureau, and probably the most powerful man in the whole organisation.

I sometimes wondered in those days whether all was well with Gaullist headquarters; one heard rumours of leakages of information, of personnel being transferred for 'unreliability', of friends of General Giraud (suspected of attachment to Vichy) finding posts at Carlton Gardens... Officer's girlfriends often got jobs in secret information, on no other qualification than their looks; I felt that the war was not being taken seriously enough by these people, especially when reading the illegal papers, sifting the news, and talking to the resistance leaders who occasionally turned up to report, having braved unheard-of difficulties and hardships in the maquis.

Back From German Internment Camp

YOUNG CAMBRIDGE WOMAN'S ESCAPE

"French Counting on Britain"

Miss Stewart

THE story of how a young Cambridge woman escaped from a German internment camp in France by crawling through a hole in barbed wire, was told to a "Cambridge Daily News" representative a few hours after she had arrived back at her home on Saturday evening.

Miss Frida Stewart, daughter of Dr. and Mrs H. F. Stewart, of Girton Gate, Huntingdon Road. is the young woman concerned

With Miss Rosemary Say, of Hampstead, she succeeded in making her way through France and Spain, eventually returning to England by plane from Lisbon.

When France was over-run by the Nazis, Miss Stewart was working for a refugee committee in Paris. "I tried to get out," she said, "but it was difficult to get a conveyance, and with about 4,000 other women I was seized by the Germans. I was interned, and for five months was kept in a military barracks used as an internment camp. The conditions there were very bad, both in hygiene and in food. When I was moved to another camp the hygiene was a bit better, but food was still scanty And you can imagine that we were greatly cheered by the Red Cross parcels which arrived from time to time.

FRENCH PEOPLE HELPED.

In the camp Miss Stewart met Miss Say, and they decided on their bid for liberty. "We escaped by crawling through a hole in the barbed wire round the camp," she went on, "and made our way through occupied and unoccupied France to Marseilles. All the time the French people helped us, and everywhere we found they are just counting on Britain to relieve them. Some of them even said they wished they were coming to England with us."

At Marseilles the two girls had to wait some time for their papers to get into Spain, but eventually they arrived and the girls reached Lisbon, from where they flew back to this country In London they had, to use Miss Stewart's own words, "a nasty shock" when they saw the effects of the bombing. As for the future, she hopes very soon to take up some form of work to help the war effort.

Miss Stewart was educated at the Perse School, and afterwards did various forms of social work. She spent two years at the Manchester University Settlement, lectured with the W.E.A. in Yorkshire, and organised entertainment for Basque refugees.

WORK FOR WAR REFUGEES.

When war broke out she worked on the entertainments side of the Y.W.C.A. and went abroad to work for war refugees in Paris. From May to December. 1940, she lived with an English friend who had married a Frenchman, and also attended lectures at the Sorbonne. She was left alone by the Germans until all the English were rounded up because of a disclosure that someone was using the wireless to give away information.

Local press report on Frida's escape.

After the Allied landings in North Africa in the autumn of 1942, we all thought it was the start of a final assault, and would soon be followed by a second front in Europe; we expected de Gaulle to fly to Algiers, and proclaim the Free French government there, and we started arranging imaginary offices which we would occupy there. To our surprise, the whole sad and sinister story of Admiral Darlan followed: a pro-German Admiral was installed in power, and though his time in office was short, it was enough to show the sort of betrayal that could take place even in a moment of victory. No sooner was Darlan out, than the pro-Vichy Giraud stepped in. De Gaulle was fuming and furious. It was several months before he succeeded in getting to Algiers, and in the meantime confusion and distress prevailed among the French, for whom things were becoming more and more desperate.

The Nazis were deporting hundreds of thousands of workers to forced labour in Germany – '*400,000 hommes doivent être livrés au Moloch hitlérien avant la fin du mois de juin*,'[55] said *Libération* on 6th June 1943. The housing and food situation was appalling owing to Allied bombing, and to German requisitioning: '*Les Allemands réclament 2,000 tonnes de beurre par mois*,'[56] was a typical news item from *Combat* in August 1943. '*On meurt de faim dans les prisons de France*,'[57] in *Étoiles* of September 1943. Hostages were being shot in mass reprisals for acts of sabotage, atrocious punishments doled out to whole universities and institutes and factories which had shown some resistance.

Yet the opposition was stronger and better supplied and organised than seemed possible under those conditions. The *Maquis* was attacking, the workers were sabotaging, the women were helping heroically, taking messages, hiding agents, looking after their homes single-handed, fighting too. It was almost intolerable to be sitting in an office in comfort and safety; but by this time I was anchored by family ties, husband, baby and flat, and could only help the French by trying to publish the truth about their struggle, and their desperate longing for the British landing and the second front in France.

The winter of 1943-1944 was a long one; we waited

anxiously for news of invasion in Europe, while our armies crawled up the leg of Italy, prior to the attack on the 'soft underbelly' which Churchill had promised.

It was bad enough in England; but it must have been undiluted hell in the occupied countries, in starving Warsaw, Copenhagen, Brussels, Amsterdam and beyond conception in Leningrad, shelled and besieged since 1941 without light, food, coal...

Spring came at last, although it seemed as if it never could come again. And with it, the defeat of the Germans at Stalingrad, the rising of the Italian partisans, the arrival of the Allied armies on the Brenner pass, and at the ports of Marseilles and Toulon. At the end of May, we waited every night for news of the second front. On 5th June, the radio announced the '*Mille six centièmes et dixième jour de la lutte du people français pour sa libération.*'58 The following day, the 1,611th of their struggle for freedom, the long-awaited announcement reached the people of France: This morning, at 5 am, British forces landed at a number of points on the north coast of France. From the underground, the partisans and *franc-tireurs* (snipers) of the *maquis* came out into the open.

The long nightmare was over – whatever was to come would now happen in broad daylight.

Chapter 25 – Nazis on the Run

The dawn is woven with bright threads
The innocents have reappeared,
Light with purity, white with anger,
With the strength of their undying justice,
The strength of a land that is purged.

Paul Éluard, *Au Rendez-vous Allemand*

Although the Normandy landings were not the end of the war by a long chalk, they were, we felt, the beginning of the end. Britain had at last joined the Resistance movements, and the Nazis were really on the run. From that day it seemed that Hitlerism was finished and we could start seriously thinking about 'after the war', about building peace and going forward to the Good Society which would refuse to tolerate racialism, militarism, oppression, inequality.

In England we celebrated two events, VE day with dancing in Trafalgar Square, and with the milling crowds which invaded Clubland as though they knew that the West End belonged to them now and not just to the upper income group. And when VJ day came, we celebrated again, not fully conscious of the price that had been paid for the rapid surrender of Japan or the full size and threat of the mushroom cloud which rose over Hiroshima.

Two events that followed the end of the war in England were symbolic, we felt, of the shape of things to come: Labour's sweeping success in 1946 on a programme of social reform which promised education, health and security to all; and the Festival of Britain, planned mainly by young people and carried out in the post-war spirit of unlimited optimism. The palaces and pavilions on the South Bank flaunted their gaiety and the New Look in the face of the ruins and bombed sites around, and seemed a foretaste of what England could be if her people made up their minds to it.

With modern technology and science on the side of peace we could do anything we pleased! Marvellous buildings, theatres, schools, housing estates, hospitals, would spring up: with the unlimited skill of trained workers and automation in our industry there would be prosperity and plenty, and leisure for everyone.

All over Europe the same sort of dreams were being dreamed by the people who had lived through the years of fascism and war; in the Eastern countries, the foundations of socialism were laid, and reconstruction went ahead firmly and fast. In the West, Germany was restored (with unlimited dollars) and France and Italy struggled to their feet under the same direction as before. For the people of Spain and Greece, hope stirred. But the dreams evaporated all too soon; and now the reality has to be faced: health and education and reconstruction have been surrendered to the needs of a possible war; industry, science and manpower have largely been directed to armaments; homes are broken up while speculative building runs riot. Conservative government has produced chaos and stagnation behind a façade of commercial TV and showy advertising.

The reforming zeal of the thirties may be forgotten and despised today; but the need for that spirit of enthusiasm and determination is greater than ever, and the reward for unity and action will be real and lasting peace. The young left-wingers of the '30s fought fascism when fascism was strong and controlled most of the world; today – thanks partly to the sacrifices of the anti-fascist and their friends – two thirds of the world have been freed and transformed and are on the side of peace and social progress.

Youth today must decide to go forward along the road to disarmament and friendship, refusing to be misled by propaganda and lies if it can understand who are its friends, and ally itself with them; and I think our young people understand this, in spite of mountains of hostile propaganda, millions of lies.

The Aldermaston marches which have become famous all over the world are an indication of this; and the thousands of young men and women, from every corner of the country, with their banners and bands and guitars, singing all along the road

243

from the Weapons Establishment in rural Berkshire to the Government offices in Whitehall, with the greatest demonstration in our history greeting them in London – these offer real hope for our future.

The Easter March shows that Youth is determined not to be swindled out of its heritage, and that it has chosen the best way – doing what it believes right, hand in hand with whomsoever believes the same.

The middle-aged and elderly may throw their hands up in horror at the youth of today, like my elderly relatives in the thirties; but they should be clapping their hands in admiration at the young for their energy and devotion and joie de vivre, at a time of greater strain and stress than ever faced them before.

Under the shadow of the nuclear menace, the young people rock and roll, jive and swing, sweat to get through harder tests in school and college, and work, more than ever their parents had to endure. They travel to the ends of the earth, they mix and make friends on equal terms with Russians, Africans, Chinese, they speak and write and publish newspapers proclaiming their ideas to thousands. We never lived so fully nor had such a challenge to face. Our lives were comparatively simple; we had more enemies, but things were black and white, less confused by the constant assault of massive hostile propaganda.

But youth in the thirties had one thing in common with the lively young people of today; we were in the right; and we were on the winning side. And so are they.

Afterword by Angela Jackson

Babies, Books and 'Ban the Bomb'

Memoirs end but life goes on. For Frida, who died aged 85, this meant almost another fifty years of continuous activity. During the Second World War Frida married B.C.J.G. Knight, a scientist and man of letters who shared many of her political concerns. By 1951 they had four children, and soon afterwards moved from London to Reading where Jonathan, as he was known, became the first professor of Microbiology at the University. Patience Edney (née Darton), who had been in Spain as a nurse during the Civil War, vividly remembered the arrival of Frida's first baby. As a close friend and neighbour, she called in to see Frida on her way home from work to find her rushing round as usual but grumpily complaining of indigestion. This resulted in a dash across London in the blackout to get to the hospital in time as Patience, a trained midwife, recognised the imminent arrival of an infant.

Like many other doting mothers, Frida made notes on the progress of her baby, Sofka, recording the usual anxieties over feeding and delight at first smiles. However, there are probably not many other mothers who would offer as an explanation for the premature arrival of their infant that, 'She chose to arrive three weeks early to be in time for the October celebrations and the recapture of Kiev by the Red Army', calling her after St. Sophia, the patron saint of Kiev.

Also during the war years, Frida's first book, *Dawn Escape*, was published. The book gives a more detailed account of her escape from the internment camp than the memoirs, and includes reproductions of drawings she made of camp life. The publication of the book followed front page newspaper articles about her return to England and a radio broadcast about her escape. Never missing an opportunity to raise funds for an important cause, Frida spoke at meetings, this time in aid of the Free French, telling how 'the French people risked their lives to befriend her.' However, determined that the Spanish people should not be forgotten, she devotes a whole chapter of *Dawn Escape* to her impressions of Spain during the return journey to England, giving an account of the conditions there under Franco. A lengthy extract is included here as there are few accounts written from a British woman's perspective of life in Spain at that time.

We heard on every side the same story, of illness and undernourishment and even death from lack of food. In our third-class carriage to Barcelona, our companions told us pitiful stories of starvation and want among their friends. In Barcelona I found the outside appearance very little changed. Las Ramblas, the main avenue, seemed still very animated and full of colour, crowded with people, the flower stalls piled high with mimosa, roses, and violets (I couldn't help wondering whether this was meant as a suggestion of the Popular Front Flag)...

We called on a cousin of Pujol's (a Catalan refugee friend of mine in Marseilles), who lived up a dark staircase in a little back street. They fell on our necks when we introduced ourselves as friends of Pujol – it was rare that anybody sympathetic to their cause visited them from another country – and they were wild for news. 'We listen in to London,' said the daughter of the house, 'but we don't get nearly enough news.' Letters often do not arrive or are held up by one of the censorships, and recent first-hand news of friends abroad is greeted with great joy.

José had been in prison as a result of his activities in the Spanish republican army, and had since lost his job. He was haggard and worn with hunting for work, but had managed to find a part-time poorly paid occupation. His son was a young architect who offered to take us round Barcelona and up to the Stadium.

We went by tram to the city's park and walked up the road, through the gardens where the shrubs were bursting into leaf, and up to the Stadium, where we sat on a terrace and looked at the view of Barcelona lying below us in a blue haze. 'I'd give all this to go to England,' said the boy. 'Life is impossible here. Culture has been killed. Look at the books, at education, at science. There is nothing.' He told us how the church had taken over

248

responsibility for education and even censored the films... The Catalan cultural movement, of which Barcelona had been so proud had been crushed. Officially they were not allowed even to talk the language – which did not prevent it being spoken all over the place, but still....

We caught the evening train to Madrid, sad at what we had seen but consoling ourselves with the thought that the capital *must* be more cheerful. What a hope! It was raining when we got there. Perhaps that was partly why it seemed so desperately sad and gloomy. But even when it cleared up, people still looked grey and wan and worried – quite unlike the *madrileños* of pre-war days, or of the crowds, cheerful, confident and determined, of 1937. It was difficult to find the way about the town: the names of the streets in many cases had been changed, the 'Cibeles' (*Castellano*) to Avenida Generalísimo Franco, the 'Gran Via' to 'Calle José Antonio' and so on. We made our way down to the Puerta del Sol, feeling sadder every moment. But there were no *milicianos*, no blue *monos* (the Republicans' battledress), no ambulances parked in the middle of the square, no tough International Brigaders, none of the feeling in the air of excitement and effort. Only the harassed-looking men and women, tired-faced soldiers in brownish uniforms, and the cars of the wealthy, which on closer inspection turned out to be mainly Fiats and Mercedes Benz.

We took one of the yellow trams – one of the few things in Madrid which have not changed – to the outskirts of the town, to see what had become of the University City after three years' 'peace.' Little appeared to have changed since the days after the heavy fighting in 1936; the streets had been cleared of the debris which was strewn about at that time, and the telegraph poles set up again. Apart from that, the general appearance of the place was exactly as it had been on the hot day in July 1937, when I passed the spot and visited the trenches nearby. Building had started on a few blocks of new flats to the north, but the big university buildings were untouched, as they had been then. The 'Clínico' hospital stood, as it did just after the Asturian miners dynamited it (a week before my last visit), to blow up the tenacious Moors, a gaunt three-walled skeleton against the blue

249

distance and transparent amethyst silhouette of the sierra.

In the garden of the *Casa (Facultad) de Filosofía*, a boy in overalls was working. We spoke to him and he told us he had just got the job, after being released from two years' prison for republican sympathies. He had fought in the trenches on the front during the war. 'I probably met you here,' I said. 'Let's hope next time we meet it will be a happier time for Spain.'

Although she knew she ought to have been delighted at the prospect of continuing her journey home, she writes, 'But in fact, my heart was so firmly rooted in Madrid that it was like being torn in half to be carried off in the Portuguese express.'

In an interview for a local newspaper Frida said that after her marriage she had settled to the 'boring life of an academic wife'. But married life for Frida never conformed to the traditional pattern. She remained essentially a political person, her horizons never narrowed to the domestic or to the social. Her children remember how she would be constantly bashing away on the typewriter at one end of the kitchen table while they ate, writing articles for newspapers, plays and books. After the war, when her work for the Free French had ended, her involvement with the peace movement began, taking her abroad to conferences working as a translator. Her notes on these travels record her impressions of the countries she visited, enjoying both the welcome the delegates received from their hosts and the chance to see and learn more about countries such as Sweden and Ceylon. In a letter home from the World Disarmament Congress in the Soviet Union she writes,

> This is all so exciting that words will in fact probably fail or be illegible. We sit and do our translating under a huge plate glass window through which all the gold minarets of the Kremlin are winking at us – no other word for their lovely shiny glimmering. The Congress Hall is inside the Kremlin wall, and in the intervals people wander round the gardens; the hall itself is superb, and vast – people on the platform look tiny but I recognised various eminent

250

people... and in the front row of the audience – Titov and Gagarin, looking exactly like their pictures, broad grins and all.

When it was announced in 1958 that the USA was to be allowed to build four missile bases in Britain, Frida joined The British Campaign for Nuclear Disarmament. Along with thousands of others, she participated in the Aldermaston marches to register her protest. A photograph of Frida at this time shows her in the long column of marchers against the Bomb, striding purposefully onwards, a campaigner not to be deterred by cold or discomfort. Her children became accustomed to their home being a meeting house for planning the next move in the fight for Peace, and to the fact that cooking *cordon bleu* meals was not high on the list of their mother's priorities! Frida never doubted that exciting projects, such as arranging a Peace Concert with the world famous singer, Paul Robeson, were much more important than housework.

But life had not been only conferences and campaigns. In the random assortment of her papers, at first glance there is little that sheds light upon her emotions as a woman. Her energies seem directed ever outwards, not inwards for self indulgence or self pity. One tragic event does however reveal how she reacted to her own personal suffering. Two letters from Frida refer to the death of her baby boy, Billy, in 1946. The first is written to her doctor the week after the inquest, asking for information concerning the number of babies who die from asphyxiation in their bedclothes, as Billy had done. She writes, 'It seems to me a danger that is underestimated in all books addressed to mothers – in all the text books I ever read on mothercraft it was never stressed at all.' The second letter is to the Editor of *The Times*, to make others aware of the danger. 'The general public is not aware of the frequency of these cases, and it is only if one has oneself suffered the loss of a beloved child in this way (as I have myself) or know of friends thus bereaved, that one realises that such fatal accidents can so easily happen.' With typical concern for others and to try to ensure that some good can come from her own grief, she thinks of positive actions to prevent these accidents recurring in the cold British winters, warning 'careful mothers, who naturally pile on blankets to keep their babies warm,' that this can have fatal results, and calling for the welfare clinics to ensure that information about this 'insidious and unforeseen danger' is available to every mother. Frida must have been thinking again of the loss of Billy during her last illness, reminding me that she had five babies, not just four.

Right to left: Frida with siblings, Margaret, Ludovick, Katharine and Jean.

In between bringing up Sofka, Frances, James and Robert and campaigning for causes, there was somehow still time to write a book which, although based on a historic event, reflected some of her own concerns about modern society and the oppression of dissenters. *The Strange Case of Thomas Walker; Ten Years in the Life of a Manchester Radical,* published in 1957, is a vivid and scholarly account of the persecution and trial of a merchant, Thomas Walker, which took place towards the end of the eighteenth century. Because of his outspoken and relentless condemnation of the political and social evils of his time, Walker became the victim of smears, boycotts and false accusations. Nevertheless, despite financial ruin he remained a firm believer in civil and religious freedom for all. Reviews of the book were highly favourable but a novel, *Teacher on Trial,* based on her work as a teacher of English and music in Reading was never published

As her children grew up, Frida became deeply involved with another book, *Window on Shanghai* published in 1967. This was a compilation of letters from China written by her daughter, Sofka, who lived and worked there as a teacher of English for several years, before and during the Cultural Revolution. Hundreds of letters were exchanged between mother and daughter, Sofka writing in great detail of her daily life and feelings about the Revolution, and Frida responding with enthusiasm and love, revealing a depth of maternal affection which might otherwise have remained unrecorded. On two occasions Frida visited China, staying for six weeks in 1966, and for three months in the winter of 1973. Her first journey there was made on the Trans-Siberian railway, arriving in Peking just before the Cultural Revolution began. In her recollections of those visits she emphasises the positive changes that took place for many Chinese people.

> At last came the joy of journey's end, my daughter's welcoming hug and introduction to the 'reception committee' on Peking station platform, beneath the benign gaze of Marx', Engels', Stalin's and Mao Tse Tung's giant portraits. These huge posters were the outward and visible sign of New China's socialism; they surprised me at first, but turned out to be an element of the landscape, along with *Da ze baos* (Great Character Posters) exhorting us to 'Put Politics First!' and 'Serve the People!' and with Mao's propaganda blaring out in many public places and on most forms of transport at all hours... Peking in August 1966 was very hot and slightly jittery – in that the streets and parks seemed to be populated by restless young people coming or going to political group meetings; they would settle down into circles for their discussions which were based on the *Little Red Book* of Mao's sayings, which was a must for everybody. This

season of political discussion meant that all the youth were deeply engaged and it was not easy to find a young guide or taxi driver. But we did not recognise these early signs of the coming storm which was going to break in the next week, with the announcement of the Cultural Revolution. By then Sof and I had left Peking to tour the central countryside.

She arrived in Shanghai greatly impressed by her tour, which included the warrior tombs outside Xian, Mao's historic army base at Yenan, temples, hospitals and communes.

We arrived in Shanghai in early September to find it rejoicing in the Cultural Revolution spirit. The streets were plastered with *Da ze baos*, and during most of the day were blocked with processions and demonstrations – more carnival than revolutionary in spirit. There was in those early days very little rowdyism, and nobody foresaw the wrongs to come later; I left China feeling that all would be well; Mao's wisdom and understanding would prevail. Perhaps I was too optimistic; but many of my friends and my daughter certainly supported the Cultural Revolution in those days, and saw the positive side as well as the destructive. When I hear our Chinese friends, students and visitors to Europe, today describe the years 1966 to 1976 as 'disastrous', I know it is partly true – but what was achieved before then and even during those years, should not be dismissed out of hand.

During her second visit she saw the work of the Evergreen Commune which supplied Peking with vegetables all year round, and watched operations being carried out under acupuncture in the hospitals. The adventure of lecturing in the University was only surpassed by her most vivid memory, the warm welcome she received from Chou en Lai.

The University of Peking was open to students, but only to politically reliable applicants; so when I was invited to speak about 'Life in Britain' to the department of English, I addressed a crowd of Red Army men one day, and a

254

contingent from the Navy the next (presumably anyone in the armed forces was a trustworthy Maoist!) It felt strange trying to explain the Western way of life to the sea of red-starred khaki or blue caps, and I did wonder how much they took in!... The high point of my three months in China was Women's Day, March 8ᵗʰ 1973, when all the 'foreign friends' working in Peking were invited to a banquet in the Great Hall. Many of them had recently suffered rough treatment: David Crook, solitary confinement; Rose Smith, enforced exile; others, long-term imprisonment. Chou en Lai welcomed them back, apologised for the injustice and wrongs done to such good friends, and promised redress. He toured the hall, shaking hands with every one of the four hundred guests (he even said 'How do you do' to me in English – what a moment to remember!) assuring us of better times. We felt then that what remained of the Cultural Revolution was safe in Chou's hands; I thought the great achievements were safe too: the Communes, Da Chai, socialist education and medicine, women's rights – some of which I had seen developing so splendidly. Alas, Chou died in 1976, and Mao soon after, their work uncompleted.

On her return, Frida did her best to promote better understanding and friendship between China and Britain. She joined the Society for Anglo-Chinese Understanding, and also wrote articles for journals and newspapers based on the detailed diary she kept during her visit and Sofka's letters.

As the years passed, other books and plays on subjects close to Frida's heart followed and were accepted for publication, *University Rebel: The Life of William Frend (1971), Beethoven and the Age of Revolution (1973)*, and *The French Resistance (1975)*. The development of sacred and secular music in Cambridge from the Middle Ages to modern times was explored in her book, *Cambridge Music (1979)*. Although it is not about radicals or resistance like her other books, true to her political nature she finishes on a campaigning note, calling for people to fight resolutely for generous aid to the Arts from central government. The product of much diligent research into the 1972 building workers' strike and the subsequent Shrewsbury trials remains in manuscript form, considered by publishers as 'too political' for the mass market.

Her vision of worldwide peace and a just society led to her involvement in campaigns concerned with the Vietnam War, Greece and Chile. Frida came from the generation of English grass roots activists who, after the initial war cry, 'We must form a Committee,' could mobilise others to join the cause. Her return to Cambridge when her husband retired, is remembered by a member of the Cambridge Communist Party as 'the arrival of a new driving force in Cambridge politics.' At first she joined in the protest against welfare benefit cuts and in campaigns on local issues. When it was announced in 1979 that Cruise missiles were to be based in Britain, she helped to found 'Cambridge Against the Missile Bases'. Soon there were over a thousand active members who arranged frequent large meetings in and around Cambridge and attended mass rallies and demonstrations. She was one of the instigators of the Cambridge Peace Council and as Secretary during the 1980s, she helped to co-ordinate the efforts of the eighteen member organisations.

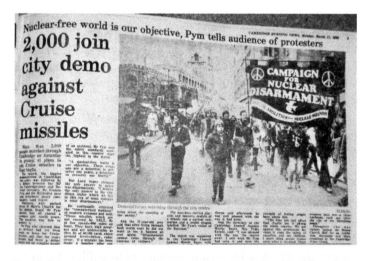

Press article on the demonstration organised by Frida as Secretary of the Cambridge Council Against Missile Bases, including a quote, "I was pleased with the way the march went . . . We are against this programme because it risks the safety of ourselves and our children."

Women's involvement with the peace movement specifically questioned and rejected male militarism, and from 1981 onwards, thousands of women from the camp at Greenham Common were arrested for their protest activities. Frida enthusiastically supported the stand made by the Greenham women and visited the camp. She wrote of 'a foray into Trident country' with the Scottish CND, along the Clyde to the Gareloch, where the Polaris nuclear submarine was based, and then on to see the residents of the Faslane peace camp who were monitoring the movements of Polaris warheads and protesting against the development of the base as a site for Trident. She still manages to introduce a note of optimism in her report, despite the threat of nuclear annihilation.

> It was somehow a sentimental journey for me, remembering the idyllic holidays as a child at Rosneath, opposite Helensburgh – now looking straight across the loch to the Polaris base. My great-grandfather who named his house *Achnashie* ('Field of Peace' in Gaelic) would be horrified at the desecration of the lovely scene – I certainly was! The drive along the shore of the Gareloch is beautiful, even in the wild weather. As we drove through the eye of the storm to the gate of the base it was a shock to come upon the barbed wire fencing and military outposts. On the other hand it was a good surprise to find the six or seven brightly painted caravans of the Faslane peace camp a few yards along the same road, standing cheerfully on the grass among the bushes, and the inhabitants warming themselves inside and welcoming us with cups of tea and camp gossip. They don't like the wet weather and they appreciate visitors, as the days can be boring; but the spirit is fine.

Discoveries in long-buried letters and faded documents

In the weeks following Frida's death, I spent hours in the attic rooms of her drafty old house, trying to put her vast, haphazard collection of paperwork into some sort of order, hoping one day it could be archived properly and made available for future researchers. Among all the notes and drafts for books were copies of letters giving glimpses into more personal aspects of her life. For example, a letter to her old friend in Germany, Luise, includes a plaintive maternal plea regarding her children who had all, unsurprisingly with Frida as a role model, grown up to reject nine-to-five jobs and quiet lives in suburbia. After completing their university studies they all left England, first Sofka to China, then Frances to work overseas for several years, teaching in Nepal, Japan, Equador and Nicaragua, Jimmy went to live in France and play his guitar at rock concerts, whilst Rob spent two years in Argentina. She wrote,

> Why are my offspring all so wayward and unconventional?? I'd love to have happily settled children, in good bourgeois jobs, producing gorgeous grandchildren – but not a hope of that! I do envy you and all proud grandmothers!

The children returned eventually and grandchildren arrived, but so did a great sadness with the death of Sofka. By this time living in England, Sofka spent many years suffering from schizophrenia which eventually became too much for her to bear. Despite Frida's efforts and a desperately worried letter to the doctor asking if there were any other possible methods of treatment for her daughter and offering all the family support possible, this was a battle lost. Sofka's tragic suicide happened years before I met Frida and she spoke of it just once to me. It was the only time I saw her look defeated.

Advancing age and health problems did not prevent Frida from working for causes. The question, 'How are you?' was given a cursory response in her eagerness to hear your news and discuss the latest world events, then plan what was to be done next. When I came across her mother's obituary in a cutting from the Newnham College Roll, I discovered how much Frida resembled Jessie, of whom it was written, 'Many friends from four generations delighted in her company, and the wary learnt to greet her, not with conversational enquiries as to her health, but with – "What have you been reading?"' Frida would have been pleased to know that in character, she matched the description in other ways too, especially when her mother is seen as combining, '...extreme modesty with a ruthless determination to get her own way' and as 'a deeply compassionate character, with a strong and effective social conscience, stemming from a family of liberal traditions.' It is clear from the memoirs that admiration for her mother and the strong family tradition of concern for others had a great influence on Frida's innately resolute character.

Hand-written notes recalling childhood memories from the First World War reveal Frida's early sensitivity to both beauty and sorrow.

> The garden was dug up to make a potato patch. There was a hen run where the flower beds had been and I remember the birds leaping up to pick the pink rosettes of the cherry trees. And I will never forget the thrill of picking up eggs – brown, warm, living – distinct from the cold white stone one which (they said) encouraged the hen to lay; nor the tragedy of dropping the morning's harvest at the door, the sticky yellow disgrace of it... Another infantile thrill was the arrival of a family of rabbits – how we peered through the wire trying to make out the tiny bundles of fur – it was useless telling us that mother rabbit would devour her young if they were disturbed – we had to experience the sad happening before we would believe it. The deaths of the tiny rabbits scarred my five year old heart. I believe small children feel these things far more than anyone imagines.

Many early letters written by Frida had been preserved and through them it was possible to catch glimpses of her developing character and interests. A letter to 'Darling Daddy' from a twelve year old Frida, complete with graphic illustrations for emphasis, clearly shows her lack of enthusiasm for the academic traditions of her family, as she laments, 'But this week it'll be beastly EXAMS. I'm sure to do frightfully badly (worst luck) and I shall have to revise pages and pages, (because I *mustn't* get into the remove).' Determined as she is to try to study and avoid failure, it is clear that music and Italian paintings with 'floppy fat ladies' are much more to her taste.

In her memoirs, Frida says little about the serious illness that had confined her to bed as a teenager, writing instead about the General Strike that was taking place at the same time. But the numerous letters written to her family from Longworth Manor, her grandfather's house where she was being nursed, show that her love of music, literature and art was growing, though her drawings of the antics of her kittens and the people at the Manor are amusing rather than indicative of artistic promise. The whole environment was one of intellectual stimulation, with plenty of time to enjoy games of chess with grandfather, heated debates about the merits of favourite poets with 'nurse', and to read newspapers with diverse political perspectives because 'Mummy says it's good for me to see both sides of things.'

As a young woman, Frida's abilities to organise and to relate to people were soon recognised by others. References kept from Manchester University Settlement praise her drama productions and record that her 'vigour and initiative have been remarkable,' noting her 'charm of manner and youthful enthusiasm.' Mrs Stocks, representing the Settlement Council, comments on how stimulating and educative Frida's productions were and observes, 'She has a singular capacity for making outside contacts. Thus when she produced Purcell's *Fairy Queen* last Summer – a daringly ambitious and surprisingly successful production – she appeared to draw auxiliary talent from as far afield as London, Oxford and Cambridge.' Mrs Stocks sees this as a result of Frida's 'singular persuasiveness of manner,' a quality that was to be used to great effect to raise support for the Spanish Republic and the refugees. Francesca Wilson, who established the children's hospital in Murcia where Frida worked, wrote of the sudden influx of typhoid patients in all stages of fever, delirium and sickness. In this situation of working under great pressure, she describes Frida as 'a perfect brick' – high praise indeed in the vocabulary of the day.

There is no doubt that Frida considered her time in Spain

as a life-changing experience. On an old scrap of paper, undated but written in the rather shaky handwriting of her later years, is a brief summary of her life which begins, 'The most significant moment in my life was the day the ambulance took me across the border into Spain.' This retrospective perception of the Spanish war as a key event in her life is not surprising if the depth of her feelings are understood. A letter from Madrid to her sister, Margaret, describes the atmosphere of determined resistance that prevailed in 1937, 'You can't think what the pull of Madrid is! If only you could come out and see you wouldn't dream of wiring anyone to come home! And get the Joint Committee to send me back as soon as possible for it's the only place in the world just now to be.'

The defeat of the Republic and the plight of the refugees in France affected her deeply. She tried to publicise their situation by writing numerous articles for appeals and letters to newspapers. In one of these articles entitled *Evacuation from Argelès*, her strong emotional response to the situation is clear. The scene is described through a conversation between Frida and an old Spanish soldier, divided by the wire fencing of the camp.

> 'Why do they evacuate the camp?' I asked.
> 'They hope the summer visitors will come back; it used to be a famous resort. But,' said he, looking round, and sniffing, significantly, 'it will never be the same Lido again. The shore is poisoned.'
> I was to agree that I personally would not choose the *Plage d'Argelès* for a seaside holiday this summer, but perhaps I have been too close to the camp to be unbiased. Perhaps the strand is not so much poisoned physically as morally and spiritually. It is not so much the typhoid germs, or the lice, the latrines or the smell of bad fish that poison the camp – the wind, that has harried the men all these weeks, will blow away smell and bugs and germs – but the knowledge of what the place has been, the ghost of the past of the *plage*, with its scenes of misery and ill-treatment of the finest people in the world, that would make it unbearable to stay in, ever again.

Her frustration at the slow procedure for helping the refugees is poured out in letters to her mother in which she says she is unable to think of anything other than the camp and the courage of the men, who try to keep their spirits up by organising classes and concerts.

> It's desperately depressing that we can only get out the tiniest fraction of them and I feel very ineffective fiddling around with our list of 500, and our card indexes. The Home Office is being unbelievably slow in giving permission for even our 60 names. By the way, Carmen's friend is on the list and I hope will be through in a very few days but it's in the lap of Whitehall and the Gods... It makes me wriggle with anger and shame to have all this dangling; and always having to say '*mañana*' when one's asked 'When shall we go?'

'Carmen's friend' was the refugee Silverio de la Torre, who, with his wife and little boy Fernando, was to be sponsored in England by Frida's parents and live with them at Girton Gate for over two years.

Refugees at Girton Gate. Back row: 4ᵗʰ from left, Frida's father, Hugh; 6ᵗʰ from left, Frida's mother, Jessie. Front row, left, Fernando de la Torre, the refugee whose family had been sponsored by the Stewarts to come and live in England.

Frida was cheered by the departure of the 2000 refugees to Mexico and the 'hair-raising four days, getting the people collected and on to the boat; more emotionally exhausting than anything I have ever experienced.' Although thinking that the scene at the quay side needed Tolstoi at least to do it justice, she does note the funny moments too, when the Duchess of Atholl tripped over the improvised coffee canteen on the quay and later when 'the General found himself with two family-less infants in his arms on the deck, and a choice of 1500 parents in the crowd!' Frida was hoping to go to Mexico with the refugees if there was enough room on the boat and lightheartedly wrote to her father enclosing an application form for him just in case he wanted to come too. Years later, the Duchess of Atholl wrote to Frida recalling the day of the embarkation and the soap sculpture of the Republican soldier she had been given, still carefully kept. Frida told me how sad she felt when her own soap sculptures eventually disintegrated. To both the Duchess and Frida they represented the spirit of the people in the camps who, despite their defeat in Spain and an uncertain future, still struggled to keep morale high.

This attitude was mirrored by Frida's own approach to life. Her belief in socialism and the promise offered by Communism suffered hard blows but was not extinguished. After the break up of the Soviet Union, she explained to a friend how the commitment to her ideals remained unshaken.

The 1989 events were certainly unexpected, and to me, for one, distressing because I saw that socialist governments had failed to win hearts and minds and to satisfy people's needs; it's obvious that bad mistakes were made – over-centralising, heavy-handed bureaucracy, censorship – and that ambitious, self-seeking leaders used power for their own ends – as did Napoleon, Cromwell, and many others in history... I don't blame Communism for the evils of Ceauçescu or Stalin, any more than I blame Christianity for the Inquisition or for Cromwell's crimes, or the Crusades... Can you imagine turning your back on the Ninth Symphony, just because it's been badly performed? Well, I can't! What is great and good does not turn out to be paltry and rotten because the wrong people got hold of it and misinterpreted it! Communism has not yet had an adequate performance, and we'll have to wait and work at it long and hard before this can happen.[59]

Her faith in socialism was reinforced by a visit to Cuba in 1992 when she joined in the May Day celebrations in Havana. Although frailty forced her to resort to the wheelchair, photographs show her looking happy, shaded by a big palm leaf, perhaps thinking of ways to support the Cuban people when she got home. By winter that year, there she is in a photo taken in Cambridge Market Square, wrapped in a thick coat and huge scarf at a stall raising funds for medical aid for Cuba, having founded the Cambridge Cuba Solidarity Campaign. Other photographs in the local newspaper show her with a walking frame on wheels, supporting the miners by protesting against the closure of the coal mines and, labelled as 'Frida, the woman who dared to fight Franco and Hitler', in an article written by a reporter who came to get a little information about a Peace Council meeting but instead produced a double page spread about Frida's life. She acted like a catalyst on people around her, one bureaucrat asking 'Who is this Frida Knight who keeps ringing me up and asking me to do things?' A much younger friend of Frida's felt guilty remembering how, in the winter of 1993, she chose not to make the uncomfortable gesture of sitting up all night in the cold Market Square as a protest against homelessness, only to see a picture in the local paper the next day of the elderly Frida, huddled in blankets, doing just that. Lanterns for the annual Hiroshima Commemoration were made at Frida's house and she would go to the Ceremony to watch them float down the River Cam, whatever the weather, whatever her aches and pains.

The writings of the artist and socialist, William Morris, became a great inspiration and consolation to Frida during this period. The shaky handwritten notes left scattered near her high-backed winged armchair revealed that the project of organising events in Cambridge to commemorate the centenary of his death kept her busy during her last year. If asked how she could continue to hold on to her optimistic belief in socialism she would often say that she knew William Morris was right in believing that it might not happen for a hundred years but that in the end socialism would come because there is no other system that will keep the world going. She greatly admired Morris because his socialist ideals were combined with an intense love of beauty and nature which permeated his work as a designer. He was the subject of the last of the many articles she wrote for the *Morning Star* in which she draws attention to him as a 'hero of socialist activity', agreeing wholeheartedly when he wrote, 'Let us work to set our shop ready by tomorrow's daylight, so that the civilised world, no longer greedy, strife-full and destructive, shall have a new art and a glorious art, made by and for the people as a happiness of the worker and the user.'

Some years earlier, inspired by Morris, Frida had written a musical play based on his leaflet entitled, *Useful Work Versus Useless Toil,* linking this idea with the plans of the shop stewards at Lucas Aerospace to create socially useful goods, such as kidney machines, instead of arms. I found her draft copies of this unusual musical work, written especially for the Clarion Singers and premièred at the Birmingham May Day Festival in 1981. Frida and her sister Katharine, a pianist, had long been involved with this choir, founded in 1940 by a doctor, Colin Bradsworth, who had served with the International Brigades. He had been so much impressed by the power of songs in the struggle of the Spanish people that when he returned he decided to form a choir to promote the cause of Socialism through music. Frida shared these aims and wrote several scripts and sketches for the choir. Music always ran like a bright thread through her life and from the book of Spanish songs she edited to raise money for the Basque children to organising a Peace Council concert with Paul Tortelier, the cellist, she used it whenever she could to promote her belief in peace and justice.

Friendships: old and new, near and far

Frida loved causes because she loved people and practical action to help them in some way was always her speciality. One newspaper cutting in her collection concerns a councillor from Cambuslang in Scotland who intended to visit Cambridge. As he reached the last number on his list and his last hope of finding accommodation, he misdialled the number and found himself speaking to an unknown elderly Cambridge lady, who had driven an ambulance from Cambuslang that the local miners had donated for use in the Spanish Civil War. Frida, of course, offered him accommodation for the duration of his visit, which was gratefully accepted. Another friendship formed!

Friends were constantly coming and going in Frida's home. Through my research on British women and the Spanish Civil War, I became one of these many frequent visitors. She would insist that I share her 'meals on wheels', sitting at the table next to the poster of a beautiful Cuban beach, amidst a jumble of mementoes from other lands, drawings from her grandchildren, newspapers and letters. Sometimes we went out together, and a trip with Frida was always fun because she was so interested in new experiences, in seeing changes, and enjoyed chatting to complete strangers. We were friends, separated by many years but linked perhaps because we both belonged to idealistic generations. In the thirties they had believed in the possibility of rebuilding society through political action, in the sixties some of us thought all you needed was love! I like to remember Frida on our last visit together to the International Brigade Association annual ceremony at their memorial in London's Jubilee Gardens. Frida, as usual rejecting the wheelchair in favour of arduous independence on crutches, sat in front of the speakers on a folding chair and, as the speeches were rather long and the sun very hot, I was glad we had brought it with us. But Frida was used to lengthy political speeches and didn't seem to mind at all. She was pleased to see old friends, especially Fernando, the Spanish refugee who had lived with her family as a child so many years before. We all went for lunch afterwards, where

Frida and one of the Brigaders, Sam Russell, began to make plans for a memorial to the International Brigade in Cambridge. This idea had initially been proposed during the Spanish war on the death of the Cambridge graduate and poet John Cornford, and was now long overdue. Frida never gave up easily and proposed a new attack on those in authority in Cambridge hoping to add to the sixty memorials already in place in Britain that remind people of the fight against fascism in Spain.

When I think of her that day, tiny as a little twisted olive tree that has somehow survived extremes of weather, I can understand why the 'Aid Spain' campaigns in England were so successful. Women predominated in this extensive grass roots action. They sometimes did not share political views or even religious beliefs. Some, like Frida, came from liberal intellectual backgrounds, many others had grown up in extreme poverty and a surprising number were titled ladies. But they were all determined to work together for the particular cause of Spain, whether motivated by anti-Fascism or a belief in democracy and the right of the Spanish people to keep their elected government, or simply by a wish to alleviate suffering. Can this broad phenomenon justifiably be called a 'movement', when it lacked either an institutional or a political basis? Women like Frida and many of her contemporaries certainly viewed it as such, choosing to disregard their differences in favour of co-operation. They successfully organised a system based on loose affiliation which co-ordinated the efforts of the bewildering array of committees involved with the Republic and the Spanish people. Their movement was certainly unified in spirit, if not in the traditional, perhaps more male orientated, formal hierarchical style, and the success of their efforts can be judged from the huge amounts of money raised, and the participation of so many ordinary people in the various campaigns.

Frida's work for the cause of Republican Spain was valued highly by Bill Alexander, former Commander of the British Battalion in Spain and Honorary Secretary of the International Brigade Association. He had referred to her as 'at least an honorary Brigader', and considered her to be someone who 'used her unlimited energy and talents to the full, working for

Peace and Liberty.' On her death he wrote of the significance of her role for the Brigaders.

> Frida's part in help to the Brigaders, herded in the camps in France, made a deep impression on me. I was home, free and at least able to eat, speak and fight in World War II. But her efforts must have lifted the spirits of all our Comrades who faced the grimmest conditions with little light and hope. Frida's activities, little known and sometimes dangerous, helped many to eventually find their way into the Resistance Movement – adding a new dimension to the World War against Fascism.

When we gathered in Cambridge to celebrate her life, there were many speakers, each given a few minutes to say a little about one of the many aspects of Frida's life. It became clear that the symbolism inherent in her work to help the Spanish Republicans was also recognised by others who had not known her personally. Fernando, always grateful to Frida and her family for their generosity to him as a refugee, quoted to the assembled crowd from a letter he had recently received from Spain. It had been written by a Republican veteran who had read one of the newspaper articles describing the ceremony to scatter Frida's ashes by the *Puente de los Franceses*. He wrote of his feelings towards those who came from other countries to fight in Spain.

> I told you then and I tell you now, what a deep emotion we all felt at home reading the article. My wife, whose brother had been killed near there, cut it out to show to our children. We all read it with tears in our eyes. Frida's life and her solidarity with the Spaniards who were fighting fascism, as well as the heart-warming wish to blend her ashes with our soil where she and thousands of like thinking people had fought, helped us to believe again that humanity had not entirely lost its way. Frida and the Brigaders, offering their lives to us, also told us that love of justice is not dead. We anti-fascist Spaniards, although we were risking our lives, were doing so for ourselves, for our well-being, for our dignity. What Frida and her

comrades did, their altruism towards people unknown to them, was sublime. Dear friend, with these lines I want to tell you, and those who feel and think like Frida, the deep feeling of gratitude from someone who also fought at the fronts where the Brigaders fought, against Franco, for liberty and democracy.

The meeting in remembrance of Frida was, above all, a happy occasion. Music was provided by the Clarion Singers and musicians who performed extracts from Purcell's *Fairy Queen*, and Mozart's *Magic Flute*. We all sang Paul Robeson's words to *Ode to Joy*, much loved by Frida for their egalitarian sentiments. I spoke about her involvement with the Spanish Civil War and her work in the refugee camps. The last speaker was the former leader of the Campaign for Nuclear Disarmament in Britain, Bruce Kent. He made us laugh with his recollections of Frida's humour. Although he believed that Frida had been capable of many things, he said one thing she could never have become was Poet Laureate, and proceeded to illustrate this by reading examples of Frida's funny verses. These were usually written for special occasions such as family birthdays or CND anniversaries, to make grandchildren laugh or to lighten hearts during an arduous campaign. Finally, after warmly praising her work in the peace movement, he used the words of Bernard Shaw to capture the essence of Frida's fighting spirit: 'Some people see things as they are and ask, "Why?" Others dream of things that never were and ask, "Why not?"'

Afterwards, reading through Frida's papers, I discovered the outline for another book she intended to write, *Let's Make Peace*. She writes,

> All my life, peace and war have been the main preoccupations. I've been involved in campaigning for as long as I can remember. What I'd like to put across, through my personal experience, is the possibility and the need for understanding and friendship between people, whatever their social system, race or class.

She would have been pleased if her memoirs, although

269

describing only the first half of her life, were to contribute to this aim in some small way.

As I dug ever deeper into the old files of letters, I found more of Frida's poems written out in rough on yellowed scraps of paper. These poems are unlike her others, they are poems searching for a way to give meaning to tragedy, for acceptance of loss. They are undated but must surely have been written after the death of someone she loved dearly. Her life inspired others to fight for ideals; her message in these unfinished lines is to love life itself.

> Never love strongly man or child
> Never feel things too deep
> Never disarm your heart and mind
> (...)

> What, and not know the joy of love,
> The pleasure of response?
> Not let my feeling unfold and flower
> Nor my heart sing and dance?

> Never, if you would not be hurt
> Life's harsh to those who care
> Keep to yourself and be intact
> Your suffering to spare

> I'd rather live and love in full
> Than stint and poorly fare
> And if it hurts, when all is done
> I've still got riches here.

A Note on the Sources of the Poems

Most of the poems used to preface the chapters were selected by Frida herself. Every effort has been made to identify the correct authors and the original publication dates and media. All extracts, whether under copyright or in the public domain, have been reproduced here for transformative purposes under the principle of 'fair dealing'. Should anyone object to the use of any extract in respect of which they are the copyright holder, the publisher will endeavour to substitute it with a suitable alternative as soon as possible after receiving notice of such objection.

The poems are listed below in the order the appear in the text.

Frances Cornford (1886-1960), *A Glimpse*, first published in *Country Life*, Volume 52, Part 1, 1922.

Thomas Betteron (1635-1761), *The Fairy Queen*, first performed Dorset Garden, London, 1692.

T. S. Eliot (1888-1965), *East Coker*, included in *Four Quartets*, Harcourt, London, 1943.

John Gay, (1685-1732), *The Beggar's Opera*, first produced London, 1728.

W.H. Auden (1907-1973) and Christopher Isherwood (1904-1986), *The Dog Beneath the Skin or Where is Francis?, a play in three acts*, Faber and Faber, London, 1936; a version of this poem was first published as *The Witnesses* by W.H. Auden, *The Listener (Poetry Supplement)*, 12th July, 1932.

T. W. Higginson (1823-1911), *Heirs of Time*, The Cry for Justice: An Anthology of the Literature of Social Protest, Upton Sinclair, New York 1915.

Roger Oldham (1871-1916), *A Manchester Alphabet*, Manchester, 1906.

H.H. Lewis (1901-1985), *Farmhand's Refrain,* Poetry, Vols. 53-54, Modern Poetry Association, 1939.

Robert Nathan (1894-1985), *Ethiopia,* Selected Poems of Robert Nathan, Albert Knopf, Michigan, 1935.

Rex Warner (1905-1986), *Hymn,* first published 1933; republished in *Poems,* The Bodley Head, 1937.

Stephen Spender (1909-1995), *Port Bou,* Collected Poems, Faber & Faber, 1955, first version *Port Bou – Firing Practice,* published in *New Writing,* 1938.

W. S. Landor (1775-1864), *The Foreign Ruler*, The Works and Life of Walter Savage Landor, Vol. VIII, Miscellaneous poems, ed. John Forster, Chapman & Hall, London, 1876. Purists will delight in noting that strictly speaking the title should be spelled *The Foren Ruler* as per the poet's original intention.

W.H. Auden (1907-1973), *Spain,* Faber & Faber, London, 1937.

Rex Warner (1905-1986), *The Tourist Looks at Spain*, published in *New Writing*, ed. John Lehmann, Vol. IV, Autumn 1937, Lawrence and Wishart, London, 1937.

Jack Lindsay (1900-1990), *Look at a Map of Spain on the Devon Coast (August 1937)*, Republished in *Poesía inglesa de la guerra española, El Ateneo*, Buenos Aires, 1947.

Alec McDade (1905-1937), *There's A Valley in Spain*, republished in *Poets from Spain, British and Irish International Brigaders on the Spanish Civil War*, ed Jim Jump, Lawrence & Wishart, London, 2006.

Rex Warner (1905-1986), *Arms for Spain* published in *Poems For Spain*, ed. Stephen Spender and John Lehmann, Hogarth Press, 1939.

Miguel Hernández (1910-1942), *Recoged esta voz – Gather this voice,* Translated by Inez Pearn and Stephen Spender, published in *New Poetry,* 1937.

John Cornford (1915-1936), *A Letter from Aragón*, published in *Left Review, II, No. 14*, November 1936.

Louis MacNeice (1907-1963), *Out of the Picture* from *Collected Poems*, Faber & Faber, London, 1949.

Herbert Read (1893-1968), *Inbetweentimes* from *Thirty-Five Poems*, Faber & Faber, London, 1941.

M. Jean Prussing, *September 2, 1939*, Poetry, Vol . 55, The Poetry Foundation, London, 1939.

Louis Aragon (1897-1982), *Le Crêve-Coeur*, Gallimard, Paris, 1941; translation by Louis MacNeice published in *New Writing and Daylight*, Summer, 1943.

Aileen Palmer (1915-1988), *The Dead Have No Regrets* (1939), published in *Poets from Spain, British and Irish International Brigaders on the Spanish Civil War*, ed Jim Jump, Lawrence & Wishart, London, 2006. Thanks to Jim for suggesting we include this poem here.

Walt Whitman (1819-1893), *To A Foil'd European Revolutionnaire* published in *Leaves of Grass* (2nd edition), Fowler & Wells, New York, 1856.

Paul Éluard (1895-1952), *Au Rendez-vous Allemand*. Éditions de Minuit, Paris, 1945, translated by Frida Stewart [?], undated, previously unpublished.

Frida Stewart (1910-1996), *Never Love Strongly Man or Child*, undated; previously unpublished.

Notes

[1] *Pour sa vie et son bonheur* = Wishing her a long and happy life.

[2] *Ah! Ces chères petites Anglaises!* = Ah, these sweet little English girls!

[3] *Aaah! Je te tirerai les oreilles!* = Ah, I'm going to tweak your ears!

[4] The second siege of Vienna by the Turks in 1863.

[5] *Wahrheit ist wahr! Deutsch ist die Saar!* = The truth will out! The Saarland is German!

[6] *Nichtaryer mussen den Saal lassen.* = Non-Aryans must leave the hall.

[7] The 1934 Unemployment Act led to the establishment of the Unemployment Assistance Board. A household means test was also introduced, which was abolished in 1941.

[8] The miners are: Bill Locke, Charles Page, George Wright, Jim Lee and Alan Milburn. Students: Ernest Roth, Frida Stewart, Roger O'Tournay, Arthur Cobb, Johanns von Giehel, Joseph Joachim and Ludwig Lienhart. Thanks to Mark Whyman for this photograph sent to him by Frida for inclusion in his book *Heartbreak Hill*, Cleveland County Council & Langbaugh-on-Tees Borough Council, 1991.

[9] Rex Warner, *Hymn*.

[10] *¡No pasarán!* = They shall not pass!

[11] *¡Madrid será el tumbo del fascismo!* = Madrid will be the burial ground of Fascism.

[12] *Je ne bombarderai jamais Madrid... il y a des innocents* = I shall never bomb Madrid... there are too many innocents.

[13] 'Blue Bird' was the name of Sir Malcolm Campbell's car, famous for breaking the land speed record.

[14] *Bonne chance et bon retour* = Good luck and safe journey.

[15] *El hidalgo inglés* = The English gentleman.

[16] FAI – Iberian Anarchist Federation.

[17] POUM – Unified Workers' Marxist Party.

[18] *Agrupémonos todos en la lucha final, el género humano es la internacional* = Let's work together in the final struggle, the human race is the *Internationale*.

[19] *El frente de la Libertad* = The front line of freedom.

[20] Exact numbers of volunteers are not known, but estimates put the total number of volunteers throughout the course of the war at around 35,000.

[21] Note from the author – see Koestler, *Spanish Testament*, Left Book Club Edition, 1937, pp. 100-116.

[22] *Jesu Cristo fue Socialista* = *Jesus Christ was a Socialist.*

[23] Arthur Koestler gives details of the treatment of Republicans in Seville in *Spanish Testament*, pp. 86-88.

[24] *Los niños ingleses* = The English children.

[25] Robert Capa and Gerda Taro were the *noms de guerre* adopted by the photographers, Endre Ernő Friedmann, from Hungary and Gerta Phorylle, a German of Hungarian origin.

[26] *Writers Take Sides*, Foreword, New York, 1938.

[27] *¡Aquí la voz de España!* = This is the Voice of Spain!

[28] *The Basque Children in England*, Yvonne Cloud (Kapp), Gollancz, 1937.

[29] *Tous les laboristes britanniques ne sont pas comme ça, nous savons* = We know that not all the British Labour Party members are like that.

[30] *Betrayal in Central Europe: Austria & Czechoslovakia: The Fallen Bastions*, G.E.R. Gedye, Harper, 1939.

[31] Ibid.

[32] Katharine, Duchess of Atholl, *Working Partnership*, 1958.

[33] Barcelona was eventually occupied by Franco's forces on 26th January 1939.

[34] *Que vous interesserait sûrement* = Which would surely be of interest to you.

[35] *Stalin c'est un autre Hitler ou pire* = Stalin is another Hitler, or worse.

[36] *Je savais qu'il y aurait quelque chose de louche!* = I knew there'd be something fishy!

[37] *Drôle de guerre* = phoney war.

[38] *Que voulez-vous, c'est la guerre!* = What do you expect? There's a war on!

[39] *Les Communistes seront mis a raison* = We'll bring the Communists under control, c.f. Livre Blanche, 1939.

[40] *Droits de l'Homme* = Rights of Man.

[41] *Deuxième Bureau* = French military intelligence agency.

[42] In camera (i.e. behind closed doors).

[43] *Au nom de la République Française* = In the name of the French Republic.

[44] *Assasins! – Tortionnaires! Bonnet au Poteau* = Assassins! Torturers! Put Bonnet in the pillory!

[45] *C'est l'anglais qui vous a fait cela* = It's the English who did this to you.

[46] *La France a perdu une bataille – elle n'a pas perdu la guerre* = France has lost a battle: she hasn't lost the war.

[47] *À bas les Nazis, vive Thorez* = Down with the Nazis, long live Thorez.

[48] *Marchons, marchons, qu'un sang impur abreuve nos sillons!* = Let's march, let's march! Let their impure blood irrigate our fields!

[49] *Deutschland, Deutschland über Alles – nicht wahr?* = Germany, Germany for everyone – isn't that true?

[50] *C'est le premier pas qui coûte* = The first step is the most difficult.

[51] *Una perita, señorita* = Any spare change, miss?

[52] *Nous, nous ferons mieux que ça!* = We can do better than that!

[53] *Un vraiment grand homme* = A truly great man.

[54] *Á mon cher camarade* = To my dear comrade.

[55] *400,000 hommes doivent être livrés au Moloch hitlérien avant la fin du mois de juin* = 400,000 men must be delivered into the Hitlerian hell by the end of June.

[56] *Les Allemands réclament 2,000 tonnes de beurre par mois* = The Germans are demanding 2,000 tonnes of butter a month.

[57] *On meurt de faim dans les prisons de France* = People are starving to death in French prisons.

[58] *Mille six centièmes et dixième jour de la lutte du people français pour sa libération* = The one thousand six hundred and tenth day of the French People's struggle for their liberation.

[59] Frida joined the Communist Party in 1936. Her activities were monitored by the Security Services from 1940 until her file was closed in 1951. The National Archives KV 2/2374.

Angela Jackson: Books

British Women and the Spanish Civil War (Routledge/Cañada Blanch Centre for Contemporary Spanish Studies, London, 2002. Revised edition, Warren & Pell, Barcelona, 2009). Published in Spanish as *Las mujeres británicas y la Guerra Civil española* (University of Valencia, 2010).

Beyond the Battlefield: Testimony, Memory and Remembrance of a Cave Hospital in the Spanish Civil War (Warren & Pell, Abersychan, 2005). Published in Catalan as *Més enllà del camp de batalla: Testimoni, memòria i record d'una cova hospital en la Guerra Civil espanyola* (Cossetània Edicions, Valls, 2004).

Warm Earth (Pegasus, Cambridge, 2007).

At the Margins of Mayhem: Prologue and Epilogue to the Last Great Battle of the Spanish Civil War (Warren & Pell, Abersychan, 2008). Published in Catalan as *Els brigadistes entre nosaltres: Pròleg i epíleg a l'última gran batalla de la Guerra Civil espanyola* (Cossetània Edicions, Valls, 2004).

Prelude to the Last Battle: The International Brigades in the Priorat 1938/Preludi de l'última batalla 1938 (Bilingual edition, Cossetània Edicions, Valls, 2004).

Antifascistas: British and Irish Volunteers in the Spanish Civil War (with Richard Baxell and Jim Jump, Lawrence & Wishart, London, 2010). Published in Spanish as *Voluntarios Británicos e Irlandeses en la Guerra Civil Española* (Pamiela, Arre, and Editorial Piedra de Rayo S.L., Logroño, 2016).

'*For us it was heaven': The Passion Grief and Fortitude of Patience Darton from the Spanish Civil War to Mao's China* (Sussex Academic Press, Brighton/Cañada Blanch Centre for Contemporary Spanish Studies, London, 2012). Published in Spanish as *Para nosotros era el cielo. Pasión, dolor y fortaleza de Patience Darton: de la guerra civil española a la China de Mao* (Ediciones San Juan de Dios, Barcelona, 2012).

Also available from The Clapton Press:

BOADILLA by Esmond Romilly
The nephew that Winston Churchill disowned describes his experiences fighting with the International Brigade in the Battle of Madrid. Written on his honeymoon in St. Jean de Luz after he eloped with Jessica Mitford.

MY HOUSE IN MALAGA by Sir Peter Chalmers Mitchell
While most ex-pats fled to Gibraltar in 1936, Sir Peter stayed on to protect his house and servants from the fascists. He ended up in prison for sheltering Arthur Koestler from Franco's rabid head of propaganda, who had threatened to "shoot him like a dog".

SPANISH PORTRAIT by Elizabeth Lake
A brutally honest, semi-autobiographical novel set in San Sebastian and Madrid between 1934 and 1936, portraying a frantic love affair against a background of apprehension and confusion as Spain drifted inexorably towards civil war.

SOME STILL LIVE by F.G. Tinker Jr.
F.G. Tinker was a US pilot who signed up with the Republican forces because he didn't like Mussolini. He was also attracted by the prospect of adventure and a generous pay cheque. This is an account of his experiences in Spain.

THE YOCCI WELL by Juana Manuela Gorriti
A love story, ghost story and gothic horror rolled into one, the action of this brilliant novella spans 25 years, encompassing the Argentine War of Independence and the brutal civil wars that followed. Published now for the first time in English.